Valerie Russell is a qualifie[...] [...] [...]
freelance writer by profess[...] [...]
and countryside writing, a[...] [...]
takes her own photograph[...]

C000128501

WILDLIFE WALKS OF BRITAIN

VALERIE RUSSELL

GRAFTON BOOKS

A Division of the Collins Publishing Group

LONDON GLASGOW
TORONTO SYDNEY AUCKLAND

Grafton Books
A Division of the Collins Publishing Group
8 Grafton Street, London W1X 3LA

A Grafton Paperback Original 1990

Copyright © Valerie Russell 1990

A CIP catalogue record for this book
is available from the British Library

ISBN 0-586-07441-4

Printed and bound in Great Britain by
Collins, Glasgow

Set in Bembo

All rights reserved. No part of this publication may
be reproduced, stored in a retrieval system, or
transmitted, in any form, or by any means, electronic,
mechanical, photocopying, recording or otherwise,
without the prior permission of the publishers.

This book is sold subject to the condition that it
shall not, by way of trade or otherwise, be lent,
re-sold, hired out or otherwise circulated
without the publisher's prior consent in any
form of binding or cover other than that in
which it is published and without a similar
condition including this condition being imposed
on the subsequent purchaser.

CONTENTS

PREFACE

In choosing these walks I have endeavoured to include as many different habitats as possible while keeping them within the capabilities of the average person, like myself, who is interested in natural history. Only one walk (the Beinn Eighe Mountain Trail) requires above-average fitness.

There may be some surprise that none of the walks is longer than eight miles. This is quite deliberate, as these are natural history walks – not walks designed primarily for exercise or to admire the view. I feel that plenty of time is needed to look at and for the various species, to identify them if necessary, and indeed, to find the many that have not been mentioned in the text. Some walks are described in more detail than others, to cater for different tastes and different levels of experience.

Most of the walks are on nature reserves. There are two reasons for this. Firstly, I am conscious that it is all too easy to destroy the very habitats we wish to preserve by encouraging too many people to visit them. Nature reserves are, in general, geared to having visitors. Secondly, so many of the best places, fortunately, *are* reserves. I would, however, reiterate the plea made at various points in the text: please keep to the paths in reserves where this is particularly requested.

Although I have drawn attention to various rarities (such as the natterjack toad, for example, on p. 134), I have done so only where these species are already mentioned in the literature available from the reserve or the managing organization, or on information boards on the reserves themselves.

The map references are from the Ordnance Survey series.

SOUTH-WEST ENGLAND

8 Dawlish Warren
9 Exmoor – Cloutsham
10 Exminster Marshes
11 Kimmeridge Bay
12 Studland Heath
13 Cheddar Gorge
14 Bridgwater Bay

1 Portreath Rocky Shore
2 Loe Bar
3 Predannack Cliffs
4 Place
5 Red Moor
6 Kilminorth Woods
7 Dunsford Daffodil Walk

Portreath Rocky Shore

SUMMARY A scramble over granite rocks rather than a walk, but for anyone interested in seaweeds this is a fascinating place, as there are well over thirty species in a comparatively small area.

APPROXIMATE LENGTH OF WALK ½ mile.

BEST TIME All year.

LOCATION Portreath is on the Cornish coast, about three miles north-west of Camborne on the B3301. (203)655454.

If possible, start the walk at low water mark spring tide, beyond the end of the jetty. This is reached by going down the steps from the car park and walking out on the rocks.

The seaweeds described in this walk are ones seen during the summer, but would not necessarily be seen in the same places – or indeed be seen at all – in the winter. This is because the position and appearance of some varies according to the season. Some of the green seaweeds, for instance, such as *Enteromorpha* and *Ulva*, show some degree of migration down the shore in the winter, while some of the red weeds may migrate in the opposite direction. Obviously it is not the individual plants that move; it is the spores, which settle in different places while the old plants die back. Some seaweeds, such as Irish moss or carrageen (*Chondrus crispus*) and *Gigartina stellata*, die back in the winter, leaving little but the discs attached to the rocks. Other seaweeds disappear altogether. These movements are probably induced by variations in temperature and light.

The conformation of the shore is such that there are three main areas of fairly high rocks, the largest of which surrounds the end of the jetty. On the landward side of this, and again, immediately below the jetty, is quite a large rock pool, and on the landward side of that there is another area of high rock. The remainder of the shore shelves down to the water. This conformation has influenced the distribution of the seaweeds.

The rocks around the end of the jetty are very exposed, and are subjected to the full force of the sea as the tide comes in. As a consequence, the seaweeds found there are tough ones that can withstand the conditions. Before looking at the species in detail it is perhaps helpful to take an overall view of how the seaweeds are distributed. The high rocks, particularly around the end of the jetty, are exposed to wave action and, because of their height, are also exposed to the air for quite long periods. They therefore support only those seaweeds which are able to withstand those conditions. Bladder wrack (*Fucus vesiculosus*) is found in some quantity, but so is a variant which does not have any bladders and is a much shorter, tougher plant.

In crevices and on landward-facing slopes – which are to some extent protected from the fiercest wave action – knotted wrack (*Ascophyllum nodosum*) and spiral wrack (*Fucus spiralis*) are present, while the pool offers sheltered conditions for some of the red seaweeds, and also for some of the more delicate green seaweeds which cannot stand being exposed to the drying air.

On the lower rocks, a definite zone of serrated wrack (*Fucus serratus*) appears above the kelps (*Laminarians*). The latter are the lowest on the shore – indeed, they are only just visible at low water.

As they are exposed for the least time, it is logical to start by looking at the kelps. Those present are dabberlocks (*Alaria esculenta*), which have a yellowish midrib and a long, thin, yellow-brown frond with slightly wavy edges; oarweed

(*Laminaria digitata*), with a thick, round stipe (stem) which broadens into a wide blade, which in turn is divided into a number of strap-like fronds; sea belt or sugar kelp (*Laminaria saccharina*), which has a long, leaf-like frond with crinkled undulations over its surface and wavy edges. Finally there is batters (*Sacchoriza polyschides*), with a very distinctive hold-fast (the rootlike structure by means of which seaweeds are attached to the rocks). It is a collarlike, knobbly structure from which arises a stiff stipe with wavy edges, leading to a blade that divides into many strap-shaped fronds.

Above the kelps is the zone of serrated wrack, another brown seaweed, easily recognized by its flat fronds with serrated edges. Also above the kelp zone there are a number of other brown seaweeds, but these are less numerous than the serrated wrack. They include sea thong (*Himanthalia elongata*). These long (several feet), thin, leathery, flattened fronds are branched, and arise from buttonlike structures, which are often found on their own or with just the beginnings of the long frond showing.

Near the sea thong, and also higher on the shore, are specimens of another, much smaller brown seaweed, *Cladostephus verticillatus*, which does not have a common name. It is a rather stiff plant, about 15 cm (6 inches) in length, much branched, and with each branch bearing whorled, spiny branchlets. In the same area of the shore or a little higher up, link frond (*Scytosiphon lomentaria*) is found. Although a brown seaweed, the colour is more of a yellow-green, and the plant looks just like strings of very tiny sausages. The 'sausages' are hollow, and rather slimy. Another brown seaweed of the lower shore found at Portreath is *Desmarestia aculeata*. This is a large plant of 60–180 cm (2–6 feet) in length, and is found in the spring and summer only. It is dark brown, but becomes green when out of the water (which does not happen often). It has a main stem from which side branches bearing very fine filaments grow.

Immediately below the jetty on the high rocks the two kinds of bladder wrack already mentioned can be seen. There is the common one, with the familiar paired bladders on either side of the midrib, and the variant which does not have bladders.

There are numerous rock pools of varying sizes at Portreath, but the most interesting is the very big one between two outcrops of high rocks by the jetty, in roughly a middle shore position. The seaweeds that thrive here include many of the reds, whose special red pigments enable them to utilize the low-intensity light of the sheltered habitat where they are usually found, i.e. under other seaweeds, in deeper water, in shade and in crevices. There is, for instance, a good growth of the beautiful *Corallina officinalis*, which is more pink than red; it feels quite brittle to the touch, due to calcium and magnesium salts in its much-branched fronds. Inspection with a hand lens will show that the main stem and branches are a series of tiny, articulated (jointed) sections. Another very common red weed in the pool is Irish moss (carrageen), another branched plant, but flatter and without the brittleness of *Corallina*. It is about 10–15 cm (4–6 inches) long, and although it is deep red in the water it takes on a greenish hue if exposed to the air. Both *Corallina* and carrageen are at their best in the summer, and are much reduced in the autumn and winter.

One of the red weeds, *Porphyra umbilicalis*, has a wider range than most reds. It can sometimes be found high on the rock, where it merges into the sandy shore, but also extends down into the middle shore. It is a deep red, membranous (and, if stepped on, extremely slippery) seaweed, which is more widespread in some years than in others.

There are about fifteen other red seaweeds to be found – some in the large pool, others in the smaller pools or under the brown seaweed on the middle and lower shore. Hardly any have common names – so for the naturalist armed with a field guide, the following may be seen: *Rhodymenia pseudopalmata*, *Heterosiphonia plumosa*, *Ahnfeltia plicata*, *Furcellaria fastigiata* (*lumbricalis*), *Catenella repens*, *Rhodocorton*, *Gastroclonium ovatum*, *Laurencia pinnatifida*, *Laurencia obtusa*, *Plumularia elegans*, *Ceramium*, *Porphyra umbilicalis*, *Gigartina stellata*, and *Lomentaria articulata*.

One of the most attractive of seaweeds is the small green *Bryopsis plumosa*, found occasionally in some of the deeper pools. No more than 10 cm (4 inches) long at the most, this delicate plant looks just like a miniature Christmas tree, with branches coming from a main stem. Other green seaweeds found at Portreath include the sea lettuce (*Ulva lactuca*), and the long tubular *Enteromorpha*. A few plants of the very dark green *Spongomorpha arcta* grow in pools on the middle and lower shore.

Although the seaweeds are the most obvious forms of life at Portreath, there are also several animals. Right down on the lower middle shore, under and among the weeds and clinging to the rocks, are flat periwinkles (*Littorina littoralis*), which favour the bladder and knotted wrack particularly. On the upper shore, and especially in the cracks and crevices of the rocks near the jetty and in the jetty itself, are the very small, rough periwinkles (*Littorina saxatilis*) and the equally tiny, blue-black periwinkles (*Littorina neritoides*). Both these latter creatures are modified for the long periods of exposure to the air by the possession of a lung.

Mussels are found on the lower to middle shore, and, where there are mussels there are likely to be dog whelks, which prey on them. A few top shells are present. In the rock pools are two species of anemone. The common red beadlet anemone (*Actinia equina*) is there in profusion, and there are also a few of the delicately coloured mauve and green snakelocks anemones (*Anemonia sulcata*). The latter, as will be noticed, cannot retract their tentacles; they are usually found in the more sheltered pools, where they are not normally exposed to the air. The beadlet anemones, however, cling to rock surfaces in a variety of situations, and protect themselves to some extent from desiccation by retracting their tentacles and reducing their overall surface area.

Loe Bar

SUMMARY A short walk to and on the sand and shingle ridge known as Loe Bar, with Loe Pool which is cut off from the sea by Loe Bar. The actual distance covered is short, but a detailed inspection of the unexpectedly rich flora is included, and the walk is quite time-consuming.

APPROXIMATE LENGTH OF WALK 2 miles.

BEST TIMES Spring, summer.

LOCATION Near Porthleven, Cornwall. SW639259.

From the car park near Porthleven follow the pathway marked 'Loe Bar', which leads along the cliffs. On the way a certain amount of gorse is growing, with celandine (*Ranunculus ficaria*) and common scurvy grass (*Cochlearia officinalis*). After about a mile, the track leads down to the shingle and sand ridge of Loe Bar. On the way down it can be seen that the bar runs parallel with the coast. It has been built up only over the last 100 or so years by the action of the sea, and now joins two headlands and encloses the freshwater Loe Pool on the landward side. The slope of the bar is steepest on the seaward side where there is little vegetation, and it slopes gently down to the pool to landward; on this slope, most of the plants are found.

The bar itself is composed of fine pebbles or shingle, with an increasing (but never high) proportion of organic material as the pool is approached. From an ecological viewpoint the top of the bar can be regarded as a shingle ridge, and in this case one that is unstable and is constantly being reworked by wave and wind action. Thus one of the principal problems confronting the plants right at the top of the ridge is that of obtaining and retaining water. Although the shingle would appear not to contain any moisture, in fact warm moist air off the sea is drawn through the sediment of the bar by upward convection currents, especially at night. Condensation takes place on the cold pebbles to form dew, which is then available to the plants.

Nutrients for all the plants are provided by decaying vegetation, which comes from the pool and from seaweed washed up by the sea or blown about the bar by the strong winds.

Nevertheless, the top of the bar is a hostile environment, well within reach of salt spray from the sea, and exposed to strong, moisture-evaporating winds, so the plants need to be well adapted. A walk to the far end of the ridge shows a large area of sea sandwort (*Honkenya peploides*), which is well suited to these conditions. As can be seen, it is a ground-hugging succulent, with fleshy, yellow-green leaves, and small, whitish flowers. To avoid the worst of the winter gales, the upper flowering parts die back after the seeds are shed, and winter buds form on the underground part of the stem. It spreads by means of seeds, but also by vegetative means with shoots that are protected from the shingle by hard scale leaves. This enables it to grow up again when, as often happens, the whole plant is buried. Sea sandwort can also, it seems, store water in very large cells just under the leaf surface. The water can, if necessary, be withdrawn by the underlying photosynthetic tissue.

Other plants growing on or near the top of the bar include sea kale (*Crambe maritima*), sea holly (*Eryngium maritimum*), and yellow horned poppy (*Glaucium flavum*). Most of these plants have deep and/or spreading roots which anchor them firmly and remain in touch with the water supply.

Moving down almost to the edge of Loe Pool, one of the

plants which grows close to the water is ribwort plantain (*Plantago lanceolata*). It has a rosette habit which enables it to survive the winds, but it is not salt-tolerant, and it appears to require the richer nutrients found in the humus by the pool shore. A plant also found on the landward side of the bar, although further from the water than the plantain, is rest-harrow (*Ononis repens*), which cannot tolerate salt, possibly because it has nitrogen-fixing bacteria in its roots. However, it is able to evade burial in the shifting sand because of its highly branched habit and sticky glandular leaves which form a turf-like covering over the ground and act as a windshield.

Other plants which may be found, principally on the landward side of the bar, include yarrow (*Achillea millefolium*), sand couch grass (*Agropyron junceiforme*), thrift (*Armeria maritima*), sea beet (*Beta vulgaris*), sea bindweed (*Calystegia soldanella*), birdsfoot trefoil (*Lotus corniculatus*), creeping cinquefoil (*Potentilla reptans*), sea campion (*Silene maritima*), curled dock (*Rumex crispus*), and the moss *Tortula muraliformis*. Around the fringes of Loe Pool, water mint (*Mentha aquatica*), sea rush (*Juncus maritimus*), and hemlock water dropwort (*Oenanthe crocata*) can be seen.

The pool is a good place for birds, with tufted ducks, mallard, cormorants, gulls, teal, pochard, shoveler, golden-eye and gadwall.

Return to the car park along the same route.

Predannack Cliffs

SUMMARY A cliff walk on the Lizard Peninsula, but one that is notable for its plants rather than for sea birds.

APPROXIMATE LENGTH OF WALK 2 miles.

BEST TIMES Spring, summer.

LOCATION Park in farmyard at Predannack Head near Mullion. SW660163.

Leave the car park by the pathway signposted to Predannack cliffs. In the farmyard wall, navelwort/wall pennywort (*Umbilicus rupestris*) is growing, and further on, by a five-barred gate, there is a stand of common fleabane (*Pulicaria dysenterica*). After a couple of hundred yards, branch off right where the signpost says 'Footpath to cliff'. The track is bordered by gorse, bramble and some stunted elder, with red campion (*Silena dioica*) growing between. Hard fern (*Blechnum spicant*), and also some polypody fern (*Polypodium vulgare*), grows in among the brambles and in crevices on the stony bank. Note the profusion of lichens growing on the branches of the gorse.

After a short distance, a notice board explains fully about the reintroduction of summer grazing in an attempt to halt the invasion of scrub and coarse grasses, and thus encourage the return of many of the wildflowers and grasses for which the cliffs were once known. Continue on over a lovely stone stile by the gate, and come to a track off to the right. This leads down the hill across the gently sloping cliff, which is covered with rough grass, gorse and ling (*Calluna vulgaris*) and bell heather (*Erica cinerea*). Outcrops of rock have bright patches of lichen, principally the brilliant orange

Xanthoria. In spring, this relatively protected part of the cliffs is a colourful scene of violets, spring squill (*Scilla verna*), lesser celandine (*Ranunculus ficaria*) and wild thyme (*Thymus drucei*).

At the bottom of the hill is a tiny stream which runs down to where the cliff drops steeply to the shore. The bed of the stream is, in places, thick with watercress (*Rorippa nasturtium-aquaticum*), and on the banks the brilliance of red campion makes an attractive show. Another feature here and in the general vicinity is the presence of betony (*Betonica officinalis*), with its reddish-purple flowers. It is interesting to note the height of this plant in these surroundings, and compare it with the stunted growth of the same species growing on the more exposed cliff top later in the walk.

From the stream, return up the hill and rejoin the original path, which leads round to the left and, after crossing a stile, a field, and another stile, emerges onto the rough heather and grassland of some of the most exposed parts of the cliffs. The views of the dramatic Cornish coastline are impressive, and as always on cliff walks, care must be taken if venturing near the edge.

It is immediately obvious that the plants here have adapted to the hostility of their habitat, where they not only have to survive frequent gale-force winds, but air that is always salt-laden. The heather is short and tough, and a brief search shows that in among the more common species is the unique Cornish heath (*Erica vagans*), found in considerable quantities on the Lizard. Cornish heath is in flower from July to September, and is distinguished by the very prominent brown anthers that protrude from the mouth of the globular pink-to-lilac flowers.

Also present are ox-eye daisy (*Chrysanthemum leucanthemum*), betony, knapweed (*Centaurea sp.*), saw-wort (*Serratula tinctoria*) and devil's-bit scabious (*Succisa pratensis*), clinging closely to the ground in unusual dwarf forms – thus preventing excessive loss of moisture by reducing the surface area of their leaves exposed to the drying winds. Other plants, such as juniper and dyer's greenweed (*Genista tinctoria*), have adopted a slightly different protective mechanism; they occur in a creeping instead of an erect form.

This is one of those walks where it must be left to the individual to choose how far to go, as the route is part of the South-West Peninsula Long-distance Coastal Path. All the plants that have been mentioned can be seen in a walk totalling about two to two and a half miles.

Place

SUMMARY For the lover of shore life there can be few
richer areas than this small inlet which faces on to the
Porthcule river estuary. It has rocky, sandy and
slightly muddy shores with an enormous range of
species, all within an area of about thirty acres. This
walk is primarily one for low tides, preferably low
spring tides, when all the species mentioned can be
seen.

APPROXIMATE LENGTH OF WALK Variable – about 1½
miles.

BEST TIME All year, but spring tides reveal the most
species.

LOCATION By Place Manor on the Porthcule River,
south of Truro. (204)856322.

From the jetty, go down onto the shore of the inlet and to
the sandy section in the middle. It is, in fact, an area of sand
and mud, the constitution of which varies somewhat from
year to year. However, the presence of lugworms (*Arenicola
marina*, see p. 230) can readily be seen by the wormcasts on
the surface of the sand.

A quiet, gentle approach to the shallow water of the
estuary at low spring tide will probably reveal the lovely
sight of a number of tube worms feeding. The head end,
which is surrounded by a rosette of flowerlike, filamentous,
beautifully coloured gills, protrudes from the surface of the
substrate, and can be seen if the approach has been quiet and
the creatures have not sensed any footfalls. Those likely to
be seen are the peacock worm (*Sabella pavonini*), which
constructs its tube of mucus and fine sand grains; *Myxicola
infundibulum*, whose tube is made of transparent jelly; and

the sand mason (*Lanice conchilega*), with a tube of fine shell fragments.

From the sandy inlet, move on to the area of solid rock on the right of the inlet and, further round, of boulders on a gravel and sand substrate. Here, the rocky shelves with damp overhangs provide a habitat for an enormously rich and varied fauna. Large areas of rock are covered with a dense incrustation of sponges such as *Sycon coronatum*, and with the purse sponge (*Grantia compressa*). There are also many other creatures on and under the rocky shelves. Anemones are there in plenty – including the common beadlet anemone (*Actinia equina*), and the very attractive plumose anemone (*Metridium senile*) which may be orange, salmon-pink, creamy-white or brown, and with a dense crown of tentacles which give it a 'feather duster' appearance.

The beautiful colonial star sea squirt (*Botryllus schlosseri*) can be found under some of the overhangs. This looks like a thin encrustation of jelly, in a range of delicate blues, oranges, yellows and greens, with starlike patterns on the surface. Sea squirts are primitive creatures consisting of little more than a bag-like body with one opening through which oxygen and food enters and another through which waste products are passed out. Much larger individual sea squirts with a body up to 10–12.5 cm (4–5 inches) long are also found here.

These sedentary species are browsed upon by a variety of other animals such as the sea lemon (*Archidoris pseudoargus*), which is a strange-looking sea slug with a ring of gills on its back. The much more attractive mollusc, the cowrie (*Trivia sp.*) is another predator.

Looking under the movable boulders is always tremendously enjoyable, and a whole host of animals can be found under those at Place. Small eels can be found beneath a great number of smaller rocks, as well as many specimens of the ragworm (*Nereis diversicolor*). A wealth of crustaceans is revealed, including a number of squat lobsters. The larger ones should be treated with respect, as they are quite prepared to use their formidable claws. They are, however, rather 'fun' creatures and, if disturbed, will suddenly straighten out the abdomen and then bend it again, so that it moves backwards at a remarkable rate. The crabs found may include the fiddler or velvet crab, which threatens by sitting on its tail and holding up its nippers. Also present are hairy porcelain crabs, which are well adapted to life on the shores, being flattened and able to attach themselves to the rock by walking legs which end in spines, thus preventing them from being washed away.

Hermit crabs are also present, and live, according to their size, in the shells of periwinkles or whelks. One of the crab's front legs is larger than the other, and this is used for closing off the entrance to the shell. Like any other creature, crabs grow, and because they have a hard carapace ('shell'), this has to be moulted to allow for the growth. This is a dangerous time for any crab, as the body underneath is soft and easy prey for predators. For the hermit crab, moulting often includes having to find a larger shell in which to live.

Some hermit crabs may be found with a sea anemone (*Calliactis parasitica*) living on their shell. This partnership is of mutual benefit, and is known as commensalism. The anemone, instead of having to stay in the same place as it would if attached to a rock, moves round with the crab, and thus has a wider area over which to feed. The crab benefits from the anemone, which, it is thought, offers it some protection by using the stinging cells on its tentacles against predators.

One of the most remarkable creatures found under the rocks on the lower shore is the bootlace worm, whose Latin name of *Lineus longissimus* is particularly apt. It is an immensely long, deep-red/brown-coloured, unjointed worm, which is usually found coiled up. Attempting to pick it up can be disastrous (for the worm!) as it tends to break, but it commonly measures over 4.5 m (15 feet) in length.

These are just some of the species found in this area, but it is by no means an exhaustive list. Moreover, as time spent on this shore is limited by the state of the tide, a move to the far side of the inlet is recommended.

Walk around the little headland and go down near low-water mark on the sandy shore. This is a good place to find razor shells (*Ensis spp.*). There are plenty of empty ones about, but the presence of the living animal is indicated by a little hollow in the sand with a small opening. It is possible to dig them out, but they can burrow down so quickly with their powerful muscular foot that this can be an unrewarding pastime. A much easier method of encouraging them to appear (which should not be over-done) is to place a little salt over the burrow. The animal is extremely sensitive to increased salinity, and within a matter of seconds the shell comes popping up above the surface of the sand.

Another burrowing creature is the heart or potato urchin (*Echinocardium causdatum*), which lives in a burrow lined by mucus. This cannot be extracted by the salt method; it can only be found by digging – and again, please do not dig up more than one. Offshore in this area is a large bed of eel-grass (*Zostera*). It is unique in this country in being a marine flowering plant. It has to be said that it tends to *look* a little like a grass, with its long, narrow leaves. The flowers are produced on special fertile branches, and do not look anything like an ordinary land flower. Both male and female flowers (which are on the same plant, but separate) are very much reduced, and are contained in a kind of sheath towards the base of the fertile branches. Neither has petals, and the female consists of just an ovary and two stigmas, while the male is just a single anther with two long filaments. When the flowers are released into the water they stay under the surface, where fertilization occurs.

Return to the car before the tide comes in too far!

Red Moor

SUMMARY A Cornwall Trust for Nature Conservation
reserve on what was formerly an open-cast mining
site. The mine left large holes and depressions, the
deeper of which have filled with water over the years
and become a series of nine ponds. The damp
depressions have developed into willow carr, and there
is a large area of heathland. The reserve is visually
unspectacular, but more than makes up for this by its
wide range of habitats within a comparatively small
area. There is a waymarked Nature Trail, sections of
which can be very wet, so waterproof footwear is
advisable.

APPROXIMATE LENGTH OF WALK 1¼ miles.

BEST TIMES Spring, summer.

LOCATION Turn off the B3268 Bodmin/Lostwithiel
road south of Lanhydrock House. Cars should be left
on a small triangle of land, ref. SX077624, to avoid
blocking the narrow Cornish lanes.

From the car, walk down the road marked 'No Through
Road' for about 100 yards to the reserve entrance on the
right, indicated by a notice board. Immediately on entering
the reserve, a broad pathway leads through a small, dense
woodland in which willows are the dominant species in the
wet ground on the right, and moss and lichen-encrusted
oaks, with some small hawthorn bushes, on drier ground on
the left. The relative poorness and acidity of the soil is
indicated by the stunted growth of the trees.

In the drier areas under the trees, bracken is growing, and
also some great woodrush (*Luzula sylvatica*). In spring,
primroses (*Primula vulgaris*) are present in considerable numbers. It is worth giving this common but delightful plant

more than just a passing glance. Examination shows that in almost every population there are two distinct kinds of plant. In one type, the flowers are 'pin-eyed', in which the stigma on the tip of the style is clearly visible at the entrance to the corolla tube. In the 'thrum-eyed' variety, it is the anthers which are visible, and the style only reaches half-way up the corolla tube. This is a device which helps to prevent self-pollination, and so ensures maximum seed-setting.

Post One of the Nature Trail is found a short distance along the path, and just at this point there are a number of common polypody ferns (*Polypodium vulgare*) growing on tree trunks. The character of the woodland has changed slightly, with more hazels appearing, and in spring bluebells (*Endymion non-scriptus*) are present. One of the more common woodland butterflies – the speckled wood – may be seen, its brown wings with white spots giving some degree of camouflage in the dappled sunlight coming through the trees. Surprisingly, these delicate creatures are highly territorial during courtship, and will attack other butterfly intruders on their patch and drive them away in an upwardly spiralling chase.

On the left is the open water of one of the ponds, which is a good place to see frogs and toads moving to the water to spawn in early spring. A careful look (the water is very deep!) may reveal the spawn – that of the toad being a double row of eggs in a long strand of jelly which is usually wound round the stems and leaves of water plants. This contrasts with the mats of spawn laid by frogs in the open water. Also near the pond is a willow with a good example of the grey-green beard lichen (*Usnea sp.*) growing on a bough.

By Post Two, the habitat has begun to change to heath-land, especially on the left, with gorse, cross-leaved heath

(*Erica tetralix*) and ling (*Calluna vulgaris*). Post Three follows almost immediately, and it is interesting that in the booklet describing the Nature Trail, the area on the left is described as 'almost bare ground left by ploughing . . . notice how quickly the Mosses, Lichens and Heathers have appeared . . .' Clearly, much more growth has taken place since that was written but, as the booklet notes, those mosses, lichens and heathers were the first stage in a succession of plant growth (see p.136) which occurs on bare ground, and they have been added to considerably by the next stage – with grasses, gorse and brambles. The final or climax stage of the succession, represented here by small hazel trees, is woodland. In this area, there may be summer migrant birds such as the grasshopper warbler (its presence signalled more often by its unique 'fishing reel' song than by an actual sighting), and the tree pipit.

A little further on, the path can be very muddy and wet, so a boardwalk has been provided. From this, it is easy to look down to the right into a very marshy area with willows, under which are growing many clumps of rushes and some patches of bog moss (*Sphagnum*). The single, straplike fronds of hart's-tongue ferns (*Phyllitis scolopendrium*) are also present, and on fallen boughs some examples of the blackish, flaccid fungus *Exidia glandulosa*.

On the right, a short distance along the path, a large expanse of open water is glimpsed through the trees on the right, and another, smaller one on the left. Around the fringes of the latter is a stand of common reed (*Phragmites australis*) and, in midsummer, the rather unusual-looking purple-red flowers of the marsh cinquefoil (*Potentilla palustris*). The plant with broad flat leaves lying on the surface of the water is pondweed (*Potamogeton*), and extending out into the pond is a good growth of common reedmace (*Typha latifolia*).

After just over a quarter of a mile, by a small shed at Post Five, turn off to the right and follow the track to a small picnic area. This is another place where frogs and toads may be seen. At the right-hand top of the picnic area a narrow track, which in spring is lined by greater stitchwort (*Stellaria holostea*), leads down to the largest pond (already glimpsed from the far side). On branches of the nearby gorse bushes is the bright orange jelly-fungus known as golden jelly, or, less attractively perhaps, as yellow brain fungus (*Tremella mesenterica*). Plants growing at the pond edge include water mint (*Mentha aquatica*) and the five-petalled yellow flowers and spearlike leaves of the lesser spearwort (*Ranunculus flammula*). There are newts in the pond, and they can sometimes be seen in the shallower water. Birds such as moorhens, coots and mallard may be seen or heard on the various ponds or in the fringing vegetation.

From the left-hand corner of the picnic area, follow the path across an area of bog. This is characterized by the presence of species of bog moss and, in the rather drier areas, clumps of hair moss (*Polytrichum*), as well as tussocks of purple moor-grass (*Molinia caerulea*) and varieties of rush.

Remain on the track, ignoring, for the time being, a sharp turn to the left, until Post Eight is reached, and, if suitably clad in waterproof footwear, continue a little way beyond this point, passing under a willow tree with common poly-pody fern on a bough overhanging the track. In this area the habitat changes once more – from bog to woodland, with small oak trees. A short walk leads to a little bridge over a narrow neck of the pond. There is a very nice example of the bright green *Thuidium tamariscinum* moss on the bank on the right, its delicate structure almost fern-like in appearance, although on a very small scale. There are a number of holly bushes among the oaks, and nest boxes have been provided to encourage such birds as tits.

Return to Post Eight, noting another area of tussocky purple moor-grass on the right, among which the purple-pink southern marsh orchid (*Dactylorhiza praetermissa*) is relatively common, and devil's-bit scabious (*Succisa pratensis*) is abundant. Patient watching in this area may be rewarded with the pleasure of seeing one of the Reserve's specialities – the nationally uncommon marsh fritillary butterfly. The fritillary caterpillar feeds on the scabious plant, and the butterflies themselves are on the wing during late May and early June. They have orange-red and yellow markings on a black background on the upper sides of the wings, with lighter markings on the undersides. Some fascinating facts have been discovered about this species. It has been found that when the young black caterpillars emerge from hibernation in a communal web and bask on its surface in the spring sunshine, absorbing the sun's energy, their internal temperature may rise up to 37°C. Even more remarkable, perhaps, is the discovery that the amount of damage done to the caterpillars by parasitic wasps varies according to how much sunshine there is, which in turn affects the sex ratio of the butterflies each season. Lack of sun leads to the pupae of the parasitic wasp hatching late in the spring – too late to attack many of the nearly fully grown caterpillars. However, female caterpillars take slightly longer than the males to develop, and this delay may result in them being attacked by the wasps, thus leading to the emergence of fewer female than male butterflies.

Before reaching the boardwalk leading back towards the picnic area, bear right, across a quite extensive expanse of moorland. The principal plants here are heathers and gorse on the right, and on the left where the land drops away and is much wetter, the heath which is typical of a wetter environment, the pale-pink, cross-leaved heath (*Erica tetralix*) with its diagnostic whorls of four leaves, together with patches of bog moss. On the right particularly, birds associated with open moorland, such as yellowhammers and linnets, may be seen – the yellowhammers conspicuous as they perch on the tops of trees or shrubs. After Post Nine another boardwalk leads, still across some moorland, to Post Ten. On the right of this is a small clump of stunted oak trees, under which is a group of large granite boulders. These can be reached (with a bit of a struggle due to an overgrowth of brambles and some tall moor-grass tussocks), and the lichen, *Parmelia caperata*, which grows both on the boulders and on the trees, can be examined.

Continuing along the path, there is a pond on the left – one of a series of three – which is covered with pondweed and duckweed (*Lemna spp.*), and fringed by reedmace and common reed. On the bank are some plants of the now comparatively rare royal fern (*Osmunda regalis*), whose fronds die down in winter leaving a distinctive mound of roots, rhizomes and dead frond bases, from which the new fronds shoot again in spring.

At Post Twelve, there is a memorial plaque to three founding members of the Cornwall Trust. Face away from the memorial, and instead of following the clearly defined path between two ponds, bear very slightly left and follow an ill-defined track (about twenty yards along which there is a Nature Trail sign) round the edge of the large pond to a clearance on the bank. From here, an excellent view is obtained of the extraordinary raft of plants which all but obscure the water of the pond. The large, reddish centre of the raft is bog cotton (*Eriophorum sp.*), easily recognized in summer by its white seed heads. In the foreground is a fine expanse of marsh horsetails (*Equisetum palustre*). Around the edge of the pond are the usual plants such as reeds and rushes, in which sedge warblers and reed buntings may be seen – and almost certainly heard.

Returning to the memorial plaque, rejoin the pathway and follow it over the bridge between the two ponds to Post Thirteen. There is a bracket fungus on a stump just before the bridge, and some beard lichen on the trees. The track leads across an area of mixed heathland and bog, and among the bog moss there are a number of the insectivorous sundew plants (*Drosera rotundifolia*).

As the pathway approaches the main track there is an interesting piece of ground on the right, where the furrows made by the old farming practice of cleaning the plough-shares in the underlying gravel are clearly visible beneath and between the heather that is beginning to grow.

Just after Post Fourteen a T-junction with a main track through the reserve is reached. Turn left on to this, and follow it between high gorse bushes to Post Fifteen. Some distance along, the path is flooded in all but the driest weather, and a boardwalk leads over it. On both sides is some willow carr, with beard lichen growing on some of the trees. Water mint and rushes may be seen in the marshy ground, and the clearing of trees on the left to encourage the growth of marsh plants has been rewarded with the appear-ance of gipsywort (*Lycopus europaeus*) and more southern marsh orchids. From this point follow the pathway back to Post Five and on to the gate.

Kilminorth Woods

SUMMARY An unusual combination (though less so in Cornwall) of woodland, flooded river valley and estuary. A really delightful walk with a good range of species. The area is managed by Caradon District Council, and is a conservation site of the Cornwall Trust for Nature Conservation. There are waymarked walks and information boards. The going is steep in places and muddy, but not very rough.

APPROXIMATE LENGTH OF WALK 2½ miles.

BEST TIMES Spring and summer.

LOCATION On the west bank of the West Looe River at Looe, Cornwall. (201)235538

From the car park walk up towards the wooded hill. The River Looe is below on the right, and a number of waders are usually present, including redshank, dunlin and oyster catcher, with some herring gulls and black-headed gulls, and one or two mute swans and herons.

Just below the woods are Woodland Walks signs; follow the metalled road along above the river to the first of the information boards. This explains that the reserve is a gently sloping, flooded river valley known as a rias. It also describes the opposite bank of the river, where the action of the salt of the estuarial water has made a very neat, straight edge to the tree line.

The nearby trees are mostly oak and birch, with a few polypody ferns (*Polypodium vulgare*) growing on them and on the bank on the left side of the road. Continue along the road, where the bank is covered with hard ferns (*Blechnum spicant*) and ivy. There are a number of beech trees on the right.

The main part of the walk starts behind a boat yard, where a very steep flight of steps leads up into the wood. Another information board explains about the practice of coppicing, which continued in these woods up to World War II. From the top of the steps follow the path, which for much of its length is flanked by moss-covered banks. ˙

Kilminorth is an excellent place in which to examine the four-layered structure of a natural woodland. These layers consist of the ground layer of mosses and fungi, the field layer of ferns and herbaceous plants, the shrub layer or understorey of, for instance, hazel, bramble, holly or haw-thorn, and finally the tree layer or canopy of mature trees. All four layers are present at Kilminorth, but not necessarily in every wood; even where they are all present, they may not be clearly defined. For example, in a beech wood the canopy is so dense when the trees are in leaf that little, if any, field layer is able to develop.

In this wood, the tree layer is principally sessile oak, but there are also ash, birch, sycamore, beech and a few Scots pine. The shrub layer or understorey is represented by hazel, holly, hawthorn, and some of the smaller birches. There is great variety in the field layer, with many species of herba-ceous plants and ferns. The ground layer, too, is well developed, with great carpets of mosses.

A short distance from the top of the steps the path divides; follow the one leading down the hill. The wood here is predominantly oak, and under it is a field layer of bilberry (*Vaccinium myrtillus*), bluebells (*Endymion non-scriptus*), dog's mercury (*Mercurialis perennis*) – almost invariably an indicator of old woodland – hard ferns, male and lady ferns (*Dryopteris filix-mas* and *Athyrium filix-femina*) and a profuse growth of great woodrush (*Luzula sylvatica*), while on the ground there are patches of the red-stemmed moss, *Rhytidiadelphus*. On the banks there are some beautiful examples of the fern-like moss, *Thuidium tamariscinum*. There is a lovely view of the river through the trees – at times it appears to be a glorious, deep green colour.

Continue steeply downhill until the next information board is reached. This gives some details of the non-flowering plants to be seen. On a number of the dead or dying birches, the birch polypore fungus can be seen. It forms a knob-shaped bracket, greyish-brown on top and white with pores underneath. This fungus is responsible for the death of the tree by sending threadlike hyphae through the cracks in the bark into the sapwood, causing it to rot. The greeny-yellowish scaly-looking lobed lichen *Parmelia caperata* grows on the trunks and boughs of many of the trees.

Where the path divides once again, ignore the blue-marked one which goes up the hill, and remain on the red one. Further along, as the path dips down towards the river, another information board is found. This gives details about the salt marsh which is visible except at high tide. If the tide is suitable, go down the little track on to the marsh – hart's-tongue fern (*Phyllitis scolopendrium*) is growing on the side of the steps, and there is some common scurvy grass (*Cochlearia officinalis*).

Take great care on the marsh, as there are some deep holes hidden under the vegetation. The various zones are clearly visible (see Cuckmere Haven, p. 97). The plants on this particular marsh include the green seaweed *Enteromorpha* at the bottom, followed by glasswort (*Salicornia sp.*), and annual seablite (*Suaeda maritima*). Towards the top is some thrift (*Armeria maritima*) and sea arrow-grass (*Triglochin maritima*), an indication that this part is covered by water for less than about fifty hours a year.

Return to the main path, where a few hundred yards along there is another information board by a road, describing the birds of the estuary. These include herring gull, kingfisher, curlew, redshank, heron and dunlin.

Go through the gate on to the road and turn left. The road winds up the hill between banks with hart's-tongue fern, mosses, dog's mercury, and some beech hedge. About a quarter of a mile along the road there is a sharp turn off to the left, signposted 'Woodland Walk, Picnic Area, Bridle-way'. Take that route, and note the mosses and ferns on the high bank on the right. Another notice gives information about the woodland birds, such as the blue and great tits, nuthatch, great spotted woodpecker, and jay, and the possibility of seeing or hearing a buzzard soaring over the tree tops.

This is another mixed woodland, with some beeches on the right, but it is a little drier and there are fewer ferns than in the previous one. A little further along, the track opens out into a clearing with some large rocks (and a litter bin), with wood sorrel (*Oxalis acetosella*) on the surrounding banks, and some more hard fern. Further on again, a board gives information about the animals and insects which might be seen. The mammals include the grey squirrel, wood mouse, bank vole, and the badger.

Between Posts Nine and Ten of the Trail keep an eye on the ground, where pieces of dead wood or bark coloured a bright blue-green may be seen. This is a sign of the presence of the fungus *Chlorospenium aeruginascens*, and the colour is given by the hyphae which invade the wood. Much more rarely, the small-stalked, cup-shaped fruiting bodies of the fungus are seen. Along this section there are a few foxgloves (*Digitalis purpurea*) and a thick growth of brambles.

About a mile from the start the track leads downhill, and

then quite sharply to the right and up a few steps. This section adjoins the ancient monument known as the Giant's Hedge. It is a linear earthwork which runs through the wood and consists of a high bank and ditch. Follow this along, and after about one and a quarter miles from the start, the three waymarked paths meet. In a few hundred yards there is a picnic area. Carry on past the litter bins and up the hill past another Giant's Hedge notice, and come to the final information board, describing the measures taken to conserve the oak woodland.

Turn left down the hill, and along the pathway note the presence of bilberry and some ling (*Calluna vulgaris*). The track leads down to the road and thence to the car park.

Dunsford Daffodil Walk

SUMMARY A delightful walk at almost any time of the year, but a real joy in spring when the wild daffodils, which are the outstanding feature of the reserve, are in flower. Managed by the Devon Trust for Nature Conservation.

APPROXIMATE LENGTH OF WALK 2 miles.

BEST TIMES Spring for the daffodils, but summer and autumn are also interesting.

LOCATION 8 miles west of Exeter on the B3212. SX 805883.

From the car park adjacent to the Steps Bridge Hotel turn left down the road past the hotel, over the bridge, and into the wood through the gate on the left.

The path leads beside the River Teign and through a mixed woodland of silver birch, oak and ash with holly and hazel understorey. The dominant feature at this point is the river, which is fringed by alder and hazel, with a most attractive view looking back towards the arch of the bridge. On the right, wall pennywort (*Umbilicus rupestris*) grows in crevices in the rock wall, while on the river bank the first of the wild daffodils (*Narcissus pseudonarcissus*) can be seen. On the far bank, in the grounds of the hotel, daffodils grow in great profusion and are a lovely sight.

Remain on the riverside pathway until it branches by a Devon Trust notice board. Take the left-hand path by the river, soon passing another notice which draws attention to the problems of erosion of the river bank and asks the public not to stray from the pathways. The track gradually diverges from the river, and on the left there is an area where the

Trust has reintroduced the practice of coppicing in an effort to increase the amount of light reaching the woodland floor, thereby encouraging the growth of more wild flowers. Some holly and bracken grow in among the trees, and the coppicing has certainly encouraged the daffodils, which carpet the ground in their hundreds, together with wood anemones (*Anemone nemorosa*). Where brambles have grown up among some grasses, chiffchaffs and willow warblers nest.

After about half a mile, the track converges with another and leads through a deep wooded gorge, made even more attractive in spring and early summer by a mass of bluebells (*Endymion/Hyacinthoides non-scriptus*). A variety of woodland birds frequent this area – blue and long-tailed tits, wrens and, from April until about July, a few pied flycatchers and redstarts. After another half mile, the path leads more directly away from the river and through a more open area, where coppicing has not been practised for some time. The lack of growth underneath the trees is obvious, as are the old trees which have died, fallen and decayed. Great spotted woodpeckers take advantage of some of the dead and dying trees which are still standing for nesting. On the woodland floor, the occasional wood-ant nest provides food for the birds. Here, too, the wood warbler may be seen or heard – recognizable by its yellow-green upper parts, white underside and yellow breast, but more especially by its lovely musical trill. On the right, up the side of the hill, the ground under the trees is a brilliant yellow carpet of daffodils, and the banks by the pathside are covered with bracken and with hart's-tongue fern (*Phyllitis scolopendrium*). The delicate clover-like leaves of wood sorrel (*Oxalis acetosella*) gradually unfold. Buzzards often wheel overhead – perhaps prospecting for a nesting site in the top of one of the taller trees.

Further along, the woodland becomes even more diverse,

with sycamore and an understorey which includes a few
specimens of alder buckthorn, spindle, wild cherry and crab
apple. At any point along the valley, the early-morning or
late-afternoon visitor may glimpse fallow deer. They feed
on the flood plain, where their footprints ('slots') are often
seen in the mud, but they spend much of their time high
above the valley in the woods.

After just over a mile the valley opens out into the river
flood plain, where small clusters of hazel, silver birch,
blackthorn and holly are set among grasslands and where
daffodils grow in even more profusion. Green woodpeckers
frequent the more open area, probing deeply for ants.

The river banks support many alders, whose cone-like
fruits are eagerly taken by siskin and redpoll in the winter.
A quiet and stealthy approach to the river may be rewarded
with the sight of small shoals of brown trout, or even the
much larger sea trout. For the entomologist the river can be
a real joy, with sometimes literally thousands of mayflies,
and a good population of damselflies, including the exquisite
demoiselle.

Wetland plants, too, are common. Early in the year marsh
marigolds (*Caltha palustris*) make a welcome splash of colour,
followed closely by the white flowers of the strongly smelling wild garlic (*Allium ursinum*), and later still by meadowsweet (*Filipendula ulmaria*), which in spite of its somewhat
umbel-like appearance is a member of the rose family.
Hemlock (*Conium maculatum*), water dropwort (*Oenanthe
sp.*), hemp agrimony (*Eupatorium cannabinum*) and Indian
balsam (*Impatiens glandulifera*) may also be seen.

The limit of the reserve is reached at the road, and the
return should be made along the outward path until a
signpost saying 'Public Bridleway' is reached, where the

upper track to the left may be followed to add variety to the walk. This passes through more mixed woodland of hazel, silver birch, oak and some beech, and eventually rejoins the path near the exit gate.

Dawlish Warren

SUMMARY A sand dune, beach and bird walk in a
marvellous reserve, culminating in a hide overlooking
one of the best bird estuaries in southern Britain.
Managed by Teignmouth District Council.

APPROXIMATE LENGTH OF WALK 3 miles.

BEST TIME All year, but particularly good for waders
and wildfowl in winter.

LOCATION Dawlish Warren, Devon. Car park
through the tunnel under the railway. SX981787.

From the car park walk through the beach huts to the reserve
visitor centre, which has interesting displays. At the end of
the beach huts, the wide open area behind the dunes is
known as Greenland Lake and was once a tidal lagoon, now
largely dried out. Fortunately, from a nature viewpoint, it
has been colonized by reed and scrub and supports an
exciting range of plants, one of which, the warren or sand
crocus (*Romulea columnae*), is found nowhere else in Britain.
Its tiny, bluish flowers grow among the short grass, and
bloom in April. Orchids are also a feature of this area, with
southern marsh orchids (*Dactylorhiza praetermissa*) flowering
in May and June. In early September or even late August
autumn lady's tresses (*Spiranthes spiralis*) blooms, with its
blue-green leaves and spirally twisted spike of inconspicuous
white flowers smelling of coconut. From June to September
the lovely yellow evening primrose (*Oenothera biennis*) makes
a colourful show.

On the far side of the lake area, away from the dunes,
thick scrub has grown up, and the wetter areas contain reed,
alder and sallow. Many small birds nest in this, or use it as

shelter during migration times. In the summer, resident dunnocks, wrens and blackbirds mingle with chiffchaffs, whitethroats, blackcaps and willow warblers. Reed and sedge warblers are quite common in the wettest area.

A good number of butterflies are on the wing, including the small copper, and migrant species such as red admiral, painted lady and clouded yellow. In late summer evenings, the strident, high-pitched sound of the great green bush cricket is heard. This is a striking, bright-green insect which lurks in thick, bushy vegetation or reeds. If disturbed, it is much more likely to run away than to fly or hop.

After investigating the lake area, climb up on to the marram-covered dunes which line the sandy shore. From this vantage point an enormous number of seabirds may be seen, according to the time of year. Cormorants and shags are always present, and large numbers of gannets pass by offshore. During the summer, many sandwich terns are present, while in winter common scoter, and, less frequently, velvet scoter may be spotted flying low over the water some distance out.

Go down on to the beach and walk along to the left. In winter, sanderlings are often seen, scuttling along the water's edge like little clockwork toys. After rough weather, a number of intriguing objects are always washed up, both here and further round towards the point. Shells are common – fan shells, cockles, razor shells, oyster shells, tower shells, and the occasional spiny cockle – while crab carapaces (usually of shore crabs, but sometimes of spider crabs), are also washed up. Jellyfish are frequently stranded, as are sea squirts, which look like shapeless blobs of greyish jelly. Autumn is the time for starfish, and the autumn gales also bring in some of the large seaweeds.

Return to the top of the dunes, and about three-quarters

of a mile from the car park the track leads inland, near to the golf course. Before long, a large hide comes into view ahead and to the left. In among the more stable dunes there are numerous yellow-flowered tree lupins (*Lupinus arboreus*), an introduced plant which has to be controlled, as it shades out the sand-stabilizing marram grass if left to spread.

After a short walk around a sandy bay, the two-storeyed hide is reached. Entering a hide and opening the flaps is always exciting, but this one is particularly so. It looks out over a huge sweep of sand, mudflats and salt marsh which in winter is a feeding ground for thousands and thousands of waders and wildfowl. It is an absolutely fabulous place at almost any time of the year. In summer, it is an excellent viewing post for terns; there is a large colony of breeding sandwich terns, while smaller numbers of little and common terns can also be seen, and the much rarer roseate and Arctic species are sometimes present. Dunlin are always in evidence, as are gulls, and enormous flocks of oystercatcher, whose total population numbers several thousand.

During autumn and winter, the variety is infinite. In addition to dunlin (with the possibility of seeing the little stint or curlew sandpiper among them), and oystercatchers, there are turnstone, knot, bar-tailed godwit, grey plover, a few greenshank, ringed plover, sanderling, curlew, redshank, and, on a few occasions, a black-tailed godwit. Coming and going all the time are enormous flocks of dark-bellied Brent geese, and in the deeper channels further out in the estuary red-breasted mergansers can be spotted. As the tide rises, the waders come closer and closer to the hide, and a really superb close-up view can often be had of all these marvellous birds.

Return to the car park along the same route.

Exmoor: Cloutsham

SUMMARY A circular walk, following a waymarked Nature Trail, which takes in many of the habitats of Exmoor. It is primarily woodland, but includes a section of open moorland, farmland and a stream, with a great variety of plant and animal life. There is a steep (but not rough) climb up the side of a coombe near the end of the walk.

APPROXIMATE LENGTH OF WALK 4 miles.

BEST TIMES Spring, summer.

LOCATION Starts at Webber's Post car park, on the main road over Dunkery Hill. SS902439.

From the car park at Webber's Post follow the Nature Trail signs down the road towards Cloutsham. There are splendid views of the moor from this section of road, with Exmoor's highest point, Dunkery Beacon, standing out on the horizon to the south. On the other side of the coombe, or valley, is Horner Wood. Bracken is thick on both sides of the road, with a mixture of gorse, heather and bilberry, and some yellow tormentil (*Potentilla erecta*) underneath. Further down, some oak trees grow by the roadside.

After a short distance a signpost leads off the road on the left to Cloutsham. Follow the narrow track up the hill through some more bracken, with a few silver birch trees. In among the bracken and at the path's edge the pale-yellow flowers of cow wheat (*Melampyrum pratense*) add colour to the scene from May to September. It is a semi-parasitic plant, attaching itself to the roots of grasses from which it obtains minerals and water.

As the path dips down the hill, an attractive little stream is met, its edges fringed with mosses and ferns, herb Robert (*Geranium robertianum*) and the yellow flowers of golden saxifrage (*Chrysosplenium oppositifolium*). As the path descends quite steeply into a valley, the surroundings become more wooded, with lichen-encrusted oaks, some rowan, and more silver birch. There are small holly bushes, and one or two very big holly trees. Polypody ferns (*Polypodium vulgare*) are growing on the branches of some of the oak trees.

Signpost Two of the Nature Trail is reached in this beautiful valley, down the sides of which a number of small streams wend their way. The valley floor is thick with hair moss (*Polytrichum sp.*) in places. There are also many hard ferns, some bracken, foxgloves (*Digitalis purpurea*), and rushes. In this area there are a number of dead and dying trees, many of which have been blown down in storms, unable to form deep roots in the shallow, stony soil. On the right, as the path climbs out of the valley again, there is a big bracket fungus on a tree trunk. The presence of many gnarled old oak trees indicates that this is ancient woodland, probably undisturbed for many centuries.

Follow the National Trust sign down the hill to the right, descending a very steep and stony track. Cross the stream, noting the delicate fern-like *Thuidium* moss growing on the banks. The valley becomes even more heavily wooded here, and the ground is covered in bracken and bilberry. Follow the track down to the road, turn left, and cross the footbridge over the ford, then go into the wood on the right of the road, where there are some huge pollarded oaks. Follow the road signposted to Dunkery Beacon, keeping an eye on the stream on the left, which could be a good place for dippers.

After a short distance, there is a sign on the right saying 'Cabinet Walks'; ignore it, stay on the road, noting the sallow, the ash on the stream side, and the foxgloves and herb Robert on the road and on the stone wall. There is a large picnic site on the left, and, shortly, a trail signpost up a very steep lane to the right – follow this. The track leads up towards Cloutsham Farm and was formerly used by horse-drawn carts. The lane is flanked by some hazel trees, and there is a large spreading holly tree on the left. Navelwort/wall pennywort (*Umbilicus rupestris*) is growing in the stone wall, and there is also some red campion (*Silene dioica*). At the top of the lane a tarmac road is reached; turn right, and in about twenty yards there is another Nature Trail sign, leading to a gate. Enter, turn right, and go through another gate into a field, from which there are splendid and extensive views down the heavily wooded coombes to the sea, and even, on a clear day, across the Bristol Channel to the Brecon Beacons in Wales.

Follow the bank along the field edge and through the gate at the end, into an area where there are some ornamental conifers which were planted in the nineteenth century. A seat has been placed under a Douglas fir, which is Post Five of the Nature Trail. Among the trees on the left slope of the hill are many hawthorn bushes, while on the right there are fewer hawthorns in an area of moorland with foxgloves, gorse, heath bedstraw (*Galium saxatile*) and sheep's sorrel (*Rumex acetosella*). Whinchats and stonechats frequent the moorland in the summer, and occasionally a ring ouzel may be seen. Yellowhammers are often present, using the gorse or hawthorn as a song post.

Follow the trail as it leads down the hill to the left through a dense, ancient oak woodland. Many of the trees are covered with honeysuckle and ivy. The latter is very much at home in the shade of the woodland, and it is not difficult to see that this climbing plant has two types of leaves. Those on flowerless stems usually have from three to five lobes, while those on stems which bear flowers are not lobed, although they may have a wavy edge. In some instances the bark of the honeysuckle has been stripped – mostly by mistle thrushes for building their nests. The trunks of some of the oaks also have large patches of the lobed, greyish lichen, *Parmelia caperata*. Lichens are unique plants in that they consist of two organisms – a fungus and an alga – living in a close association (symbiosis). The algal partner possesses the green pigment, chlorophyll, so is able to manufacture the food for the whole structure by means of photosynthesis; the fungus, which in almost all species forms the greater part of the lichen, produces the fruiting bodies, and in most cases protects the algal portion of the plant from heat, drought and excessive light.

In this and other parts of the walk, signs of the famous Exmoor red deer and of sheep may be present. The most obvious signs are footprints. Those of deer are known as slots, and are not always easy to distinguish from those of sheep, as both have cloven hoofs. However, the overall outline of a deer's hoof is rather rounder than that of a sheep, i.e. the line of the outer edge is curved more symmetrically towards the tip, whereas that of the sheep is more elongated, with a flatter outside edge, giving a nearly rectangular outline. In really clear marks, the round pads under the heels on the deer's feet can be seen; these are lacking in the sheep. Size can be a help, as the slot of a fully grown stag may be up to 10 cm (4 inches) long and 9 cm (3½ inches) wide, while that of a sheep is rarely more than about 5 cm (2 inches) long and 4 cm (1½ inches) wide.

As the path descends the hill through the wood, with an increasing number of ferns (male ferns in particular) among the trees, and mosses (principally hair moss) by the trackside, the sound of rushing water is heard, and becomes louder and louder until a wide, boulder-strewn stream comes into view. Keep to the left at the bottom of the hill towards the ford (this should be Post Six, but the number was missing when I was there). There is a ford ahead, and a footbridge which initially is hidden from view among the trees. Cross the bridge, and follow the pathway to the left, downstream through the lovely wooded coombe – an enchanting place. The stream is well-known for dippers and grey wagtails, while woodland species include redstarts, wood warblers and the two spotted woodpeckers. In the coarse grasses by the side of the track there are many plants of common sorrel.

This is one of the best places on Exmoor for deer, although it requires considerable stalking skill actually to see them. However, on the right of the pathway (Post Seven) there is a very wet, boggy area where signs of the animals are frequently seen. It is a favourite wallow, where both stags and hinds come in spring to wallow in the mud when their winter coats are irritating them. In the autumn the area is used by stags at the time of the rut (mating season) when the heavy manes they have grown become soaked with the mud. When using the wallow, a deer almost always urinates into it, then stirs it up with hoof or antlers before lying in it and rolling, first on one side and then on the other. It then rubs its head and neck on the side. As can be imagined, the smell is strong, and unattractive to all but other red deer!

From the wallow, continue along the bottom of the coombe to the next footbridge where, in a delightful little glade, grey wagtails and dippers may be seen, in and around the stream. Return to the Trail sign by the wallow, which points up the hill. The path climbs quite gently to the right, passing a number of coppiced oaks with holly and bracken underneath. In the more open areas a certain amount of gorse is growing. At a signpost to Webber's Cross, turn very sharply right on to what is known as Tucker's Path (named after the huntsman of the Devon and Somerset Staghounds in the early years of this century). This path zigzags steeply upwards through bracken and gorse, with some foxgloves, and a few small specimens of rowan and holly. At the top there is a seat at a T-junction. Turn right, and then take the left-hand fork which leads through a plantation of mixed-age Scots pine (the seeds for the younger trees having come from the older) and birch, with bracken, cow wheat, grasses, bilberry, some ling (*Calluna vulgaris*), and foxgloves growing underneath. Further along on the right is a typical forestry plantation of pine – all the same age, planted in rows so close together that no light can penetrate, hence there is little or no vegetation underneath. Stay on this pathway until the Webber's Post car park is reached.

Exminster Marshes

SUMMARY A longish walk, first along the sea wall from Powderham Church to Turf Lock Hotel, then across the Exminster Marshes and back via the Exeter ship canal bank. A varied route, with a host of birds and, in spring and summer, many interesting water plants.

APPROXIMATE LENGTH OF WALK 8 miles.

BEST TIME All year.

LOCATION Park by Powderham Church, off the A379 a mile south of Exminster. (192)973844

From Powderham Church, cross the road and go through the gate to follow the path beside the railway line. On a high tide the fields on the left are likely to be a mass of waders – oystercatcher, lapwing, curlew, godwit, redshank, snipe and a few dunlin. After a couple of hundred yards, cross the railway line at the marked crossing (with great care, as this is a main line) and continue along the top of the sea wall. Look out into the estuary, especially at low tide, for more waders, notably ringed plover and dunlin, and various wildfowl, including mallard, teal, and shoveler. In winter flocks of Brent geese can almost always be seen.

This can be a tremendously exciting section of the walk, with flocks of waders getting up from the mud flats or the fields and flying low over the sea wall. Similarly, the Brents can suddenly take to the air and stream up or down the estuary, honking as they go – a wonderful sight and sound. Do not be surprised, either, if a seal's head appears in one of the channels – they are quite common winter visitors. Around the sea wall itself some small birds might be seen –

reed buntings are not unusual, and meadow and rock pipits sometimes forage on the shore. From November until early March the lucky walker may just see the real speciality of the Exe Estuary, the wintering flock of avocet. Their favourite haunt is in the channels near Topsham on the opposite side of the estuary, but sometimes they feed near the Turf Lodge Hotel, which is about two miles from the start of the walk.

Go down on to the road at the left of the hotel, cross the stile and walk diagonally across the field towards the railway. Once, most of the fields through which the walk goes were real marshes, but they have been drained, and are now probably more accurately described as grazing water meadows. Many meadow plants have been lost, but there is still much of interest in and around the channels and drainage ditches, and the meadows still attract many birds.

Keep to the right of a small stand of trees, in which buzzards often sit, and go towards the gate and stile into the next field. Snipe are likely to get up anywhere in this area, as it is very wet, and their erratic darting flight and short alarm call are easily recognized. Head across the field towards some iron railings on a little bridge which crosses a small stream. In this stream and in any of the waterways ahead there are plenty of plants to see in spring and summer, and, of course, where there is water there is the possibility of dragonflies and damselflies – indeed, the meadows support nearly twenty species. The dragonflies most likely to be seen are the large, green southern aeshna, while the common blue and the azure damselflies are both present.

The wetland and water plants include water dropwort (*Oenanthe sp.*), and the floating frogbit (*Hydrocharis morsus-ranae*). The latter has leaves like miniature water lilies, with a diameter of about 2.5 cm (1 inch), and the flower, which is about the same size, has three white crinkly petals with a yellow spot near the base of each. Although the plant does not root on the bottom, it spends the winter on the bottom as a detached bud.

Also likely to be seen on the water's edge in the marshes is the very handsome flowering rush (*Butomus umbellatus*), which has an umbel of rose-pink flowers, each flower about 2.5 cm (1 inch) across. It is tall (up to 1.2 m (4 feet)) with stout, grass-like leaves.

Having crossed the little bridge, keep to the right of the stream and parallel to the railway until the next stile, which leads into another field; cross this, and by means of another stile and a gateway enter a vehicular grassy track. A few reeds grow by the fence on the left, and reed buntings can occasionally be seen. Come to a white wooden gate, turn right and walk about 100 yards to a lane; follow it down past an industrial complex (Devon Transport) until quite a broad expanse of water leading into a ditch is seen on the left. Cross the reed-filled ditch into the field by means of a single plank bridge with an iron railing.

A great many birds may be seen in these water meadows, depending on the time of the year. During the autumn and winter almost any of the estuary birds may use the meadows as a high-tide roost. Redwings and field-fares spend much time in the hedgerows between the fields, feeding on the hawthorn and other berries, while, much more rarely, a ruff or a golden plover may be spotted. Midwinter is a rewarding time, when common and green sandpipers may be seen in some of the ditches, and perhaps a jack snipe. The real excitement of the area occurs with the arrival of exceptionally cold weather, when Bewick's swans often put in an appearance and some white-fronted geese may also be seen. With all these birds present, hen harriers and short-eared owls are sometimes about, and peregrines and sparrowhawks are always a possibility too. Keep on through the marshy fields, crossing several small bridges, until a stile is reached, and a pathway leads up on to the canal towpath.

In spring, house martins (of which there is a breeding colony at the Turf Lodge Hotel), swallows and sand martins arrive, and in late April or early May, migrating whimbrel are almost always seen somewhere in the area. Yellow wagtails arrive in about April, to join the resident greys.

Once up on the towpath, turn right back towards the Turf Lodge Hotel. The fringing reed of the canal is a good place to see reed and sedge warblers, both of which breed here, as do moorhen and coot. Continue on past the hotel and back along the sea wall to Powderham Church.

Kimmeridge Bay

SUMMARY A rocky shore, rich in species, and part of the Purbeck (Dorset) marine wildlife reserve. Of some geological interest. (NB The cliffs are very dangerous, with constant rock and shale falls, and should not be approached.)

APPROXIMATE LENGTH OF WALK 1 mile.

BEST TIMES Plenty to see throughout the year; low spring tides are most rewarding.

LOCATION Near the village of Kimmeridge on the Isle of Purbeck in Dorset. SY909788.

From the western (right-hand) end of the cliff-top car park, steps lead down to the shore, which at this point consists of boulders and dark sand with large banks of strand-line seaweeds. About fifty to sixty yards west along the beach the widest and longest of a number of flat, cement-stone ledges reaches out into Kimmeridge Bay at right angles to the shore. Over 100 yards of this are uncovered on a good low tide, and a walk along the ledge reveals a wealth of marine species.

Seaweeds are present in abundance, and the wracks in particular demonstrate how seaweeds grow typically in more or less clearly defined zones on a rocky shore. Highest of all on the shore, and not very plentiful at Kimmeridge, is the channelled wrack (*Pelvetia canaliculata*). As it is highest on the shore it is exposed to the air for long periods, and has several features which enable it to resist desiccation. For instance, it has a high oil content and, when compared with the wracks further down the shore, its fronds are smaller and shorter, exposing less surface area to the drying atmosphere.

As can be seen, it is often dry and black, with its fronds curled inwards to form the channel from which comes its common name. This curling also helps to prevent water loss (note that the channelled side is almost always facing downwards), but even so, the species may lose up to sixty-five per cent of its water content during the long exposure of neap tides.

Immediately below, and sometimes intermingling with the channelled wrack, is a small band of flat wrack (*Fucus spiralis*). This plant is usually slightly longer than channelled wrack and, although it lies flat on the rock, if picked up it tends to twist, hence the name *spiralis*. It, too, can resist desiccation, but rather less successfully than channelled wrack.

Much more conspicuous as one walks out along the ledge is the zone of bladder wrack (*Fucus vesiculosus*), with its twinned bladders, one either side of the midribs on the fronds. This seaweed grows on both the horizontal and vertical surfaces of the rock. The bladders give it great buoyancy, enabling it to float very near the surface, and thus exposing it as much as possible to the light required for the food-manufacturing mechanism (photosynthesis) to proceed. Bladder wrack is stronger than either channelled or flat wrack, and is able to survive in the rougher waters of the lower shore.

Abundant in the shallow pools further down the shore and in the shallow water on either side of the ledge is an extensive zone of serrated or toothed wrack (*Fucus serratus*). It, too, is very strong, and is adapted to live in the lower light intensity of the deeper water – but like bladder wrack it cannot survive desiccation.

In the pools about halfway along the ledge the green seaweeds put in an appearance. The locally common *Codium tomentosum* is an attractive plant, with its branched fronds which are circular in cross-section, and feel spongy and felt-like to the touch. Moving aside the serrated wrack sometimes reveals the very dark green filamentous tufts of *Cladophora*, and, further away from the shore (and also under the serrated wrack) may be seen the pink and deep-mauve patches of the encrusting seaweeds, *Lithothamnium* and *Lithopyhylum*. The hard, chalky layers of these two plants give the appearance of being part of the rock itself. Some of the more distant pools are lined with the beautiful red-to-pink tufts of coral weed (*Corallina officinalis*), with its characteristic chalky skeleton. Also in some of the pools is the distinctive, much-branched, light-brown rainbow bladder weed (*Cystoceira tamariscifolia*), the tips of many of the fronds showing a brilliant, blue-green iridescence under the water.

On either side of the ledge in the deeper water are some of the larger brown seaweeds or kelps which are rarely, if ever, fully exposed to the air, even at low spring tides. Principal among those at Kimmeridge is the oarweed (*Laminaria digitata*), easily recognized by the much-branched and tangled holdfast which attaches it to the rock. From the holdfast, a smooth, flexible, cylindrical 'stem' or stipe leads to the broad frond which is divided into a number of ribbonlike blades. Also present, but further down the ledge, is the very similar *Laminaria hyperborea*, distinguished from oarweed by its rough, stiff stipe, and more fan-shaped frond. Another large weed is furbellows (*Saccharina polyschides*), which has a massive, hollow, knobbly holdfast, and a broad, frilly-edged stipe leading to a much-divided frond.

Attached to rocks, and swaying gently with the movement of the water, are the thin, unbranched fronds of bootlace weed or mermaid's tresses (*Chorda filum*), while the undivided broad, crinkly fronds of sugar kelp (*Laminaria saccharina*) lie over the submerged rocks. The protrusion of the ledge far out into the bay affords a delightful and quite rare glimpse of these larger seaweeds actually growing in their habitat, rather than washed up and dried on the shore.

There are, of course, a number of marine animals to be seen on the ledge. Throughout its length, on both horizontal and vertical surfaces, the common limpet is present in some numbers, while on and among the wracks (particularly the serrated wrack) flat periwinkles (*Littorina littoralis*) are present. They come in a variety of colours – orange, olive green, red, black, and yellow – the latter two being the most usual at Kimmeridge. On the fronds of channelled wrack (and others) are the tiny, white spiral tubes of various species of tube worm (*Spirobus spp.*).

Red beadlet sea anemones (*Actinia equina*) are relatively common in the pools, on vertical rock surfaces just above low-tide mark, and in the shallow waters either side of the ledge. Remaining covered by water are the very lovely, delicately coloured snakelocks anemones (*Anemonia sulcata*), with their mauve-tipped, pale-green tentacles. In spite of their static and plant-like appearance, anemones are predatory animals, and it is not uncommon to see a shrimp or a limpet trapped within the tentacles.

Crabs, too, are present. In the pools, lurking among the seaweed or under small boulders, are the green shore crabs, while in the open water the deep-red swimming crabs hide among the kelps or scuttle under the boulders.

Return to the shore and continue westwards towards the point, where a wide shelf of flat rock jutting out from the base of the cliff contains some rock pools in which are various small brown seaweeds, limpets, periwinkles, and beadlet anemones. Those pools highest on the shore contain the delicate, bright-green fronds of the seaweed *Enteromorpha*, each frond being a hollow, flattened tube.

Some 100 yards further on, down near the low-water level, is an area of loose, weed-covered boulders, interspersed with stratified rock. Among the weeds is a certain amount of knotted wrack (*Ascophyllum nodosum*) – its presence a sure indication that this area of the shore is sheltered. A very rewarding, and indeed exciting, time for the marine enthusiast may be spent in this area, turning over some of the boulders where a variety of species can be found. (Please remember to replace the boulders, so as not to destroy the animals' habitat.) Crustaceans are the most obvious and, as each rock is turned over, dozens of little, shrimp-like creatures, which move almost too quickly for identification, disappear rapidly under weeds or into the sandy substrate. Easier to recognize are the crabs, most of which are common shore species, but there is also the occasional edible crab, and the greyish, broad-clawed porcelain crab whose wide, flattened nippers and rough shell edge bear short, stiff hairs. A careful search may reveal a hermit crab (see p. 17) in a winkle or whelk shell.

On the under-surface of boulders near the low-tide mark, the searcher may be lucky enough to find some of the beautiful and colourful colonial sea squirts (star ascidians), which look just like a thin layer of jelly with star-shaped patterning on the surface (see p. 16). Small starfish (*Asterias rubens*) may also be found, and the closely related brittle-star (*Ophiothrix fragilis*), instantly recognizable by its well-defined central disc, from which radiate long, extremely mobile arms (which may be shed if the animal is handled).

In this part of the bay it is quite easy to see the characteristic zoning of the various species of periwinkle – each species being adapted to the zone in which it lives. A short walk to just below the cliff (not too close) and a careful search in the

area just above the splash zone will reveal the small periwinkle (*Littorina neritoides*) nestling in rock crevices. Further
down the shore, the slightly larger rough periwinkle (*Littorina saxatilis*) is also found in crevices and among any seaweed
that has been washed on to the upper shore. Further down
again, and often under boulders, the still-larger edible periwinkle (*Littorina littorea*) lives, while, as has been seen on the
ledge, the flat periwinkle is found in considerable numbers
among the wracks of the middle and lower shore.

Along the rock-strewn shore below the widening layer of
flat rock that extends from the foot of the cliffs, more rock
pools are found, with seaweeds which have already been
seen on the ledge but with increasing occurrence of *Codium*.
At very low spring tides it is well worth walking right out
as far as possible to the most distant exposed rocks of the
point, where the big *Laminarian* seaweeds are just showing
above the surface of the sea. Here, one of the most exquisite
animals of the shore can be found on the fronds, stipes or
holdfasts of the kelps – the blue-rayed limpet (*Patella lucida*).
This small mollusc is really beautiful, with lines of iridescent
blue spots running the length of its shell.

Returning to the upper shore of the point, on the flat rock
extending from the cliff base, extensive pools are found.
Here, in addition to coral weed and the encrusting seaweeds,
there are, unfortunately, large quantities of the foreign
invader, Japanese seaweed (*Sargassum muticum*), which is
spreading along the south coast and threatening native
marine plants such as eel-grass (*Zostera spp.*). It is a much-
branched brown seaweed up to 2.4 m (8 feet) in length, with
very small leaf-like fronds and small, spherical, stalked air
bladders. There are also masses of the delicate, fan-shaped
brown weed, peacock's tail (*Padina pavonica*).

Returning along the shore line towards the car park, do

take the opportunity of looking at the geological and botanical points of interest on the cliffs. The cliffs consist of shale with prominent horizontal bands of limestone, and together they are known as the Kimmeridge Clays. These cliffs are also famous for their fossils, including ammonites and the remains of univalve molluscs, but it is *very* dangerous to attempt to dislodge pieces of the cliff in search of them. Growing on the cliff face during spring and summer are maritime plants such as thrift (*Armeria maritima*), the relatively uncommon sea kale (*Crambe maritima*), and sea campion (*Silene maritima*).

The walk concludes at the steps back to the car park.

Studland Heath

SUMMARY A beach, sand dune and heathland walk
with a wealth of wild life, and the opportunity to see
how successive ridges of the dunes have developed
over the centuries. A National Nature Reserve.

APPROXIMATE LENGTH OF WALK 1½ miles.

BEST TIMES Spring and summer for general interest,
winter for waders and wildfowl.

LOCATION Near Studland village, Isle of Purbeck,
Dorset. SZ034836.

The car park, set among the dunes, has been covered with
chalk, thus restricting the growth of acid-loving plants such
as heather. A plant introduction, which can be seen in the
vicinity of the pillbox by the car park entrance, is pirri-pirri
(*Acaena anserinifolia*), a New Zealand bur-bearing plant
which came into Britain on wool waste, formerly used as a
manure. It spreads rapidly, and needs controlling, as young
birds can be covered with the burs and eventually die.

From the car park, walk along a wide track beside the
woodland and parallel with the shore for a little way. The
woodland is a mixture of silver and downy birch, with some
sallow in the wetter parts. Along the edges the circular leaves
of marsh pennywort (*Hydrocotyle vulgaris*) can be seen, also
some wild parsnip (*Pastinaca sativa*) and sharp-flowered rush
(*Juncus acutiflorus*) – the sharp points of the flowers are easy
to see. Butterflies, such as gatekeepers and silver-washed
fritillaries may be seen along this woodland edge, as may the
common blue and emerald damselflies and sympetrium
dragonfly.

Follow one of the tracks down to the beach at Studland

Bay. The small, white chalk stack off the headland to the right is known as Old Harry's Wife and, after walking along to the left, the much larger and more famous stack, Old Harry, comes into view further inshore.

A number of shells can be found along the beach, the most interesting of which is the uncommon Pandora shell. This occurs in just two other places – Weymouth and the Channel Islands – and it is an oval bivalve with one end slightly elongated, about 2.5 cm (1 inch) long, with one flat and one convex valve. Other shells to be found include three species of razor shells, Chinaman's hat, oyster, cockle, variegated scallop, keyhole limpet, sting winkle, and an occasional cowrie. Seaweed is also washed up, including the Japanese seaweed, an introduced species which is believed to have come to this country on the hulls of ships (see Kimmeridge, p. 54) and, starting at Bembridge on the Isle of Wight, has spread alarmingly along the south coast, to the detriment of other weeds.

Offshore, various birds may be seen, including cormorants, herring and black-headed gulls, and, during the summer, terns. In winter, black-necked, Slavonian and great crested grebes and mergansers are all seen from time to time, and, more rarely, common scoter and eiders.

After about 300 yards or so, a yellow-topped post is seen at the top of the beach. This marks the start of the Sand Dunes Trail, which this walk follows. Go up through the fore dunes, where the vegetation nearest to the beach is sea lyme grass (*Elymus arenarius*), with its broad, grey-green leaves, and the smaller, narrow-leaved sand couch grass (*Agropyron junceiforme/Elymus farctus*). Both these plants are able to withstand a certain amount of immersion by the sea at high tides.

Further up into the dunes, the familiar marram grass

(*Ammophila arenaria*), which does not like immersion in salt water, plays its important role of 'fixing' the sand, i.e. helping to prevent it blowing away. Among the marram a few other plants grow, including some rather poor specimens of devil's-bit scabious (*Succisa pratensis*), hawkbit (*Leontodon taraxacoides*), the very attractive sea bindweed (*Calystegia soldanella*) with its pink and white flowers, and cat's-ear (*Hypochoeris radicata*). Several small creatures may be seen in this area, including three species of cockroach, and field grasshoppers, whose pale coloration acts as camouflage in the sandy surroundings.

The fore dunes are backed by a more continuous dune ridge, called Zero Ridge. This has developed over the last fifty to sixty years, as a result of wind-blown sand collecting around obstructions such as plants and gradually forming smaller, then larger dunes. Near the top of Zero Ridge is Post One of the Trail, and behind the ridge is a valley, or dune slack, known as Zero Slack. It is damp, as can be seen by the growth of moisture-loving vegetation such as sallow and alder, cross-leaved heath (*Erica tetralix*), a few plants of ling (*Calluna vulgaris*), rushes, and in summer, a great many sundews (*Drosera rotundifolia*). There is also a certain amount of gorse, and a few Scots pines and birches.

The Studland dunes are excellent places for observing the succession from dunes through dune heathland to woodland. Already on this walk, the beginnings of change can be seen, with the gradual replacement of marram by heather, ling and other plants (see Ynyslas, p. 236).

Follow the pathways up the other side of the slack towards the next ridge, known as First Ridge, and Point Two of the Trail. Although there is still a certain amount of marram and sand couch, ling is the dominant ground cover, and a few areas of bell heather (*Erica cinerea*) indicate a drier soil. Mosses and lichens grow quite profusely on the ground in between the larger plants. A further indication of the change towards heathland is the presence in summer of grayling butterflies, a species limited to heaths and moors. Although this brownish-speckled butterfly is relatively easy to see in flight, it has a habit, when resting, of settling on the ground with its wings closed and tipped to one side towards the sun, so that it throws little shadow and merges into the background.

Post Three is on First Ridge crest. Studland is especially important because it is one of the few places where all six British reptiles are present: the smooth and grass snakes, adder, common and sand lizard, and the slow worm. On top of this ridge is a favourite 'sunning' area for the very rare (and protected) sand lizard, and for the much more frequently seen common lizard. Both male and female sand lizards are very heavily spotted, and in the breeding season the males are a striking bright green.

Follow the path down into the next dune slack, which, as is quite obvious, is much damper than the previous one, and contains a number of pools. Post Four is by one of these. They are World War II bomb craters (the area was used for rehearsing the Normandy landings) and they now provide a rich habitat for all kinds of water wildlife. Trees are much more firmly established in this slack – mostly birch and sallow, with the odd Scots pine. There is a great deal of gorse, and much more cross-leaved heath. A few World War II pillboxes have broken up, and provide a habitat for lime-loving plants such as centaury (*Centaurium erythraea*) and hare's-foot clover (*Trifolium arvense*).

Many of the pools are surrounded by bog myrtle (*Myrica gale*) (see Harbottle Crags, p. 184), under and between which are tussocks of purple moor-grass (*Molinia caerulea*). This grass provides nesting sites for harvest mice. At various places near pools can be seen the very handsome royal fern, which is now scarce countrywide, largely due to the early collectors. It is the largest British fern, and has distinctive fertile fronds which are spore-covered and turn a rich brown in late summer.

The pools themselves contain palmate newts and ten-spine sticklebacks. Most also have a very interesting water plant, the great bladderwort (*Utricularia neglecta*). This is a rootless, insectivorous plant, which collects around the water's edge in summer. It has bushy, divided, underwater leaves bearing many bladders which trap small insects and crustaceans. The plant is able to 'digest' these creatures as part of its diet. The presence of the pools ensures that dragonflies and damselflies are present in some numbers, including the black sympetra and some rare ishneid dragonflies.

Follow the track along to the left towards Post Five – an area known as the Marsh Tip. It is noticeable that the ground becomes drier at this end of the slack, and that by the time the marker post is reached, cross-leaved heath has become quite scarce, and indeed, does not grow very much further along this track. On the way, examine some of the ling plants closely; some of them will be seen to have what appears to be red cotton wound anti-clockwise round their stems. This is common dodder (*Cuscuta epithymum*), a leafless parasitic plant that bears tiny, waxy, pinky-white flowers in summer. It is attached to the ling by suckers through which it obtains nourishment from the host. By Post Five there is a birch tree with an example of royal fern under it.

Bear right here, and walk up to Post Six on the top of Inner Ridge. This ridge was formed during the eighteenth century and, looking back towards the sea, it is remarkable just how much of a dune system has been built up in the intervening years. Facing away from the sea, look for glimpses of water through the trees ahead, and, leaving the Trail, make towards them. They are part of a large area of what is now the freshwater lake known as Little Sea. This too, has undergone changes over the years. In the seventeenth century it was part of Studland Bay, but with the formation of the dune system an area of water was cut off from the sea. Streams that run off the heath changed the water from salt to fresh, and Little Sea now offers a winter habitat for a marvellous collection of birds. These include pintail, pochard, tufted duck, wigeon, shoveler, teal, Canada goose, and mallard. The alder carr surrounding the southern part of Little Sea shelters reed warblers, buntings and water rail. Fringing plants include yellow iris (*Iris pseudacorus*), bogbean (*Menyanthes trifoliata*), water mint (*Mentha aquatica*), and greater reedmace (*Typha latifolia*), with pondweeds (*Potamogeton spp.*) on the surface near the shore, while shoreweed (*Littorella uniflora*) and small quillwort (*Isoetes lacustris*) grow under the surface.

After wandering around the edges of the lake, return to Inner Ridge and continue back towards the car park to Post Seven, which marks the end of the Trail.

Cheddar Gorge

SUMMARY This is really three walks in one, but as the first leads to the other two they can be taken as one long walk or three shorter ones. They range through rough limestone grassland, deciduous and coniferous woodland, scree, river valley and scrub. Somerset Trust for Nature Conservation reserves.

APPROXIMATE LENGTH OF WALK 6 miles when taken as one walk.

BEST TIMES Spring, summer.

LOCATION Just outside the town of Cheddar on the B3135. ST485545.

Go over the stile at Black Rock Gate into the woodland of beech, hazel and oak which clothes the steep sides of the valley. On the left is a stone wall with herb Robert (*Geranium robertianum*), wall pepper/stonecrop (*Sedum acre*) and wall or maidenhair spleenwort fern (*Asplenium trichomanes*) growing on it, both here and further along its length, while yellow archangel (*Galeobdolon luteum*) and some wild garlic/ramsons (*Allium ursinum*) can be seen beside it. A Somerset Trust for Nature Conservation board gives information about the reserve, and a holder may contain some guides. Further along is some scrub, with hawthorn, blackthorn and buckthorn – the latter is the food source of the yellow brimstone butterfly caterpillar. Along the side of the drive celandine (*Ranunculus ficaria*), cuckoo pint (*Arum maculatum*, see p. 79) and bluebells (*Endymion non-scriptus*) can be found.

Go through the next gate or over the stile beside it; if using the gate, ensure that it is closed, as there are sheep grazing on the reserve.

Flowering plants by the trackside include dog violets (*Viola riviniana*) and there is common polypody fern (*Polypodium vulgare*) growing out of the wall. By the side of the track there is an old lime kiln on the left and a small stand of larches on the right. Almost immediately after the kiln, turn left up into the old quarry – take care here, as the rock is not stable. The limestone strata of the rock are clearly visible, and it can be seen how rainwater will run away easily, down into the underground streams and rivers, thus ensuring that the valleys are almost always dry, except after really torrential rain. For the first time, it is possible to see just how steepsided the valley really is. In the quarry there are a few hawthorn shrubs, hart's-tongue fern (*Phyllitis scolopendrium*), hazel, early forget-me-not (*Myosotis ramosissima*), and some hairy rockcress (*Arabis hirsuta*) among the rocks.

Rejoin the main path, passing a cattle trough on the right. Shortly after that there is a stone stile, also on the right, with a sign 'Black Rock Nature Reserve' pointing up the hill. For those who want a shorter walk, this sign should be followed; a description of that section of the reserve is included on page 67, marked ★.

One of the most interesting areas of the walk is the steep hillside opposite that stile, which is rich in limestone plants. Among them are rock-rose (*Helianthemum chamaecistus*), quaking grass (*Briza media*), spring cinquefoil (*Potentilla tabernaemontani*) devil's-bit scabious (*Succisa pratensis*), and salad burnet (*Poterium sanguisorba* or *Sanguisorba minor*). After inspecting the hillside, return to the path and continue until a five-barred wooden gate into a field is seen on the right, and just beyond it a stile over the stone wall. This leads into the Velvet Bottom Reserve, which can also be taken as a separate walk, and it, too, will be described later (p. 65), marked #.

Continue along in the original direction, noting the dog violets and the wild strawberry (*Fragaria vesca*) on the bank. After about three hundred yards there is a wood and metal gate with a stile beside it, leading into Long Wood. On the left, just before the gate, is a piece of rough grassland with dozens of early purple orchids (*Orchis mascula*).

After entering the wood, bear right over another stile by the Long Wood reserve notice, and follow the Nature Trail sign up the hill. The woodland is a mixed one, and dates back to at least the thirteenth century. It has within its boundaries a fine range of trees, including hazel, ash, oak, sycamore, field maple and beech, with an equally varied understorey, including spindle, dogwood, elder, blackthorn and hawthorn. As will be noticed, the beech trees are, on the whole, poor specimens, and are the remains of those planted in the 1950s. The crop failed, and is now being replaced by the other species mentioned. The field layer is quite rich here, with bluebells, celandine and wild garlic. After a little way, steps have been provided to assist the steep ascent.

At Post Two of the Nature Trail turn left, and keep on through the woodland. In this area, bluebells and red campion (*Silene dioica*) grow, and also the parasitic toothwort (*Lathraea squamaria*), an unusual-looking plant with no green pigmentation and creamy-pink, two-lipped flowers on a one-sided spike. It is usually parasitic on the roots of hazels. On the left, further on near Post Three, there is a small clearing among the trees which in spring is a brilliantly coloured carpet of flowers – red campion, yellow archangel (*Galeobdolon luteum*), bluebells, wild garlic and some dog's mercury (*Mercurialis perennis*) – a really stunning sight. This lovely mixture of flowers continues for some little way under the trees by the side of the track.

Also in this area, on the left, coppicing with standards is

being practised. The majority of the trees are cut down and the shoots from the cut base are then allowed to grow. A few of the better, larger trees are left to mature as standards. This is being done to encourage flowering plants, and one of the results is the wealth of butterflies (such as orange-tipped and green-veined white) and other insects which depend on these flowers. Some of the cut material is left as food for the roe deer which live in and around the reserve.

Turn right down some steps, and then half left by a big beech tree, where there is a great show of ferns. Among those to be seen here or in other parts of the wood are male fern (*Dryopteris filix-mas*), hart's-tongue (*Phyllitis scolopendrium*), common polypody (*Polypodium vulgare*), broad buckler (*Dryopteris dilatata*) and hard-shield (*Polystichum aculeatum*). Follow the path down to the bottom of the hill, where, ignoring the signpost, turn left towards a large, fallen beech tree, which is covered in mosses, lichens and ferns. There is plenty of silverweed (*Potentilla anserina*) by the track-side, and further along there is a row of poplars, some of which have the lovely hairy *Usnea* lichen on them. Later in the year, meadow-sweet grows profusely along this valley path, and herb Paris (*Paris quadrifolia*, see Castle Eden Dene, p. 197) may be seen among the dog's mercury. The path leads back to the entrance gate to the Wood.

Return down Black Rock Drove and go over the stile on the left at the entrance to the Velvet Bottom Reserve. This reserve is owned by the Bristol Waterworks Company and is a Site of Special Scientific Interest (SSSI). It consists of a dry river valley with scattered woodland and rough grassland, and has in the past been the site of lead workings, which have influenced the flora. Since the workings ceased in the 1880s the valley has remained largely untouched.

By the entrance there is some growth of bracken, and evidence of the presence of moles. Go over another stone stile into an area of rough grassland, where there are some scattered shrubs, including wayfaring tree and hawthorn. There is some covering of ground ivy (*Glechoma hederacea*), and in spring a large patch of bluebells (*Endymion non-scriptus*) on the left. The first sign of human influence is the presence a little further on of a series of stone-built dams, of which some of the walls remain. These walls offer support to hard ferns, while there are cowslips (*Primula veris*) and dog's mercury around their bases among the bracken. Adders and common lizards are often found in the grass and bracken, especially near the walls. Plants that can tolerate a high level of lead may be found in this area, including alpine penny cress (*Thlaspi alpestre*) and spring sandwort (*Minuartia verna*).

Not far from this point, on either side of the pathway near a depression on the right-hand side, there are thousands of horsetails growing among the coarse grasses, and on the far left under some trees near the valley side, there is a glorious blaze of bluebells in the spring. As will be noticed, the trees and scrub grow more profusely away from the valley bottom and on the sides, as these areas are relatively free of lead. The scrub is being cleared in places, and these are worth inspecting where they occur along the valley, as, among the short turf that has been formed by grazing rabbits, many limestone plants are growing. These include eyebright (*Euphrasia nemorosa*), lady's bedstraw (*Galium verum*), common rock-rose, carline thistle (*Carlina vulgaris*), and common centaury (*Centaurium erythraea*), as well as early purple and common spotted orchids (*Dactylorhiza fuchsii*).

Care should be taken when walking through the coarse and hummocky grassland towards the left-hand side of the valley, as it contains quite deep, hidden holes.

Continue along the valley bottom until on the left some old lead slag heaps are seen, on which spring whitlow grass (*Erophila verna*) and herb Robert are endeavouring to establish themselves. Other than these, the area is so lead-contaminated that little grows. A short distance past the slag heap and on the same side there is a large sycamore tree, and further on again, a hut with some woodland behind it. Past this, on the dry bank on the left of the roadway in particular, are a number of plants such as white campion (*Silene alba*), tormentil (*Potentilla erecta*), hairy rockcress, lady's bedstraw and spring whitlow grass. The reserve ends at a roadway; return along the same route to the drove.

* Turn right and follow the stone wall on the left, over the stile into Black Rock Reserve. Notice the growth of maidenhair spleenwort fern (*Asplenium trichomanes*) on the wall on both sides of the stile. On the bank on the right there is some herb Robert and some lady's smock (*Cardamine pratensis*), the latter thriving in the rather damp conditions. Climb up the hill through the hawthorn and gorse scrub, where, in the little grassy glades, bugle (*Ajuga reptans*) and early purple orchids make a lovely show. Ragwort (*Senecio jacobaea*) is quite common, and on it the yellow and black cinnabar moth caterpillar is often found, while the dark green fritillary and common blue butterflies are often present on warm sunny days. Willow warblers, goldfinches and greenfinches can also be seen or heard in the scrub.

On top of the hill there are extensive views of the surrounding countryside. In spring and summer the open limestone grassland has a colourful collection of limestone plants similar to those seen on the hillside towards the start of the walk. From the summit of the hill, walk diagonally down towards a patch of nettles which partially hides a large rabbit warren. Some bracken and bluebells are also seen in this area. Continue on down the hill through thicker scrub which merges into ash, hazel and conifer woodland, with honeysuckle (*Lonicera periclymenum*) growing on the bushes. Here, dormice are known to live. Go down the wooden steps (which can be very slippery in wet weather) through the woodland to a stile which leads into Black Rock Drove; turn left back to the entrance gate.

Bridgwater Bay

SUMMARY A walk along the shore of Bridgwater Bay
– of special interest to birdwatchers because of
moulting shelducks.

APPROXIMATE LENGTH OF WALK 2½ miles.

BEST TIMES Winter and migration time; mid-summer
for moulting shelducks.

LOCATION In the village of Steart, near Cambwich.
ST278464.

From the car park by the warden's house take the track
leading down to the shore. The field on the right of the track
is often full of curlews and lapwing, and there may also be
partridges. At the end of the track, turn right and follow the
pathway by the fence and behind the very extensive
reedbeds, the haunt of reed buntings.

Keep an eye seawards, as at any time there may be huge
flocks of waders in the air. After about three-quarters of a
mile, cross a stile and follow the seaward fence of the field,
keeping close to the fence as the field is part of a farm. On
the far side of the field is the first hide, which looks out over
a scrape (a shallow pool, excavated to attract wading birds)
and from which some of the mud flats are visible, although
not at very close quarters. At migration times and during the
winter huge flocks of waders and plenty of wildfowl are
likely to be present on the mud flats. Often to be seen are
flocks of dunlin so huge that even though they are some
distance away the whispering noise of their wings as they
sweep through the air is clearly audible – a most astonishing
sound. Smaller but still significant flocks of black-tailed
godwit, redshank, curlew, and oystercatcher feed on the
mud flats, and in spring up to 1,000 whimbrel use the bay as

a staging post in their journey north. Turnstone, grey plover, and bar-tailed godwit may also be seen, but not in such numbers.

In mid-summer the most interesting wildfowl to be seen from the hide and from other vantage points are undoubtedly the 3,000–4,000 shelducks which gather to moult on this, one of just two known British sites. The shelducks' moulting behaviour is remarkable. Long before their ducklings are independent, they leave them in 'crèches' in the care of non-breeding birds, and fly to their moulting grounds. Those which moult at Bridgwater are believed to come from Ireland, while British birds migrate principally to the mouth of the Elbe in Germany.

From the first hide, turn left and follow the fence to another stile. Cross this and, noting that visitors are asked not to climb on the banks between which the track passes, proceed to the second hide overlooking a lagoon, which sometimes freezes over in winter. The third and fourth hides are also sited along this track – the third overlooking scrapes and pools, and the fourth giving good views over a large expanse of water. From any or all of these during the winter and at migration times a collection of wildfowl and some waders are likely to be seen – wigeon and mallard in considerable numbers, with smaller parties of teal, pintail and shoveler. The very lucky visitor may also see the white-fronted geese which on a few exciting occasions use the reserve during the winter.

Return to where the track leads up to the car park and, if the tide is out, continue past that turning towards the massive pile of the Hinkley Point nuclear station. After a walk of half to three-quarters of a mile, a rough car park is reached, and from it there is a marvellous view, unrestricted by reed beds, of more mud flats. There can be literally thousands of waders here: oystercatchers, curlew, dunlin, and redshank, together with the shelducks. With so many waders, peregrines are not uncommon, while merlins streak after smaller birds, and marsh harriers quarter the reed beds.

Return along the same route to the car park.

SOUTH
AND
CENTRAL
ENGLAND

1 Soudley Ponds –
   Forest of Dean
2 Crickley Hill
   Country Park
3 Martin Down
4 The New Forest –
   Eyeworth Pond and
   Studley Wood
5 Keyhaven and
   Pennington Marshes
6 Cuckmere Haven –
   Seven Sisters Country
   Park
7 Sandwich Bay
8 Barnack Hills and Holes
9 Gibraltar Point
10 Martin's Pond
11 Attenborough Pits

Soudley Ponds:
Forest of Dean

SUMMARY A peaceful and charming walk around a
small series of ponds in the Forest of Dean. An easy,
level route, some of which is suitable for wheelchairs.
A Site of Special Scientific Interest (SSSI). The ponds
were built in the 1880s as fish ponds, and support a
variety of wildlife both in the water and in the
surrounding area.

APPROXIMATE LENGTH OF WALK 2 miles.

BEST TIMES Spring, summer.

LOCATION West of Upper Soudley, Gloucestershire
on the B4227 Cinderford–Blakeney road. (162)656105

From the visitor centre, cross the road and take the path
which leads beside the ponds. Yellow irises (*Iris pseudacorus*)
grow at the water's edge, together with water forget-me-
nots (*Myosotis scorpioides*), reeds and rushes. The water is
exceptionally clear and clean (except after very heavy rain),
and the thick growth of Canadian waterweed (*Elodea canaden-
sis*) on the pond bottom is easily seen.

In the water, near the yellow irises and reeds, can be found
pond-skaters – true bugs, which have mouth parts specially
adapted for sucking the juices out of other animals – chiefly
smaller insects. They have two pairs of wings, but they
spend much of their time 'rowing' themselves across the
surface of the water by means of their long middle pairs of
legs, using the hind ones in a trailing position to help with
steering. Soudley Ponds are wonderful places for a great
range of insects and insect larvae, with caddis flies being
particularly numerous, as are dragonflies and damselflies.

From time to time, water boatmen come up to the surface for air. They differ from the pond-skaters and other water bugs by feeding almost exclusively on plant material, and spend much of their time on the bottom of the pond. Most unexpectedly for so small and insignificant a creature, the male water boatman produces a kind of 'song' to attract a female by rubbing his hairy front legs on a ridge on the side of his head.

A little further along the pond banks, alder and willow trees and shrubs are growing, while a short distance away from the water a variety of conifers have been planted – including some magnificent Douglas firs, Scots pine and cedars. There are also English oaks, and red oaks, whose large leaves have bristle-tipped lobes. The leaves turn a brilliant red in autumn, and the acorns are squat and grow in very shallow cups. A large area of beech grows towards the top of the first pond.

From time to time, leave the main path and follow some of the smaller tracks down to the water's edge, where pond weed, rosebay willowherb (*Chamaenerion angustifolium*) and water-lilies may be seen.

Follow the path to a large car park between the third and fourth ponds. Turn left and walk down the road a little way before rejoining the path by the waterside. Soon, a little causeway leads out between two of the ponds, and here the alder carr which separates the ponds can be viewed at close quarters. This wet woodland consists of willow, poplar and birch, in addition to alder, and is a splendid place for seeing birds and insects. Among the birds which may be seen here are various finches, chiffchaffs, willow warblers and long-tailed tits.

Return to the main pathway which leads along the pond edge. In late summer, white admiral and comma butterflies may be seen on bramble flowers. Towards the end of the walk, note the fine western red cedars on the right-hand side of the path. In these, and in the Douglas firs which are on both sides of the pond, goldcrests and coal tits may be seen, or at least heard. The ponds attract a number of water birds, including little grebes, moorhens, mallard and herons, while high overhead, ravens are often seen.

Crickley Hill Country Park

SUMMARY A short walk through a typical Cotswold beechwood, which gives way to chalk grassland with hazel coppice. A Gloucestershire County Council reserve.

APPROXIMATE LENGTH OF WALK ½ mile.

BEST TIMES Spring, summer.

LOCATION Off the A436, outside Gloucester, not far from the top of Crickley Hill. SO026597.

From the car park walk back down the driveway to a stile on the right. Cross this, and follow the numbered green-topped posts of the Nature Trail. The track leads almost straight into the beechwood, which in high summer is typically rather dark and consequently has little ground cover. However, a few shade-tolerant and early-flowering species are present at various times; these include celandine (*Ranunculus ficaria*), dog's mercury (*Mercurialis perennis*), wood avens (*Geum urbanum*) and dog violet (*Viola riviniana*). Spring-flowering plants include wild garlic/ramsons (*Allium ursinum*), and also bluebells (*Endymion non-scriptus*).

Some young beech trees have been planted in the vicinity of Post Three. This is necessary as beech mast does not germinate easily in the thick layer of leaf litter, so there is little natural regeneration of these beautiful trees. After Post Three bear right to Post Four, which is in a more open, grassy area, with hawthorn scrub on the woodland edge. There are a number of anthills in the grassy area, and the layers of droppings show that rabbits obviously enjoy sunning themselves on warm sunny mornings before the visitors arrive. A number of flowering plants such as eyebright

(*Euphrasia nemorosa*), wild basil (*Clinopodium vulgare*) and self-heal (*Prunella vulgaris*) grow along the woodland edge.

Continue through this more open area to Post Five where the beech woodland begins again, noting the presence of holly trees. These were almost certainly planted to give winter cover for pheasants. Keep a look out for the strange, lily-like flowers and blunt, arrow-shaped leaves of cuckoo pint (*Arum maculatum*), which has a number of other common names, including Lords and Ladies and the long-winded Kitty-Come-Down-the-Lane-Jump-up-and-Kiss-Me! The familiar long sheathing bract (known as a spathe) partially surrounds the centrally situated red spike of densely packed flowers called the spadix. This plant has a very ingenious pollinating mechanism. The lower part of the spadix (which is enclosed by the base of the spathe) is covered with female flowers, and above them are the male flowers. Above these is a ring of sterile bristles which close off this part of the plant. Pollinating insects are attracted by the smell of the flowers, push their way down past the bristles, and are trapped there temporarily. If they are carrying pollen from other flowers, this is rubbed off on the female flowers at the base. Later on, when the spathe withers, the insects are released, with pollen from the male flowers on them.

The trail now leads to Post Six, in a small abandoned quarry which has large ash trees in and above it. Here, the very shallow roots of the nearby beech trees can be seen – this enables them to flourish in the thin limestone soil, but, as can be seen in beech woods countrywide, it also means they can be blown over very easily.

From the quarry, the track leads into an area of open grassland with coppiced hazel on the left and clumps of shrub containing hawthorn, dog rose (*Rosa canina*), bramble and elder. The grassland contains a variety of flowering plants including scabious (*Succisa*), harebells (*Campanula rotundifolia*), eyebright, rock-rose (*Helianthemum chamaecistus*), betony (*Betonica officinalis*), hedge woundwort (*Stachys sylvatica*), wild basil and self-heal. These plants grow mostly on the woodland and scrub edges, where the grassland is less prone to trampling by the hundreds of visitors.

From this open grassland the track leads through an area of thicker scrub, with bramble, elder, hazel, and wayfaring tree, much of which is covered with wild clematis/traveller's joy (*Clematis vitalba*) and, in some places, with the poisonous deadly nightshade (*Atropa bella-donna*). This plant has broad, pointed oval leaves, with, at their bases, single, dull, purple, bell-shaped flowers from which a column of yellow anthers protrudes. The blue-black berries are about the size of small cherries, *and are very dangerous*.

From here, return to the car park, where perforate St John's wort (*Hypericum perforatum*) can be seen growing around the edges in summer.

Martin Down

Summary An undemanding walk that starts on the Hampshire border and continues over Dorset chalk downland, with an excellent range of typical plants, an unusual variety of scrubland, and the added attraction of nightingales in the summer. A National Nature Reserve.

Approximate length of walk 2 miles.

Best times Spring, summer.

Location In the village of Martin, Hampshire. SU058192. Approached by Sillen Lane.

Walk up one of the broad tracks through the grassland towards the linear earthwork (Bokerley Dyke) which is plainly visible directly ahead. This grassland has been undisturbed for centuries and an immensely rich downland flora has developed. Throughout spring and summer, on either side of the pathways there is a wonderful variety of chalkland plants – salad burnet (*Poterium sanguisorba/Sanguisorba minor*), squinancywort (*Asperula cynanchica*), a number of orchids, including the pyramidal (*Anacamptis pyramidalis*), early purple (*Orchis mascula*) and fragrant (*Gymnadenia conopsea*), fairy flax (*Linum catharticum*), felwort (*Gentianella amarella*), cowslip (*Primula veris*), and lady's bedstraw (*Galium verum*). The grass itself is chiefly upright brome (*Bromus erectus*) in this area. One or two small hawthorn bushes are scattered throughout the grassland.

Butterflies are a feature of the reserve, with two rare ones – the silver-spotted skipper and the Adonis blue (whose caterpillars feed only on the leaves of horseshoe vetch) – and the more usual common blue and brimstone, as well as the

Duke of Burgundy and marsh fritillaries. Marbled white butterflies may also be seen. The early-morning or late-evening visitor may be fortunate enough to see a barn owl feeding among the grassland. Kestrels are common throughout the year, and hen harriers and short-eared owls may occasionally be seen during the winter months.

As the earthwork is approached, the upright brome gives way to sheep's fescue (*Festuca ovina*), and plants such as horseshoe vetch (*Hippocrepis comosa*), kidney vetch (*Anthyllis vulneraria*), eyebright (*Euphrasia nemorosa*), and silverweed (*Potentilla anserina*) become common. Just below the dyke, to the right, there is an area where the flora is at present somewhat limited. It has recently been grazed by sheep – an important part of management which is designed to provide a proper balance of short and long grassland. In due course, the rich flora will once again be apparent in such areas.

Beyond the dyke is a plantation of conifers with some birch on the fringes. Turn right, and walk either along the dyke top or just below it. Notice the various sedges that grow among the grass, while further along there is some elder shrub – one of the five different types of scrub to be found on Martin Down. The others are dogwood, found principally on land which was ploughed during World War II, gorse scrub, on areas which were formerly chalk heath, mixed scrub, and hawthorn scrub, which is most common in the hedgerows and also in areas of grassland that have not been grazed regularly. Old man's beard (*Clematis vitalba*) scrambles over the fence and also over some of the shrubs.

Follow the dyke round until a broad track leads through a big bank of scrub, which includes much gorse and some elder. Ignore the 'No Bridleway' track going off to the right, and continue up through the scrub and out into open grassland again. Although there is still quite a good range of plants in this grassland, it is more limited than that which has previously been seen. This is a result of the ploughing of much of this northern part of the reserve during World War II, and many species have not yet re-established themselves. It shows the effect that cultivation has on such areas.

The track leads round under the bank with a fence on top. After a short distance, take the right-hand fork where the path divides and walk back down the hill in the direction of the starting point. At the next junction turn right again. Here, there is sometimes an enclosure with sheep grazing. Follow the electrified fencing downhill (heading back towards the dyke), and on to a very chalky-white rough track with a black and white post on the right-hand corner beside a thick, hawthorn-dominated hedgerow.

A short distance further on there is a meeting of tracks, with a notice on the right, 'No Vehicles Beyond Here'. Turn sharp right here and walk across the rough grassland towards the large belt of shrub. This is an area of mixed scrubland, containing a number of calcicole species such as spindle, privet and wayfaring trees, in addition to hawthorn, buckthorn, dog rose, blackthorn and bramble. It is an excellent place for birds, and nightingales are commonly heard singing here. Other species include willow warbler, yellowhammer, whitethroat and lesser whitethroat. The large stands of scrub are managed by rotational cutting to prevent encroachment on the grassland and to ensure the maintenance of healthy shrubs of varying ages.

From the scrub, return to the starting point.

The New Forest: Eyeworth Pond and Studley Wood

SUMMARY The great charm of the New Forest is the astonishing variety of habitat. This walk takes in a number of these, including Ancient and Ornamental Woodland, the bog and moorland of the open forest, enclosed woodland, and the open water of Eyeworth Pond. Stout footwear is necessary, as parts of the walk can be very wet and muddy.

APPROXIMATE LENGTH OF WALK 4 miles.

BEST TIMES Spring, summer.

LOCATION On road past The Royal Oak, Fritham, in the New Forest, Hampshire. SU228147.

From the car park at Eyeworth Pond, turn left back along the gravel road. The pond itself has a good population of breeding mallard, coots, moorhens and, in some years, Canada geese. Do not be surprised if the local fauna includes some pigs and piglets! These animals belong to the New Forest Commoners, who have the right to turn them out during the pannage season from September to December to feed on the acorns and beech mast in the woods. Eyeworth Pond is a favourite area for these animals. Near the end of the gravel track there is a patch of water-lilies on the pond, which looks quite magnificent when in flower from about June to August.

Turn right up the gravel road and follow it past some houses on the left to where some wooden 'dragons' teeth' bar vehicular entrance to the woodland. Follow the pathway into the wood, which consists chiefly of pedunculate oak and beech with holly and bramble understorey. On a large beech tree on the right just near the woodland edge are some enormous bracket fungi which have been there for many, many years.

This is Eyeworth Wood, and it is one of the Ancient and Ornamental Woodlands of the New Forest. These are unenclosed woodlands which are open to all the Forest animals, including the ponies, and contain, as the name suggests, some very ancient trees. But they also contain trees of varying ages that have regenerated naturally. Because they are subject to grazing and browsing by the ponies and the deer, the understorey and the field layer tend to be poor and consist principally of plants unattractive to these animals.

Follow the wide pathway up the slope. There is a certain amount of bracken and some foxgloves (*Digitalis purpurea*), but little else grows under the trees other than holly. It is most noticeable that many of the trees are heavily encrusted with lichens and mosses – another indication of age. At the top of the rise and on the level ground the real glory of the Ancient and Ornamental Woodland can be seen to its best advantage. There are majestic oaks, some beeches, and a few yews and silver birches, set apart by delightful glades. The soft leaf-litter underfoot gives way from time to time to wet, boggy flashes made bright by the green of bog mosses (*Sphagnum*). Keep the main pathway in view (as it is deceptively easy to lose one's sense of direction in the Forest), and wander around a little, exploring some of this lovely old piece of woodland.

There are plenty of fallen trees, which offer cover to many beetles and other insects and from which common polypody ferns grow. There is a small amount of bilberry (*Vaccinium myrtillus*). Mosses are abundant both on the fallen trees and on the woodland floor; the species most likely to be seen include cypress-leaved feather moss (*Hypnum cupressiforme*), and fork mosses (*Leucobryum* and *Dicranum spp.*). A variety of birds take advantage of the ancient and dead trees, including the greater spotted woodpecker, tawny owl, hawfinches, redstarts, and blue and great tits. Fallow deer, of which the New Forest has a large population, are frequently seen in this woodland, and even if not seen they are nearly always heard as they move away.

Eventually the track leads from the woodland out on to one of the gravel-based ridges that are so much a part of Forest scenery. Here the path leads through a very different habitat, through scrubby country with small birches and self-sown pines, holly, bracken and gorse, under which ling (*Calluna vulgaris*) and heather (*Erica cinerea*) grow. As the distance from the woodland increases, so does the amount of ling and heather. Adders are common here, while the birds that can be seen include stonechats, meadow pipits and the occasional hovering kestrel. Sometimes curlews can be heard from the boggy heath down the hill to the right.

In this area, if not before, a number of Forest ponies are almost certain to be seen. These animals belong to the New Forest Commoners, who in accordance with the rights attached to their properties turn them out to graze on the Forest. There are over 2,000 ponies within the Forest boundaries (perambulations), and they, together with the deer and cattle, have a very great influence on the ecology of the Forest. Their grazing and browsing have modified the composition of the areas where they roam. They restrict the natural regeneration of woodland to a large extent and eliminate some species altogether. On the other hand, they play a vital role in maintaining the Forest heaths, grassland and open areas, which would otherwise revert to scrub and then to woodland. Without these large herbivores the New Forest would be a very different place.

Less than a quarter of a mile on, the pathway leads through a very small woodland. There are some whitebeams just at the entrance on the left-hand side. After another twenty yards or so, beside the track on the right, there is a fox's earth. Badgers frequent this area too, coming almost certainly from a sett outside the wood.

On leaving the wood and emerging on to the open heathland, turn sharp left down the hill. There are numerous narrow pony tracks leading down through the heath, which is interspersed with small holly bushes, spreads of bracken and gorse, and more seedling pines. On the way down, look across the valley to a track that leads up the other side, and head for that. At the bottom of the hill are the beginnings of yet another feature of the Forest – a valley bog. The ground is very wet, with spreads of bog mosses and cross-leaved heath (*Erica tetralix*), while along the little stream there are horse tails, rushes, purple moor-grass (*Molinia caerulea*) and a few willows. If this area, which is aptly named Claypits Bottom, is too wet or the stream too deep, walk about 100 yards to the left, where a footbridge gives a drier crossing. Return to where the path leads up the hill through an area of denser scrub, with large stands of holly and more birch and pines. Old, straggling ling and purple moor-grass can make walking off the path difficult. Among the heather is one of the most common of the many lichens found in the Forest, the pale, grey-green, much-branched *Cladonia portentosa*.

At the top of the hill, cross one broad track (which ultimately goes diagonally down the hill again) and take the next one, leading left towards a large area of woodland. This wood, known as Studley, has recently been re-enclosed, so enter through the gate. There is a plantation of Scots pines on the left and mixed woodland, predominantly oak, on the right.

After about twenty-five yards take the turning to the right and walk down the grassy ride. It is immediately apparent that this is not Ancient and Ornamental Woodland; it shows a much greater degree of orderliness, resulting from former forestry activities. The trees in each area tend to be of approximately the same age; there are few very old ones and even fewer fallen and decaying ones. The whole effect is much tidier. There are, nonetheless, points of interest. At the bottom of the slope, look to the right over the far side of a drainage ditch; among the bracken is a very large badger sett (hidden by the bracken in high summer). Closer investigation will show it is inhabited, as there are almost always signs of new digging and very often small amounts of bracken and grass bedding near the entrance.

Because this enclosure has been open to the ponies for some time, there is not a great deal in the field layer other than bracken. This contrasts with other, older enclosures in the Forest where ponies have been excluded for many years. Evidence of the ponies' recent presence is seen on some of the holly trees, which show a distinct 'browse line' at about pony-head height from the ground – holly is a favourite winter food.

The path (boggy and wet in places) leads on through the woodland. On the left is a fine stand of beeches, younger than those in Eyeworth Wood and with little understorey. At the T-junction at the bottom of a gentle slope, turn right into a very broad ride then, after a short distance, turn left towards a bridge. Cross the bridge, and follow the broad and muddy ride up the hill, noting the many hard ferns growing in the banks.

At the top of the hill there is a Forestry gate leading into a conifer plantation. Turn left along the outside of the plantation towards another gate about 100 yards away. Go through this, back into Eyeworth Wood, and keep more or less straight ahead, following the wide path, which is not very well-defined. Where the path divides, take the left-hand fork and, a little distance along, note the deserted badger sett on the right. A little further on, this path joins the main track through the wood. Turn right on to it and back to Eyeworth Pond.

Keyhaven and Pennington Marshes

SUMMARY Primarily a sea-wall walk, with excellent views over saltings on the seaward side and marshes and a series of lagoons and pools to landward. John Gooders describes the pools in *Where to Watch Birds* as 'amongst the best in the county for waders in autumn'. A Hampshire County Council and Hampshire and Isle of Wight Trust for Nature Conservation reserve.

APPROXIMATE LENGTH OF WALK 6 miles.

BEST TIMES All year, but winter especially good for birds.

LOCATION Keyhaven Harbour, Hampshire. SU308916.

At Keyhaven leave the car park opposite The Gun public house by the top left-hand corner and walk along the road beside the harbour. The harbour itself usually contains swans, black-headed and herring gulls and, in winter, some Brent geese. A little way along on the left there is some open water, where gulls congregate. The water is fringed by extensive reed beds. Continue along the road to a signpost that says 'No vehicles 200 yards ahead'. Turn right along the path skirting the harbour; this path is part of the Solent Way. On the water's edge redshank are often present, picking among the washed-up seaweed.

As the path leads away from the harbour, a vast expanse of mud flats and saltings opens out, where in winter huge flocks of Brent geese can be seen. From time to time they take to the air and fly up or down the coast to other feeding grounds, honking as they go. The mud flats also offer rich pickings for a variety of waders such as turnstone, redshank, dunlin, and curlew, and there are almost always some shelduck. Typical salt marsh plants in this area include sea purslane (*Halimione portulacoides*), glasswort (*Salicornia spp.*), and cord-grass (*Spartina*). Further out there are areas of eel-grass (*Zostera spp.*, see Place, p. 18) on which the Brents feed. On the landward side there is scrub with birch and gorse.

After about half a mile a sea wall begins, which separates the saltings on the seaward side from Keyhaven Marshes and the series of pools on the left. Walk along the wall, or just below it where possible, and scan the marshes and pools, where a wonderful range of waders, wildfowl and other birds may be seen. Among the rarer passage migrants are curlew sandpiper, whimbrel, ruff, spotted redshank and little stint. Greenshanks are quite frequently seen, while both species of godwit, common sandpiper, and grey plover may also be present. It is a very exciting place indeed for the ornithologist, aptly described as 'a birdwatcher's bonanza'. In summer, common and sandwich tern, which breed on the nearby Hurst Spit shingle bank, can be seen overhead, and so can a few of the small breeding colony of little tern. Among the stand of reeds which fringes some of the lagoons, reed buntings are common.

After about one and a half miles there is a notice on the shore, 'Quicksands', and this is obviously not the place to explore that side of the sea wall, but it is often a good vantage point from which to watch Brent geese collecting around a breakwater and the remains of an old jetty. Remain on the sea wall, and search the surface of the sea for the ducks that are sometimes offshore – goldeneye and common scoter – while over-wintering species on the marshes include teal, pochard, wigeon, and long-tailed ducks.

The sea wall bears to the left around the northern end of Oxey Marsh, and follows the shore of an inlet, which eventually leads to a creek. In this inlet there is usually a grand collection of red-breasted mergansers in November, while great crested and the occasional Slavonian grebe have also been recorded.

Below the sea wall, a short distance along to the left, there is a five-barred gate and a stile leading into the grazing marsh. Go through this, and follow the vehicular track, which becomes gravelly, back towards Keyhaven. This marsh is often almost alive with skylarks. After about a quarter of a mile the track comes to a T-junction. Turn sharp left back to the sea wall through gorse and scrub. Turn right along the sea wall and return to Keyhaven by the outward route.

Cuckmere Haven: Seven Sisters Country Park

SUMMARY The Park has a splendid range of habitats –
chalk downland and cliffs, shingle beach, lake, river,
and salt marsh. It provides for a most interesting and
enjoyable walk following the Trail that has been laid
out. There is also a very good park centre (admission
free) with displays and exhibitions explaining the
reserve, and an extensive and excellent natural history
exhibition, 'The Living World', for which there is an
admission charge (well worth it!). As there is a
concrete road running right through the reserve from
the car park almost to the shore, this part of it is easily
accessible for wheelchairs. An East Sussex County
Council reserve.

APPROXIMATE LENGTH OF WALK 3 miles.

BEST TIMES Spring, summer.

LOCATION On the A259 between Brighton and
Eastbourne. TV519995.

A gate leads from the car park into the reserve. Follow the
track diagonally up the side of the hill, where a number of
features of chalk grassland can be seen. A short distance
along the path an area of turf has been removed from the
bank, and this shows the very thin layer of soil over the
chalk. The soil is poor in nutrients and drains well and
quickly. As a result, the plants that thrive are those best
able to survive relatively dry conditions. They do this by a
variety of means. Some, such as thyme, reduce water loss
by reduction in the number and size of leaves; others, such
as the plantains, adopt a rosette of leaves, close to the
ground, while others, such as some of the grasses, have

tightly in-rolled leaves to reduce the surface area from which water can be lost. The lack of nutrients discourages the growth of some of the larger, coarser species, as does the grazing by sheep. This is very important in the development of the typical springy downland turf found throughout such areas in Sussex and Hampshire. In the downland area, keep a lookout for the three blue butterflies – the Adonis, common and chalkhill.

The grasses commonly found are various species of fescue. The flowering herbs provide a colourful display throughout the season, and include squinancywort (*Asperula cynanchica*), salad burnet (*Poterium sanguisorba/Sanguisorba minor*), thyme (*Thymus drucei*), horseshoe vetch (*Hippocrepis comosa*), round-headed rampion (*Phyteuma tenerum*), carline thistle (*Carlina vulgaris*) and autumn gentian/felwort (*Gentianella amarella*).

On the right, note the steplike appearance of the hill below. This is formed by soil creep, thought to be due partly to the steepness of the slope, and the alternate wetting and drying, heating and cooling of the soil.

Towards the brow of the hill, a large patch of nettles, great burdock (*Arctium lappa*) and spear thistles (*Cirsium vulgare*) indicate a modification of habitat, and the reason quickly becomes apparent. This is the site of an extensive rabbit warren and also a large badger sett. The presence of these animals' droppings (particularly the rabbits') increases the organic content, and thus the nutrient value, of the soil. That suits these plants, which in any case are unpalatable to rabbits and sheep. From the brow of the hill there is a marvellous view of the valley of the Cuckmere River as it meanders towards the sea.

Continue over the brow of the hill, cross the stile and bear right across the field to another stile. Bear diagonally right again (do not follow a track downhill) and head towards a marker post. In these fields, hidden among the grasses, are clusters of both banded snails and the more local spire snail. From the marker post walk on down the hill to a stile that gives on to the road. Almost immediately opposite the stile is a splendid patch of the uncommon red star-thistle (*Centaurea calcitrapa*). This takes its name from the stiff, spiny bracts that arise just below the florets. It flowers from July to September.

Follow the track around the base of the hill to another marker post and then up the hill into a quite extensive area of scrubland. This consists of hawthorn, privet, elder, blackthorn and blackberry, with coarser grasses such as tor grass (*Brachypodium pinnatum*) and false brome (*Brachypodium sylvaticum*), which were not in evidence on the more heavily grazed downland earlier on the walk.

Among these grasses a wide variety of flowering plants can be found. Two of these, red bartsia (*Odontites verna*) and yellow rattle (*Rhinanthus minor*), are semi or partial parasites, usually on the roots of adjoining grasses. As can be seen, they do have green leaves so are able to manufacture some of their own food, but they also obtain some, probably minerals and water, from their host. These semi-parasites are able to exist independently, but in such instances their growth is usually stunted. Other flowers in this area include mugwort (*Artemisia vulgaris*), wild carrot (*Daucus carota*) and the brilliant purple-blue viper's bugloss (*Echium vulgare*).

The scrub also affords shelter and nesting sites for a number of resident birds and migrants. These include blackcap, whinchat, firecrest, whitethroat and the occasional ring ouzel, which feeds on the haws and the elderberries.

From the area of scrub, return down the hillside to the track leading past the concrete remains of gun emplacements, and on to the shingle bank at the foot of the chalk cliffs. (It is extremely dangerous to walk anywhere near the base of the cliffs, as they are unstable and rock falls are frequent.) At low tide, a brief look at the rocks on the shore reveals a number of creatures either on the rocks themselves or in the pools. Limpets are present in very large numbers, and the soft rocks indicate one or two interesting facts about their lifestyle. There are many limpet-shaped cavities, which are the scars where the mollusc has frequently clamped its shell hard down with its powerful muscles and so worn the surface away. Also on the rocks can be seen rasping trails. These are made when the limpet feeds. It moves slowly over the rock surface, scraping microscopic algae off by means of a hard, tongue-like organ, the radula, which has tiny hook-like teeth on it.

Return to the top of the shingle bank, where plants specially adapted to live in this inhospitable environment may be seen (see Loe Bar, p. 10). Yellow horned poppy (*Glaucium flavum*), sea beet (*Beta vulgaris*), mayweed/scentless camomile (*Tripleurospermum maritimum*), sea kale (*Crambe maritima*) and curled dock (*Rumex crispus*) are all there.

Behind the shingle is a flood bank. Walk along this, and look down into the area of scrub and rough grasses on the right. There are some very handsome specimens of teasel (*Dipsacus fullonum*) here, and because it is so sheltered it is a good place for butterflies such as the marbled white.

A little further to the right is an artificial lake with three islands in it, which was constructed for the benefit of birds. On two of the islands, sheets of polythene have been laid under the shingle to prevent the growth of plants, as three of the principal breeders, little and common tern and ringed plover, nest on bare shingle.

At the end of the storm wall the concrete road leads back

to the car park, but instead of taking it, cross over and continue along the bank that runs between the road and the river. Here, on the margin of the estuary, a superb area of salt marsh and mud flat has developed. It is one of the very few places I know where it is possible to see in a small area just how such a marsh has developed and how the plants in it are 'zoned'. It is, of course, best at low tide.

Basically, salt marshes and mud flats develop in places such as estuaries, where there is protected tidal water. At Cuckmere the lower part of the river is sheltered by the sea wall, where mud and silt can accumulate. This occurs chiefly at high tide when the water movement is at a minimum, and the organic particles in the river water sink to the bottom and form the mud flats. On these flats, specially adapted plants become established. They perform two functions: their roots hold the silt material together, and their upper parts enable further silt and mud to collect around them so that the level of the marsh rises and offers more material in which more plants can grow.

If the tide is out, climb down off the bank, go to the water's edge and look back towards the bank. A clear zonation of plants can be seen. Down by the water the mud is covered by a bright green seaweed. Above that is the first flowering plant, glasswort (*Salicornia sp.*). This is a strange-looking plant with swollen and jointed stems and reduced leaves. Its flower is inconspicuous, and consists of a small, fleshy disc with a central pore through which a single anther emerges during August and September.

Next in the succession is sea purslane (*Halimione portula-coides*), with its silvery-grey leaves, whose sheen is due to a coating of very fine white scales. Above the purslane is a band of sea meadowgrass (*Puccinellia maritima*), which is a true grass with narrow greyish stems and leaves, and this is followed by sea wormwood (*Artemisia maritima*), a strongly aromatic plant with narrow divided silvery leaves and drooping yellow flowers. Above this is sea beet and at the top, sea couch grass (*Agropyron pungens*).

In places, this succession of plants is compressed into a shoreline not more than ten or twelve feet deep. Among the sea couch are some plants of sea aster (*Aster tripolium*), but this grows more prolifically on the other side of the bank. All these plants are covered by sea water for varying times during each tide, and must therefore be salt-tolerant. They are known as halophytes.

In between the vegetation there are areas where there is no plant life at all. These areas may be water-filled, salt or fresh, but are frequently dry due to evaporation. They are 'pans', usually caused by the collapse of a mud wall, and the only living thing usually seen in them is the tiny, spire-shelled snail, *Hydrobia*, which provides food for many wading birds and wildfowl.

Follow the bank along to where a causeway leads down to the right and rejoins the concrete road. The river and meadows on the walk back are good places for birds. The river often has a very large flock of Canada geese on it, and there are also mute swans, the inevitable heron, shelduck, and a number of wildfowl in winter – principally teal, tufted duck and wigeon.

Towards the end, the road is flanked by hawthorn, wild rose, blackthorn, dogwood and elder, where a number of birds can be seen as well as some of the butterflies of the reserve, including tortoiseshell, red admiral and peacock.

Sandwich Bay

SUMMARY Beach and foreshore backed by low dunes with a superb collection of plants. Further along there are extensive mud flats. An easy, level walk, but can be wet in places. A Site of Special Scientific Interest (SSSI), managed jointly by the Kent Trust for Nature Conservation, the RSPB and the National Trust. The one disadvantage is the rather expensive toll to be paid to gain entrance to Sandown Road and thence to the observatory and reserve.

APPROXIMATE LENGTH OF WALK 3 miles.

BEST TIMES All year.

LOCATION Access through the Sandwich Bay Estate (toll payable). Parking at end of Prince's Drive. TR356593.

Before starting the walk it is well worth calling at the observatory, where it is often possible to watch the ringing of birds trapped on the reserve.

Enter the reserve near the information board, and immediately the richness of the plant life is apparent. This is due to the lime-richness of the sand. I cannot recollect seeing so much sea holly (*Eryngium maritimum*) anywhere else, while there are also large expanses of sea sandwort (*Honkenya peploides*), and other sand and shingle plants such as sea kale (*Crambe maritima*), rest-harrow (*Ononis repens*), and sea broomrape (*Orobanche*, see p. 104), which is parasitic on the sea holly.

Follow the pathway along the dunes behind the shore, noting the marram grass (*Ammophila arenaria*) and, some distance along, some bushes of sea buckthorn. The reserve is noted for various moths and butterflies, including rest-harrow, pygmy footmen and bright wave moths, and the migrant painted lady and clouded yellow butterflies.

About a mile along, there is a notice requiring visitors to produce either an RSPB or a Kent Trust for Nature Conservation card if asked. Continue on, passing another similar notice, and climb over a stile into a field of grazing cattle, taking care not to stray into the restricted area. There is a certain amount of sea holly growing in the sandy soil of the field.

After another stile, the path leads alongside an extensive area of salt marsh on the left, with a wonderful show of sea lavender (*Limonium sp.*) and sea aster (*Aster tripolium*). The going here can be very wet indeed. On the far side of the fence on the right are a number of delicate and attractive-looking wild asparagus shrubs (*Asparagus officinalis*). The male and female flowers are borne on separate plants, and the fruits are bright red berries. Pyramidal orchid (*Anacamptis pyramidalis*), sand catchfly (*Silene conica*), and lady's bedstraw (*Galium verum*) may also be seen here. Continue along the path, following the small Kent Trust signs through some very marshy fields. In some of these can be found the unusual and aptly named sharp rush (*Juncus acutus*) – a very tall rush, which ends in a particularly sharp spine.

The marshy ground gives way to sand and mud flats, where good numbers of waders and wildfowl can be seen in season – including both Bewick's and whooper swans, greenshank, redshank, whimbrel, curlew, Brent geese, white-fronted geese, ruff, golden plover and teal. From the salt marsh, return along the same route until the dunes are reached once more. From there, go down on to the shore, which is a happy hunting ground for beachcombers! A fascinating variety of plant and animal life is washed up, including sponges (see p. 122), hornwrack (see p. 121), piddock shells (these animals bore into the rocks), small rocks with piddock holes in them, slipper limpet shells (see p. 121), oyster shells, whelk egg cases, razor shells (see p. 18), scallop shells, and skate egg cases (see p. 122). Return to the reserve entrance and the car park.

Barnack Hills and Holes

SUMMARY This 22-hectare National Nature Reserve is
a real treasure house of limestone plants in an attractive
setting of former quarry workings. An excellent area
for butterflies and moths. No specific distance has been
set for this walk, as it is a 'wander-about' place rather
than a 'walk-through' one, but visitors are particularly
asked to keep to the major pathways (of which there
are plenty) to avoid damaging the fragile vegetation.
The Northampton Naturalists' Trust leases some of the
reserve.

APPROXIMATE LENGTH OF WALK 1–2 miles.

BEST TIMES Spring, summer.

LOCATION In the village of Barnack, near Stamford,
on the Lincs./Cambs. border. TF075046.

To appreciate fully the topography and the vegetation of
Barnack Hills and Holes, a brief outline of its history is
necessary. What is now the reserve was quarried for limestone from Roman times until the sixteenth century, and
stone from here was used to build Cambridge colleges, as
well as cathedrals and churches in Ely, Bury St Edmunds
and Peterborough. By the beginning of the sixteenth century, when the best stone had been removed, the quarry was
abandoned, but the holes from which the stone had come
and the mounds of rubble and spoil were left – hence the
unusual formation seen today. Over the intervening centuries the area has been colonized, and a shallow turf has
developed and covered the hills and holes. These in themselves are important, as the varied angles, slopes and aspects
provide a wide range of conditions which encourage a variety
of plants. Until the start of World War II the area was quite

heavily grazed and/or burned, but the cessation of these practices allowed invasion by coarse grasses, shrubs and trees. While the shrubs and trees have provided additional habitats, the increase of coarse grasses has tended to discourage the growth of the best plants. Consequently, a clearing programme undertaken by the Nature Conservancy Council and the Northampton Naturalists' Trust has been assisted by the introduction of sheep grazing during the winter months. Parts of the reserve have been enclosed for this purpose, but stiles have been provided to allow easy access throughout.

Within a few yards of entering the reserve the walker is almost certain to see the six-spot burnet moth which is usually there in great numbers on the tall scabious plants. (If, like me, you tend to confuse this with the cinnabar moth, just remember that the cinnabar has spots only on the wing edges.) These very colourful moths are colonial, hence they are frequently seen in large numbers in the same area. Both the burnet moth and its caterpillar are distasteful to predators, with the caterpillar actually secreting cyanide compounds over its body from glands.

In a good butterfly year twenty-eight species have been recorded in this area. These include the common blue, small white and small heath, the marbled white, at just about the northern limit of its range, and the chalkhill blue. The caterpillar of the blue secretes a sweet, honey-like fluid to attract ants, which 'milk' them, and help to protect them from predators, even to the extent of moving them near or into their nests. Less common butterflies which may be seen include the brown tortoiseshell, brown argus and ringlet.

Pathways lead up and down through the hills and holes, and in the grassland there is a magnificent range of chalkland plants. The most spectacular, of course, is the beautiful

Pasque flower (*Pulsatilla vulgaris*), its single, rich-purple flowers with golden anthers in bloom during April and May – especially on south-facing slopes. Horseshoe vetch and purple milk-vetch (*Hippocrepis comosa* and *Astragalus danicus*) are both present, as is squinancywort (*Asperula cynanchica*), common rock-rose (*Helianthemum chamaecistus*), and quaking grass (*Briza media*). There is a truly mouth-watering collection of orchids. The early purple orchid (*Orchis mascula*) leads the way with its spike of flowers appearing in May; the extraordinary and rare man orchid (*Aceras anthropophorum*) flowers in May and June; and pyramidal, fragrant and bee species (*Anacamptis pyramidalis, Gymnadenia conopsea* and *Ophrys apifera*) flower just a little later. Predictably, in a limestone area, there is a great show of cowslips (*Primula veris*) in the spring.

Totally parasitic flowers are not very common, but a representative of this group is found at Barnack Hills and Holes, growing on the far side of the reserve from the entrance. It is one of the broomrapes – the knapweed broomrape (*Orobanche elatior*) – parasitic on the roots of greater knapweed (*Centaurea scabiosa*). It is a strange-looking plant, as are all broomrapes. The most noticeable feature is that it is completely lacking in green parts; it obtains all its nourishment from its host, so has no need of the green pigment chlorophyll which is essential in the food-making process of photosynthesis. The plant grows up to about 45 cm (18 inches) high, with the two-lipped flowers borne on a spike. When alive this species is yellowy-brown, but the whole plant persists after the flowers have died, becoming dark brown.

There are various small trees and shrubs scattered about through the reserve – notably hawthorn, silver birch, buck-thorn, spindle, bramble, and blackthorn. Especially in the centre area of the reserve, turkey oak saplings are common. The leaves of this tree are shiny on the upper surface, with long, deep, irregular lobes; around the leaf base are straggly stipules which persist even when the leaf has fallen. The acorns are in a mossy cup covered in long, soft, pale-green scales. The more wooded areas round the fringes consist principally of ash, pedunculate oak, some lime trees and sycamore.

Clearly this is primarily a botanical walk, but for the birdwatcher about fifty species have been recorded, including breeding chiffchaff, blackcap, whitethroat and lesser whitethroat.

Gibraltar Point

SUMMARY An enthralling area of sand dunes, salt
marshes, freshwater marshes, and muddy and sandy
shores, with a vast number of species of birds and
plants. There is an excellent visitor centre which
should not be missed, and a bird observatory. A
National Nature Reserve, managed by the Lincolnshire
and South Humberside Trust for Nature Conservation,
and owned by Lincolnshire County Council and East
Lindsey District Council.

APPROXIMATE LENGTH OF WALK 2 miles.

BEST TIME All year.

LOCATION Near Skegness, Lincolnshire. TF556581.

Leave the car park by the gate and follow the road down
towards the sea. A bridge crosses the main creek on the
reserve, which is tidal and a rich habitat for wildlife. Its sides
are lined by sea purslane (*Halimione portulacoides*) and, higher
up the banks, by sea couch-grass (*Agropyron pungens*). At
low tide the barnacle-covered stones on the creek bed offer
shelter to young eels and shore crabs – the latter may be seen
scuttling about on the mud surface from time to time. Closer
inspection of the creek bed and the muddy sides shows small
depressions, which are the entrance to the burrows of
ragworms, while the white, wormlike feeding siphons of the
peppery furrow shell (*Scrobularia*) can also sometimes be seen
(see Ynyslas, p. 232).

The road passes through a wonderful salt marsh, known
as the Old Salt Marsh, which is crammed with vegetation
and also provides nesting sites for meadow pipits and skylarks, while reed buntings use the fringe of sea couch-grass
as a singing post, and redshank and dunlin probe for small

crustaceans in the damper areas and in the creek. In winter flocks of goldfinches, greenfinches, twite and corn buntings feed on the plant seeds, while predators such as kestrels, short-eared owls and hen harriers prey on them and on small mammals.

The range of plants is impressive. The marsh is at its most beautiful in summer, when the sea lavender (*Limonium spp.*) covers it with a carpet of mauve, and this is replaced a little later with the equally attractive sea aster (*Aster tripolium*). Glasswort (*Salicornia spp.*) grows in some of the barer patches, while seablite (*Suaeda maritima*) and sea meadow grass/salt-marsh grass (*Puccinellia maritima*) are also present. Sea scurvy grass (*Cochlearia officinalis*), cord-grass (*Spartina spp.*), sea wormwood (*Artemisia maritima*) and sea plantain (*Plantago maritima*) also grow in the marsh, while sea spurrey (*Spergularia spp.*) and sea milkwort (*Glaux maritima*) may be found around the edges.

At the bottom of the salt marsh, just behind a low ridge of sand dunes (the East Dunes), turn right along a white chalky track which leads past the bird-ringing laboratory. Take the steps up beside the buildings on to a track leading through the dunes. There is a Heligoland bird trap nearby. This ridge of dunes runs the length of the reserve. It began to form only after the middle of the last century, and is thus still very much in the process of formation on the seaward side. There are still no trees growing on the dunes, and the pathway leads through a scrub of elder, hawthorn, and banks of sea buckthorn (see p. 156). This scrub shelters many birds, including willow warbler, blackcap, linnet, wren and dunnock. In winter European fieldfares and redwings arrive in force and feed upon the buckthorn here and in other parts of the reserve. Flowering plants along the route include dewberry (*Rubus caesius*), viper's bugloss (*Echium vulgare*), ragwort (*Senecio jacobaea*), hound's-tongue (*Cynoglossum offi-cinale*), rosebay willowherb (*Chamaenerion angustifolium*), pyramidal orchid (*Anacamptis pyramidalis*) and, as the seaward side is approached, an increasing cover of marram grass (*Ammophila arenaria*).

After some distance, the path follows along the edge of some more salt marsh on the right. On the left, at the base of the dunes, are some plants of the poisonous, unpleasant-smelling henbane (*Hyoscyamus niger*), with its curiously coloured flowers, their creamy-buff petals spotted with purple, and with purple veins. As the track emerges on to the shore the summer warden's hut is on the right, and from it an excellent view is obtained across the New Saltmarsh and the Spit. During high tides in spring and autumn this is a marvellous place from which to see huge flocks of waders – dunlin, knot, bar-tailed godwit and oystercatcher. During the breeding season, ringed plover and little terns nest in this area – the latter are particularly carefully monitored. Because of this and the general fragility of the area, visitors are asked not to walk on the marsh or the Spit.

Turn left and proceed along the shingly shore to where a sleeper walk emerges from the dunes, marked by a trail post. In front of this is an area of mud and standing water which is gradually becoming a salt marsh. At present, it is colonized by cord grass, but as ridges of sand build up around this, sea couch-grass will move in, followed in due course by other salt marsh plants.

Continue along the shore until coming to a broad pathway that leads up into the dunes once more. Just on the left where the dunes are forming there are some evening primrose (*Oenothera biennis*) and hoary mullein (*Verbascum pulverulen-tum*). In this area there are also hundreds of ragwort plants (*Senecio jacobaea*), which in July or thereabouts are absolutely covered with the striped caterpillars of the cinnabar moth. The path through the dunes is fringed with scrub, and with large stands of rosebay willowherb and more buckthorn.

Ahead, the high dune known as Mill Hill comes into view, on top of which is a viewing platform. There is a fine and very helpful view from this, showing clearly the dune ridges and the saltings down towards the sea, and the scrub of elder, buckthorn, and hawthorn in the dune slacks.

From Mill Hill follow the pathway to the right and through more buckthorn, with sea campion (*Silene maritima*), lady's bedstraw (*Galium verum*) and more marram, to the freshwater marsh with its open water. This has been cut off from the Old Salt Marsh by a large bank. The marsh is grazed during the summer, and in the meadow grassland which this maintains are some lovely flowers such as lady's smock (*Cardamine pratensis*), cowslips (*Primula veris*), pyramidal orchids and meadowsweet (*Filipendula ulmaria*), while water dropwort (*Oenanthe aquatica*), yellow irises (*Iris pseudacorus*), and reeds fringe the water, and on it and in it water milfoil (*Myriophyllum*) and water crowfoot (*Ranunculus aquatilis*) may be seen. Dragonflies and damselflies are present in some numbers, while in the water newts and grass snakes may be seen.

High banks surround an artificial mere with islands which is overlooked by a hide. Tufted ducks, mallard, grebes, coot and moorhens are usually present, and occasionally a kingfisher may be glimpsed, while grey wagtails and reed buntings frequent the reeds and the water's edge. Waders visit in spring and autumn – redshank, spotted redshank, blacktailed godwit, common sandpiper, greenshank and the uncommon little ringed plover. The latter is differentiated from the more usual ringed plover by its all-black beak (compared with the ringed plover's red beak with a black tip), its yellow eye-ring, yellowish legs, lack of white wing-bar when seen in flight, and its size – about 15 cm (6 inches) as against 19–20 cm (7½–8 inches). In winter wildfowl such as wigeon, gadwall, teal, goldeneye and pochard have all been recorded.

From the hide, turn right and continue along the path, past a deep pool surrounded by sea buckthorn, to a car park. By the car park, go up into another dune ridge, known as the West Dunes, which were formed some 300 years ago. They have wonderfully varied habitats with wide grassy rides, dune grassland, and quite dense scrub with elder, hawthorn, and the inevitable sea buckthorn. The meadows are thick with flowers such as thyme-leaved sandwort (*Arenaria serpyllifolia*), viper's bugloss, early forget-me-not (*Myosotis ramosissima*), lady's bedstraw, dove's-foot cranesbill (*Geranium molle*), and rue-leaved saxifrage (*Saxifraga tridactylites*), cowslip and pyramidal orchid. Sea campion and dewberry grow along the edges of the dunes, while under the scrub in places there is a profuse growth of spring beauty (*Montia perfoliata*, see Snettisham, page 141). As might be expected, butterflies are common in this area, with small tortoiseshell, orange tip, meadow brown, gatekeeper, peacock, common blue, and green hairstreak all likely to be present. From the dunes, the car park and visitor centre are easily seen, and there are paths leading back to them.

Martin's Pond

SUMMARY A most interesting and unexpected nature reserve in a completely urban setting in Nottingham, just three miles from the city centre. A short walk of about half a mile, but a splendid example of conservation within a city.

APPROXIMATE LENGTH OF WALK ½ mile.

BEST TIME All year.

LOCATION Entrance in Russell Avenue off Russell Drive, Wollaton, about 3 miles from Nottingham City Centre. SK526402.

Perhaps the most astonishing feature of this reserve is the complete contrast in surroundings within a matter of just a few feet. At the entrance, one is standing in a typical suburban residential street with parked cars and neat gardens; a couple of steps through the gate, and the natural world takes over. Immediately in front is the pond itself, with a cluster of willow trees flanked by common reedmace (*Typha latifolia*) partially obscuring the open water. Take a few steps to the right, along the path that encircles the pond, and some idea may be gained of the real sanctuary for wetland plants and animals that this unusual reserve provides.

During July and August the surface of the water, especially on the far side, is covered with white water-lilies (*Nymphaea alba*), and backed by an extensive stand of reedmace – of which more later. Along the pond edge a variety of wetland plants grow, such as water mint (*Mentha aquatica*) and water forget-me-not (*Myosotis scorpicoides*), while the surface, usually in the tiny inlets where water movement is minimal, is green with the terminal rosettes of water starwort (*Callitriche spp.*).

The reserve boasts a bird list of over seventy species, with twenty-four of these breeding. Both great crested and little grebe are among the breeding birds, as is the much more uncommon ruddy duck. Woodcock, snipe, and the elusive water rail have been recorded in winter, and a real 'twitcher's special' – the spotted crake – has been seen. Anyone prepared to sit quietly and watch may see one or more of the reserve's mammals – water shrews and water voles.

Around much of the pond there are little wooden platforms extending a short distance out into the water, presumably for the many fishermen. They are equally useful for naturalists, as they provide excellent places from which to indulge in a bit of 'pond dipping'. Even a few minutes spent with a net is rewarding. Two molluscs appear to be common – the ramshorn snail (identification of the precise species is best left to specialists!), and the great pond snail. Swan and pea mussels are also present, but the former are less likely to be found as they tend to live in the mud in the deeper water. Two creatures that make many people shudder – flatworms and leeches – may also be dredged up. In the spring and early summer frog and toad spawn or tadpoles are other possibilities.

The most exciting catch of all, however, is either of the two species of newts (common or smooth, and palmate) to be found in the pond – most usually during the breeding season from February to June. As might be expected from its name, the common newt is the one most likely to be captured. Measuring up to about 10 cm (4 inches) in length, common newts are yellowish-brown in colour with dark spots, and can be distinguished from the palmate species by their spotted throats and the lack of webbing on their hind feet. The newts are most likely to be found in areas of the pond near the densest vegetation. Dragonflies are likely to be darting, hovering or flying almost anywhere on the reserve, and mayflies can be seen close to or over the water.

After a few hundred yards the path passes over what appears to be a sluice. In this area, surface water plants, such as starwort, grow particularly profusely. Following this, the bank becomes very overgrown with a great variety of plants such as rosebay willowherb (*Chamaenerion angustifolium*) in the drier parts, and marsh marigolds (*Caltha palustris*), ragged robin (*Lychnis flos-cuculi*), meadowsweet (*Filipendula ulmaria*) and some willow scrub.

A little further on, a boardwalk goes off to the left into what is arguably the most fascinating part of the reserve. The boardwalk is just above water level, and leads right through the centre of a reed swamp surrounded by willow scrub. Here, close views can be had of one of the reserve's more unusual plants – the lesser reedmace (*Typha augustifolia*). Conveniently, common or greater reedmace is also present, the two growing side by side (and in some cases they have hybridized) so that the obvious differences between them can be seen at close quarters.

Both plants grow from underground stems or rhizomes and may reach heights of up to about 2 metres (7 feet). As can be seen, the leaves of the lesser reedmace are much narrower than that of the greater. The flowering parts of the two plants are also easily distinguishable. In the common reedmace the male flowers are in a tight, pointed spike immediately above the sausage-shaped, dark-brown spike of the female flowers. In the lesser, however, the male and the female spikes are separated by some 7.5–10 cm (3–4 inches).

It is not just the reedmaces that can be seen from the boardwalk; there are also other wetland plants, such as golden dock (*Rumex maritimus*), which grows in many parts of the reserve, marsh arrow-grass (*Triglochin palustris*) with its typically arrow-shaped leaves, great willowherb (*Epilobium hirsutum*) – distinguished from rosebay willowherb by its hairy, stalkless leaves which grow in opposite pairs on the stem, contrasting with the hairless, spirally arranged, stalked leaves of the rosebay variety – and gipsywort (*Lycopus europaeus*). A delightful bonus is the chance of seeing willow, reed and sedge warblers, and possibly their nests, at quite close quarters in the willow scrub.

Return to the main path, and continue on back to the exit gate.

Attenborough Pits

SUMMARY A prime example of what can be done with worked-out gravel pits – the area is now a Site of Special Scientific Interest (SSSI). It makes a walk packed with interesting aquatic and waterside features, and includes a delightful stretch of the River Trent. The reserve, which was established in 1966, is owned by Batterley Aggregates Ltd and managed by the Nottinghamshire Trust for Nature Conservation.

APPROXIMATE LENGTH OF WALK 2½ miles.

BEST TIME All year.

LOCATION Off the A6005 in Nottingham in the village of Attenborough. SK521343.

Even before leaving the car there is plenty to see at Attenborough gravel pits. In the flooded pit by the car park dozens of wildfowl crowd the water, and many are clearly accustomed to being fed by visitors. By far the most common breeds are the resident Canada geese, mute swans and mallard, but there are also wintering teal, tufted duck, pochard, shoveler, and the occasional merganser, goosander and garganey. Moorhens and coots are common; less often seen are the grebes, but all the British species have been recorded. A few of the ducks will not be found in any handbook of British birds, being crosses between mallard and farmyard ducks!

The walk leaves the car park by way of the bridge over the ponds. To the right of the path is a stand of hybrid black poplars, while on the left hawthorn, elder, dog rose and bramble are growing. There are little tracks off to the right of the main pathway leading down to the water, and it is worth taking some of these to get a closer look at the water fowl and to be rewarded with a delightful view across to the little, tree-fringed islands. Great crested grebes often nest near the islands. Along the banks are reedmace (*Typha latifolia*), great willowherb (*Epilobium hirsutum*), sedges, water forget-me-not (*Myosotis scorpioides*) and great burnet (*Sanguisorba officinalis*). Further along the main path, nearer the water, there are alders and, on the right, ash and oak.

Where the path meets the River Trent, turn left. Just a few yards along, growing on the river bank and in the water, is a large stand of bulrush (*Scirpus lacustris*). This is *real* bulrush (also known as common club-rush), and not the reedmace that is often incorrectly called bulrush. It is very tall, with a leafless, round stem above water (the leaves are submerged) and a head of large, egg-shaped 'flowers'. Reeds also fringe the river, and water-lilies grow at various points near the water's edge, making a lovely show.

Along the river is a good place for seeing dragonflies and damselflies, such as the brown aeshna (brown body with narrow yellow stripes, yellow and black head), and the banded agrion and blue-tailed damselflies. On the left of the path a variety of trees (alder, birch, oak and hawthorn) have been planted to encourage birds to nest and to screen the ponds from disturbance. Splendid views of common terns may be had along this path, as they flight to and from their nests on a special platform that has been built for them, and great crested grebes can sometimes be seen on the river, while reed buntings skulk among the dense vegetation.

On either side of the path, depending on the time of year, a fine array of flowering plants and grasses is seen. The grasses include Timothy (*Phleum pratense*), meadow foxtail (*Alopecurus pratensis*) and cocksfoot (*Dactylis glomerata*), while tansy (*Chrysanthemum vulgare*), hemlock (*Conium maculatum* – poisonous, so take care) and common toadflax (*Linaria vulgaris*) provide colour.

After crossing the bridge over an outflow from one of the flooded pits, turn left on to a causeway known as The Bund. On the right of this, a short distance along, is a pond with several islands and some wetland, on which reed and willow grow. There is a large scrape on the right where numbers of black-headed gulls congregate and various waders such as snipe, common sandpiper, redshank and little ringed plover may be seen at migration times.

Further along, there is a small lagoon where teal often collect and herons fish in the shallow water. Towards the end of the causeway there is a sheltered area where teasel (*Dipsacus fullonum*), St John's wort and lady's smock (*Cardamine pratensis*) are among the herbs that attract many different butterflies. Among those recorded are the orange tip (whose caterpillar's food plant is lady's smock), small tortoiseshell (nettle), brimstone (buckthorn and alder buckthorn), and the small and large skippers, meadow brown and gatekeeper (grasses).

At the end of The Bund the trail leads around to the left over the works bridge. From the bridge there is an extensive view of another flooded pit, and also the gravel and sand extraction which is still going on. The flooded pit appears to be a favourite place for Canada geese. I saw about fifty of them sailing solemnly along in line astern – a lovely sight.

After the bridge the pathway goes alongside some sheltered water on the left, which is surrounded and partially covered by dense vegetation of reeds and rushes, alder and willows. Both white and yellow water-lilies (*Nymphaea alba* and *Nuphor lutea*) are there, duckweed (*Lemna sp.*), arrowhead (*Sagittaria sagittifolia*), and the small (about 2.5 cm (1 inch) across) floating fronds of water fern, which turn red in autumn. The fern has hair-like roots which hang down in the water. Other flowering plants, depending on the season, include marsh marigolds (*Caltha palustris*), yellow iris (*Iris pseudacorus*), water-dropwort (*Filipendula vulgaris*) and hemp agrimony (*Eupatorium cannabinum*). Great crested grebes may be seen here.

Continue along the pathway until it meets the Strand in Attenborough village; turn left and follow this back to the car park. Just at the corner, where the road goes into the car park, there is a stand of common comfrey (*Symphytum officinale*), recognizable by its size (about 90 cm (3 feet) tall), long, soft leaves covered with hairs on their upper surfaces, and pale, pinkish-white flowers.

EAST
ENGLAND

1 Seawick and St Osyth
2 Walton-on-the-Naze
   Shore Walk
3 Walberswick
4 East Wretham Heath
5 Winterton Dunes

6 Broadlands
   Conservation Centre
   Nature Trail
7 Snettisham
8 The Devil's Dyke
9 Wicken Fen

Seawick and St Osyth

SUMMARY The beach and the sea wall at St Osyth
provide an interesting walk, with salt marsh and beach.
In winter there are good views of Brent geese and
many waders.

APPROXIMATE LENGTH OF WALK 4 miles.

BEST TIME All year.

LOCATION Village of Seawick in Essex. TM131126.

From the car park at Seawick go down over the sea wall to
the beach and turn right. The beach consists of sand with
some shingle, and its principal interest lies in the various
shells and other objects that are washed up. One of the most
numerous shells found is the slipper limpet, which has a
curious life history. The creatures live in chains of up to a
dozen individuals, with the oldest ones on the bottom. They
actually change sex, with the lower females being fertilized
by the upper males who, as they age, become female. It is
no coincidence that many oyster shells are also found, as
where there are oysters there are very often slipper limpets.
The limpets attach themselves to the oyster shells,
smothering them and competing with them for food. They
are a serious pest in oyster beds. Also washed up are dog
whelks and cockle shells. A great many grey-fawn, flattened,
much-divided fronds about 10–15 cm (4–6 inches) long are
frequently found after storms, and at first sight look like
seaweed. However, close examination with a hand lens
shows that the surface is divided into row upon row of tiny
rectangular compartments. The fronds are in fact, one of the
sea mats, hornwrack, and each compartment contains a little

animal which feeds by protruding a ring of tentacles into the surrounding water.

Pieces of sponge are also common and they, like the hornwrack, are animals. Inspection shows that a piece of sponge consists of thousands upon thousands of tiny openings. These are embedded in a material made of a horny fibre. The openings lead into cavities lined with cells, and each cavity has two entrances – a small one through which water is drawn into the central cavity, and a large one through which it is discharged after the food in it has been extracted.

Mermaid's purses are the egg cases of both dogfish and rays – but which is which? Those of the dogfish have long tendrils at all four corners; cases up to about 5 cm (2 inches) in length, excluding the tendrils, come from the lesser spotted dogfish, while the larger ones, up to about 10 cm (4 inches) long, are from the great spotted dogfish. The cases that have points at all four corners belong to skates or the various rays, and they range in size from about 5 cm to 15 cm (2–6 inches), depending on the species. The skate egg case is the largest, and is wider at one end than the other.

After about a mile, the boundary of the Colne Point nature reserve is reached. As this is not open to the public, return along the beach to the starting point. From there, climb up on the sea wall and walk along it towards Colne Point.

On the right-hand side of the wall are cultivated fields, and on the left is a large area of marsh and saltings where waders are likely to be seen, although not in great numbers. Redshank, curlew, and ringed and grey plover are those most likely to be present. In the summer, the saltings contain thrift (*Armeria maritima*), glasswort (*Salicornia sp.*), sea campion (*Silene maritima*), and other typical salt-marsh plants, but in the winter, sea couch-grass (*Agropyron pungens*) and marram grass (*Ammophila arenaria*) are almost all that remains.

One of the best reasons for visiting this area in winter is the good views obtained of the Brent geese, and huge flocks of them are likely to be in the sky from time to time as they move about the feeding grounds nearer Colne Point. These handsome geese, smaller than the other wintering geese that come to Britain, such as greylag, pinkfoot and barnacle, belong to the dark-bellied race, which comes from its breeding grounds in Arctic Russia.

After about three-quarters of a mile, a fence across the salt marsh marks the boundary of the Colne Point reserve, but stay on the sea wall, passing a narrow road that leads to the entrance of the reserve, and continue along past some holiday bungalows. The next section of the wall skirts on the right an area of fields between it and the access road to the reserve. These fields can, on occasion, support vast numbers of waders such as curlew, lapwing, and golden plover.

A little further on, the wall begins a right-hand turn and, a short distance along, it is worth coming off the wall on the left-hand side and walking across the saltings towards the estuary. This seems to be a favourite place with the Brents, and it is possible to come across a huge flock of them quite suddenly, feeding in the very deep channels that cut through the estuary. One does, of course, get some warning that they are nearby, as there is a constant honking as they chatter among themselves, but it is not always easy to place the sound exactly. In the same area, many shelduck are likely to be seen.

Return to the wall, and after about two and a half miles from the start a sewage farm is reached on the right, where herons and pied wagtails are often seen. Nearby, autumn migrants such as wheatears and whinchats perch on the fences. Just after the sewage farm, take the small track leading down to the right from the wall to the road. Turn right, back towards the sea, and eventually rejoin the sea wall for the walk back to Seawick.

Walton-on-the-Naze Shore Walk

SUMMARY An exciting walk, especially for the bird-watcher, along the beach towards Stone Point. Hundreds of waders can be seen at quite close quarters. *This walk should be undertaken only at low tide.*

APPROXIMATE LENGTH OF WALK 4–5 miles.

BEST TIME All year.

LOCATION Walton-on-the-Naze village in Essex. TM266245.

From the cliff-top car park take the steps that lead down the very soft, red sandstone cliff to the shore. Turn left along the beach. After a short distance there are the remains of some old concrete gun emplacements or pillboxes, now covered with fucoid seaweeds (wracks), under which is a dense growth of barnacles. Out to sea, flocks of dunlin may be seen, wheeling and turning, and from time to time they come in to land on the beach or on the rocks further along the shore.

After just over half a mile or so, the lower shore sand gives way to gently shelving rock, and this continues for much of the remainder of the walk. Dunlin may often be seen on the rocks, and perhaps some grey plover. A little further on, a wire-covered groyne stretches out from the upper shore, and sometimes turnstones can be seen on it, rather unsuccessfully trying to move the stones which are contained by a wire covering. The brown seaweed, bladder wrack (*Fucus vesiculosis*) grows on the groyne, with more barnacles underneath it.

Further on again, the rocks extend higher up the shore;

note their very soft consistency. Oystercatchers may be seen in some number near the water's edge, hammering away at the mussels, while herons stalk around the rock pools or stand motionless, waiting to pounce on small fish and crustaceans.

After about a mile a causeway leads from the sea wall down to the shore. At this point or hereabouts an interesting change may be observed. Quite suddenly the beach just below the strand line is covered with huge numbers of shells (the number almost certainly varies with different winds and tides). Mussel, whelk, limpet and oyster shells lie about in their thousands. It is the most exciting part of the walk as, where the rocks further down the shore are interspersed with areas of sand, large numbers of waders collect. Ringed plover, grey plover, dunlin, godwit, curlew and purple sandpiper are likely to be seen during the winter months and, with a cautious approach, it is possible to obtain quite close views of these birds. In mid-winter little parties of snow bunting are frequently seen along the beach and groups of goldeneye can be spotted out to sea. In summer skuas are present, and make the lives of other birds, especially the common terns, a misery by their constant harassment.

Leave the beach where convenient and continue towards the Point, crossing a number of dykes (this is only possible at low tide). There is a vast expanse of saltings on the left on which greenshank and shelduck are often seen, and in winter flocks of twite may be seen almost anywhere – the males recognizable by their pink rumps and yellow beaks. One of the great sights and sounds of this walk is the large flocks of Brent geese which winter on the saltings and on the islands in Halford Water.

Having reached the Point, return across the saltings, and when possible go up on the sea wall and so back to the car park.

Walberswick

SUMMARY A fine mixture of reed beds, mud flats and
woodland, with the opportunity of seeing how reed
beds are managed for both commercial and
conservation interests. This walk can be very muddy.

APPROXIMATE LENGTH OF WALK 3½ miles.

BEST TIME All year.

LOCATION Walberswick village in Suffolk.
TM492746.

Walk down to the sea wall, on top of which is a shingle ridge.
Turn right, and keep a good lookout to sea for sea ducks such
as scoters, as well as grebes and red-throated divers. On the
right there is a flat area of pools, mud flats and shingle, where
many birds may be seen. Ringed plover scamper about on the
shingle; there may be redshank, oystercatcher, turnstone and
lapwing, and in winter small flocks of twite are often present.
After about three-quarters of a mile a National Nature Reserve
sign is reached, reminding visitors that a permit is required to
go anywhere but on the rights of way (not necessary for this
walk). Further along, away from the holiday chalets, reeds
begin to put in an appearance behind the flat marshy ground,
and shelduck, dunlin and grey plover often forage in the area
for food, while greenfinches, yellowhammers and reed buntings may be seen. In winter, snow buntings and the occasional
shore lark may be seen too.

A mile and a half along the ridge the far boundary notice
of the National Nature Reserve is reached. Almost immediately after that, turn sharp right on to a bank which runs
across the reed bed towards a water pump tower in the
distance. On either side there are extensive reed beds and

pools. Here, especially in winter, water rail may be seen, or more likely heard, while snipe may take off in their rather frantic manner. Overhead, kestrels hover, while sparrow-hawks and hen harriers are regularly seen. In winter this is a particularly good place in which to see the unusual rough-legged buzzard. It is not very easy to distinguish from the common buzzard in the field, as the diagnostic feather-covered legs are not usually visible. However, it does hover rather more than the common buzzard, and the underside of its tail is mostly white with a black bar at the tip, whereas that of the common buzzard is uniformly barred.

The reed beds are being cut in a number of places, as can be seen when crossing them. There is a management policy of rotational cutting so that there are always good young reeds for thatching, but there are also mature stands to encourage water rail, reed warblers, bearded tits and perhaps the very rare bittern. There are pools in between the stands of reeds, around which teal, shoveler, gadwall and mallard can nest, and where the marsh harrier, which breeds in East Anglia, can build its nest.

Go on past the water tower and turn right by a sign saying 'Public Footpath', then right again on to a boardwalk which goes right through part of the reed bed. At the edges a few flowering plants are often present – marsh pennywort (*Hydrocotyle vulgaris*), bogbean (*Menyanthes trifoliata*) and marsh sowthistle (*Sonchus palustris*). At the end of the board-walk, follow a track through a small wood of silver birch, Scots pine and hawthorn, with bramble, gorse and broom understorey. On the path edge in spring there is a prolific growth of spring beauty (*Montia perfoliata*, see p. 141).

Continue past another National Nature Reserve signpost and stay close to the edge of the reed bed. Turn right, down on to another boardwalk, then left, and follow the river back to the village and the car park.

East Wretham Heath

SUMMARY A fine and fascinating reserve on typical Breckland heath, with pine, deciduous woodland and meres. Closed Tuesdays. Visitors are asked to report to the warden, from whom a permit is required, at 10 A.M. or 2 P.M. There is a Nature Trail for the visually handicapped.

APPROXIMATE LENGTH OF WALK 2½ miles.

BEST TIMES Spring, summer.

LOCATION On the A1075 road near Thetford in Norfolk. TL914886.

To appreciate Breckland fully, a little background information may be helpful. It is not a natural habitat but a landscape created partly by forest clearance, partly by cultivation, and partly by the activities of sheep and rabbits. A breck was a piece of land that was cultivated to grow grain when prices were high and then allowed to revert to the original heath when the prices fell. It is a mosaic of arable land, heath, forest and grassland, all low lying and all based on chalk covered by sand or glacial deposits. The variety of habitat is largely due to the fact that the soils vary a great deal over very short distances, from, for example, pure chalk to sand.

From the warden's house, go across the field towards the clump of Scots pine. As the pines are approached, on either side of the trail there is coarse, tussocky grass, bracken, and hawthorn scrub. This encroachment of former grassland is a relatively recent development following the myxomatosis outbreaks in the 1950s. Go through the gate and in among the Scots pines, and follow the pathway to Post Two of the Nature Trail. The woodland, which consists chiefly of Scots pine, is known as the Langmere plantation, with an understorey of hawthorn and a field layer of gorse and bracken. Ground ivy (*Glechoma hederacea*) provides some of the ground layer.

At Post Three the path turns sharp left. Some stonecrop may be seen growing on the tarmac, while there is broom on both sides of the path, a very big Scots pine on the left, and some ash. Look about for signs, such as slots and droppings, of roe deer, which can sometimes be seen in the thicket on the right. Further along the path, near and around Post Four, the Scots pines offer food and shelter to a number of woodland birds, such as greater spotted woodpecker and crossbill. Examination of the fallen cones, as well as showing the presence of the crossbills when these birds are present, also proves that squirrels are in residence. The crossbills attack the cones by splitting the scales and pressing them outwards. Squirrels, on the other hand, strip off the scales, and the remains of the cone are invariably frayed.

This area is good for a variety of plants, such as bladder campion (*Silene vulgaris*), hound's-tongue (*Cynoglossum officinale*), broom, and musk mallow (*Malva moschata*) in season.

Continue along the path, which gradually rises slightly towards the top of a low ridge, noting the old wall on the right where lizards may sometimes be seen sunning themselves. As the top of the ridge is approached, a field can be seen through the trees on the right. In the field, between Posts Six and Seven, there is a deer-rutting ring. The significance of these rings, at least in the case of roe deer, is not altogether clear. The name suggests that they are used during the rutting season, but they are also used as play areas by families of roe, who run round and round for periods of up to fifteen minutes or so.

At Post Eight the woodland becomes deciduous with oak and ash, and an understorey of hawthorn, blackthorn and bracken. In it, many woodland birds may be seen. The path then leads on towards Post Nine, and between this point and Post Ten, Scots pine is once again the dominant species, with the clear area under them being very noticeable. As the Nature Trail pamphlet explains, this is due to the fact that the pine trees make the surrounding soil acid, and this prevents further pine seed germination except at the edges of the plantation. Seedling pines are being planted to replace the older trees as they die off. In this plantation and as far as Post Eleven, a little time spent just watching the tree canopy is well spent. This is the territory of the only pair of red squirrels on the reserve. Birds that may be seen here include greater spotted woodpecker, goldcrest and tree creeper.

The next section of the path leads through scrubland with blackthorn, hawthorn, and gorse, with broom on either side, and with a number of big oak trees. At about Post Twelve the tarmac remains of the old World War II runway are clearly visible, and at Post Thirteen the track turns sharp left among, in April and May, masses of brilliantly coloured broom. In this area the covering sandy soil is thin, and the underlying chalk encourages the growth of a typical field layer such as, in season, a variety of small herbs including germander speedwell (*Veronica chamaedrys*), heath bedstraw (*Galium saxatile*), viper's bugloss (*Echium vulgare*), mouse-ear hawkweed (*Pilosella officinarum*) and thyme (*Thymus drucei*). The scrub is a splendid place for birds such as whitethroat, spotted flycatcher and blackcap, while the flowers attract butterflies such as orange tip, peacock, and small tortoiseshell.

After Post Thirteen the path leads through more deciduous woodland to the hide which overlooks Langmere. The mere itself is fringed with reed canary-grass (*Phalaris arundinacea*) and golden dock (*Rumex maritimus*), while amphibious bistort (*Polygonum amphibium*), fennel pondweed (*Potamogeton pectinatus*) and knotted pearlwort (*Sagina nodosa*) all grow in the water itself. After very wet weather the water level of the mere can rise and make entrance to the hide impossible. The mere attracts an exciting variety of waders and wildfowl, such as pochard, shoveler, mallard, gadwall, teal, wigeon, tufted duck, little grebe, wood, green and common sandpiper, and redshank.

Return to the main path, and follow it through a mixed woodland of silver birch, pine, oak and ash until a gate is reached at Post Nineteen. Turn left after the gate on to a drove road. Continue along this to Post Twenty, where there is a very noticeable spread of heather on the left. This has grown up only since the laying of the North Sea gas pipeline, and covers the trench that was dug for it. Seemingly, the heather seeds lay dormant until the soil was disturbed by the workings. On the right is a line of hornbeams which were planted, and attract such birds as siskin and hawfinch, while butterflies that may be seen in this area include the ringlet and the speckled wood. Continue on the drove road almost until the A1075 is reached; just before it, turn left and proceed back parallel with the road to the car park.

Winterton Dunes

SUMMARY The main object of this walk is to 'see the rare natterjack toads which live and breed in some of the pools behind the dunes. It is a National Nature Reserve, where important conservation measures are being taken to retain and increase the numbers of the natterjack. In addition to the toads, the reserve has other interesting features, including some uncommon ferns.

APPROXIMATE LENGTH OF WALK Up to 2 miles.

BEST TIMES Spring, summer.

LOCATION Through Winterton village, about 6 miles north of Great Yarmouth. TG498197.

First, a word of warning to emphasize those which appear on notices at the reserve boundaries: there are many adders on the reserve.

From the car park (where ringed plover sometimes run about) behind the high dune ridge, go into the smaller dunes and walk away from the sea until a more open area of heather-clad dune slacks and lower ridges is reached. This area is criss-crossed with many tracks, and no attempt will be made in the description of this walk to direct walkers on to any specific one – it is far too confusing. Most of the reserve can be seen from the tops of the small ridges, so becoming lost is not a problem.

Turn right along one of the broader grassy tracks. On the far left is a woodland, in front of which is some scrub, which offers shelter to many passage migrants and breeding birds. Among the former are siskin, fieldfare, redwing, redpoll and brambling, while the breeding birds include an impressive list of warblers – garden, reed, sedge and willow – with chiffchaff and whitethroat.

As can be seen, the heathland area is a mixture of ling (*Calluna vulgaris*) and bell heather (*Erica cinerea*) and, in the many wet areas, cross-leaved heath (*Erica tetralix*). There are many pools, most of them natural, but some are bomb craters, and the larger ones are surrounded by willow. Scattered throughout the slacks, sometimes hidden among the coarse grasses, are stands of a number of uncommon ferns – notably royal fern (*Osmunda regalis*), broad and narrow buckler fern (*Dryopteris dilatata* and *D. carthusiana*), and the rare crested buckler (*Dryopteris cristata*) fern.

The speciality of the reserve, however, is the natterjack toad which breeds in some of the shallow pools – most of them some distance from the car park. Probably the best way to find them in the breeding season (April to June) is to listen! Dusk is said to be the best time to hear them, but they can also be heard at other times during the day. The croak of the male natterjack is distinctive – quite high-pitched, loud, and rasping – and the sound carries an appreciable distance. Usually one toad will start and gradually all the others join in until, just as suddenly as it started, the chorus stops. The sound is made when the toad is in the pond and throws its head back and out of the water, expanding the large vocal sac under the chin. This is done by pumping air into the sac through a slit in the floor of the mouth.

When the position of the toads has been located, approach very slowly and carefully, as it is all too easy to stand on them – not just on the adults but also on the tiny toads that may be around the edges of the pools.

Apart from the croak of the male, natterjacks are quickly recognized by the distinctive yellow stripe down the mid-line of the back. The remainder of the upper part of the body is deep olive green, and the warts have yellow, red or orange blotches on them; the underside has dense dark spots on a light background.

When the toads are moving on land they do not hop like frogs; they may give an initial short jump but then they run. (They are also called running toads.) This is because the hind limbs are much shorter than those of frogs or common toads. The short limbs also restrict their swimming ability, hence their preference for shallow pools. However, the legs are ideal for burrowing, and when the toads hibernate they dig burrows in the sandy soil. The shallowness of the water in the breeding pools can be a hazard to the natterjacks. In hot weather, the water may evaporate and the spawn or the young tadpoles and toads may die. As an adaptation to this, to develop from spawn through the tadpole stages takes only one or two months, instead of up to three months as with other frogs and toads. As a conservation measure and to increase the toads' chances of survival the Nature Conservancy Council has created a new pool at the northern end of the reserve to ensure a permanent breeding place.

Watching and listening to the toads is fascinating, but please remember that they are protected and it is an offence to disturb or to handle them.

Broadlands Conservation Centre Nature Trail

SUMMARY This is a very short walk of about a quarter of a mile, but within that short distance there is a unique opportunity to see at close (and dry!) quarters, the natural succession of plants from open water right through to woodland. 'Succession' used in this sense means the orderly sequence of changes that occur in a plant population during the development of vegetation that is left undisturbed. In still water, such as Ranworth Broad, development begins with the initial colonization of the open water by specially adapted plants, and reaches its climax on dry land with oak and other trees.

APPROXIMATE LENGTH OF WALK ¼ mile.

BEST TIME April–October.

LOCATION Car park in the village of Ranworth, Norfolk. Nature Trail at TM356149.

From the car park opposite the Maltsters public house, turn left to the junction of three roads; take the right-hand one of the two roads that lead away from the pub. The start of the nature trail is a few hundred yards down the road on the right-hand side.

Follow the boardwalk to the conservation centre which is open daily (except all day Monday and Saturday mornings) from 1 April to 31 October. It is a delightful thatched building on pontoons moored on the edge of Ranworth Broad. Throughout the walk a variety of insects may be seen on and among the lush vegetation. Butterflies include the painted lady, holly blue, comma, small and large skipper and the small copper. Moths, some of which are night-flying or more likely to be seen in the evening, are present in some numbers, with the elephant hawk, puss moth, emperor, and eyed hawk perhaps the best known. Where there is water, any one of seven species of dragonfly and three species of damselfly may be spotted. (Dragonflies are distinguished from damselflies by their generally larger size, and by their wings which, at rest, are extended horizontally on each side, while damselflies fold their wings together over their backs.) The blue and yellow striped hairy dragonfly is often seen along the Nature Trail from April till June.

The centre contains really excellent audio-visual displays and exhibitions explaining the natural history of the Broads, and should on no account be missed. From the upstairs gallery there are extensive views over the marsh and Ranworth Broad itself. Special points of interest from a conservation point of view are the wherries and a coal barge which have been sunk along the left-hand side of the Broad in an effort to stop erosion of the banks by wave action. The many small craft which use the Broads are the principal culprits.

Also from the gallery, good views are obtained of some of the birds. These include breeding herons, great-crested grebes, a colony of common terns (which nest on three artificial islands provided for them at the far end of the Broad), mute swans, coots, and water rails. The reed beds are, of course, ideal nesting sites for reed buntings and sedge and reed warblers. Other birds that regularly visit the Broad include black terns and red-necked, black-necked and Slavonian grebes. A host of other birds are present in the various habitats. The very occasional bittern has been reported but, sadly, the only one most people are likely to see here, or in East Anglia as a whole, is the stuffed one in the exhibition. In winter (when the centre is closed), waders are common; there is a huge cormorant roost, and up to 20,000 gulls of various species also roost.

Walking back along the boardwalk is the best time to take a detailed look at the plant succession. This begins in the open water with a somewhat limited selection of plants, pollution having seriously reduced the numbers. However, those which are present include various pondweeds, water milfoils, water-lilies and hornwort. Also present are mare's-tails (*Hippuris vulgaris*), so named by early botanists who believed them to be the female plants of the horsetails (*Equisteum*). In fact, mare's-tails are much less primitive plants, bearing flowers (albeit inconspicuous ones) and not spores like the horsetails.

These are the colonizing plants at the start of the succession, and some, by means of their roots or underground stems, help to stabilize the mud at the edges of the water and provide a rooting medium for the next stage – the reed fen. This consists chiefly of reeds, reedmace (*Typha latifolia*), and rushes. At Ranworth this area is cut annually to allow the growth of great hairy willowherb (*Epilobium hirsutum*), milk parsley (*Peucedanum palustre*), and marsh valerian (*Valeriana dioica*). Milk parsley is fed on by the caterpillar of the scarce and very beautiful swallowtail butterfly – a species now confined to the Broads due to land drainage elsewhere. The butterfly is on the wing from late May to mid-July, but is by no means common, and a sighting on the Nature Trail would be a triumph indeed. The inside of the reed stems acts as host to the larvae of the wainscot moth.

As some of the reeds and rushes die back annually the resulting litter, together with their underground stems or rhizomes, helps to establish a layer of peat. This offers a firmer footing for the growth of the plants of the next stage – the swamp carr. (Carr is the name given to a type of wood and scrubland formed in very wet conditions.) Here there are small bushes and shrubs such as sallow, guelder rose, buckthorn, alder buckthorn, and alder, together with ferns such as the marsh (*Thelypteris palustris*) and the broad buckler (*Dryopteris dilatata*), and some of the distinctive mounds of the tussock sedge (*Carex paniculata*). Flowering plants, including yellow irises/flags (*Iris pseudacorus*) and marsh marigolds (*Caltha palustris*), make a splash of colour in this area, and continue to grow along the trail until the habitat becomes too dry for them.

With increasing distance from the open water the peat deposit becomes thicker and more able to support larger trees until it gives rise to the next stage – the wet woodland. This is a fascinating section, with the dense vegetation under the trees giving it an almost jungle-like appearance. The alder trees are noticeably larger here, with some in excess of forty feet. The fact that some have more than one trunk points to coppicing having occurred in previous times. Also in the wet woodland are a number of ashes, and silver and downy birch. Many of the trees and shrubs support climbing plants – honeysuckle (*Lonicera periclymenum*), bindweed (*Calystegia sepium*), hops (*Humulus lupulus*), and woody nightshade (*Solanum dulcamara*).

Finally, as the end of the trail is approached, the land becomes drier and the climax vegetation (i.e. the final stage in the succession) is reached. This is the oak woodland, dominated by pedunculate or English oak, with its long-stalked acorns and almost stalkless leaves. As is well-known, the oak supports a huge variety of animals, birds, and insects. The birds most likely to be seen in this drier area are nuthatches, all three woodpeckers, willow warblers, blackcaps, spotted flycatchers, and tree creepers.

Snettisham Walk 1

SUMMARY Tidal sand, mud flats, shingle and flooded gravel pits set on the east side of the Wash. This is one of the most rewarding bird walks in England, especially in winter and at migration times, but is full of interest at most times of the year. A very good place for shingle plants.

APPROXIMATE LENGTH OF WALK 4–5 miles.

BEST TIME All year, but winter is best for waders.

LOCATION Near the village of Snettisham, Norfolk. TT648333.

Park either in the public car park by the sea wall or, if there is room, in a small pull-in just round the corner from the RSPB notice board. (There are special requests from the RSPB: (1) not to park among the caravans and chalets, which is all private property, and (2) to avoid disturbing waders, which feed close to the beach, especially in winter.)

Walk down to the sea wall (from the RSPB notice board this involves walking along a road through the caravan and chalet site). Turn left and walk along the top of the wall – not particularly easy at first, as it is loose shingle for some distance before the wall merges into a wider area of more stable shingle, backed by rough grassland. However, it has its rewards, as in spring and summer there is a fascinating range of plants, whose situation varies according to the stability or otherwise of the substrate.

The most colourful plant to be seen on the shingle is the yellow horned poppy (*Glaucium flavum*), in flower between June and September – although each flower lasts only about two days. Nearly every plant bears long, narrow, curved seed capsules – the longest of any British wild flower. Other plants of the shingle include hound's-tongue (*Cynoglossum officinale*), curled dock (*Rumex crispus*), sea sandwort (*Honkenya peploides*) and sea beet (*Beta vulgaris*), while a few plants of sea kale (*Crambe maritima*) are present. At the far end of the reserve beyond the hides and on the edge of the salt marsh, shrubby seablite (*Suaeda fructicosa/Suaeda vera*) – not to be confused with the smaller annual seablite (*Suaeda maritima*) – is found. A few plants of teasel (*Dipsacus fullonum*) are also present on the landward side of the sea wall.

Between a quarter and half a mile along, a large area of rough, sandy grassland stretches out in front of the sea wall, where the unusual and attractive little white flowers of spring beauty (*Montia perfoliata*) grow. It is easily recognized, as the flowers appear to grow up through the centre of a single, almost circular leaf. Closer examination shows that in fact the leaves are stalkless and fused in pairs. It is not a native plant, but was introduced from North America about the middle of the last century.

Just beyond the grassy patch, and especially at low tide during the winter and migration times, the astonishing extent of the bird life at Snettisham becomes apparent. The first sight of this exciting area is a moment to remember. Acre upon acre of sand and mud flat stretch out – almost to the horizon, or so it seems – and at peak times they are teeming with waders and wildfowl. The principal species are curlew, turnstone, redshank, knot, dunlin, oystercatcher, grey plover, sanderling, shelduck (which in recent years have begun using Snettisham as a moulting ground; see also Bridgwater Bay, p. 70) and mallard. Smaller (by Snettisham standards!) numbers of black-tailed godwit, ringed plover, spotted redshank and greenshank pass through in autumn.

Significant numbers of dark-bellied Brent geese are often right out on the mud flats, where their distinctive deep honking can be heard. Formerly winter visitors, the Brents now stay throughout the summer.

As a rest and change from the shingle of the sea wall, a walk along the beach reveals at least one of the reasons why some of the birds find the area so attractive. Masses of cockle and mussel shells have been washed ashore and provide food for some species, while the tiny spire-shaped shell of the snail *Hydrobia* is the principal diet of others. The tell-tale spirals of sand reveal the presence of tube-dwelling lug-worms (*Arenicola*), while further out, where visitors are asked not to go, vast quantities of other tube worms provide another item of diet.

Eventually the long line of chalets behind the sea wall comes to an end, and a better view is obtained of another exciting feature of Snettisham: the flooded shingle pits of brackish water, which is salty and alkaline. There is a long line of five pits (some of which will be seen on the return journey). Although the more distant ones are the most spectacular for bird life, on any of them good numbers of birds may be seen, depending on the time of the year. In winter, numbers of red-breasted mergansers and little grebes feed on the sticklebacks, while chironomid (midge) larvae, *Hydrobia*, and seaweeds provide food for an assortment of wildfowl – tufted duck, mallard, goldeneye, pochard, shoveler, teal, wigeon and coot. Beyond the chalets, too, shrubs of sea buckthorn grow, together with gorse.

About a mile and a quarter along the wall the first hide is reached. This gives close-up views of the fourth of the five shingle pits and more distant, but nonetheless very good views of the mud flats on the seaward side. At high spring tides in winter it is difficult to gain a seat in any of the hides, as birdwatchers come from all over the country to see the almost unbelievable numbers of birds that come to roost when their feeding grounds are covered by the sea as the tide rises. This sanctuary area is now used by some 10,000 oystercatcher, 2,000 redshank, 30,000 knot and 2,000 bar-tailed godwit. In late summer dunlin, ringed plover, sanderling and turnstone roost on the upper beach and on the pits. On the islands in the pits common terns nest, and there are also vast numbers of black-headed gulls.

Leaving this hide, follow the fence along to the left to the second hide, which overlooks the fifth shingle pit and gives yet another view of great numbers of birds. From here, turn left towards the salt marsh (to which there is no public access), and follow the fence. Little flocks of the charming snow buntings sometimes visit this area, flitting from place to place and uttering their trilling calls. It is here, too, that plants of shrubby seablite can be seen on the fringes of the salt marsh.

Keep left and cross a stile towards the third hide, which is on the opposite side of the fifth shingle pit from the second hide.

Before entering the hide climb up the dyke wall, then carefully and without standing up look over into the fields beyond. In winter this may reveal yet more of the rather special winter visitors to Snettisham – Bewick and whooper swans. It is also likely to give views of the great flocks of pink-footed geese that winter here. For anyone who is able to find overnight accommodation in the immediate vicinity of the reserve, the sight of these geese, and the wonderful sound of their conversational honkings as they fly to and from their feeding grounds at dawn and dusk, is sheer magic.

The third hide gives further views over the open water. From the hide, follow the track below the dyke over a stile, and turn left over a causeway between two of the shingle pits. This leads back to the sea wall. Return towards the car parks. For those who started from the RSPB board, return by the same route. For those who started from the public car park by the beach, follow the route towards the RSPB notice board by coming off the sea wall and walking between the rows of chalets, keeping the water of the shingle pits on the right. Towards the end of the last pit, the RSPB chalet is reached, where there is a display. From there, return to the car parks.

Snettisham Walk 2

SUMMARY An additional walk at Snettisham through part of the coastal park, and including different habitats from those in the RSPB reserve described in Snettisham Walk 1.

APPROXIMATE LENGTH OF WALK 2 miles.

BEST TIME All year.

LOCATION As for Walk 1.

Go through the gate by the car park attendant's hut opposite the club on the beach road. Follow the grassy track, which leads through rough grassland and scrub, and bear right at the yellow-topped post then right again by another similar post. On the left of this post is some shallow water merging into marshy ground.

Carry on along the grassy (muddy) track until a bank is reached with steps leading up and over it. Go over the bank and down to the reed-fringed stream, which is lined with willows, reedmace (*Typha latifolia*) and some hawthorn. In and around this area many nesting reed buntings can be heard, and also a number of warblers. Coots and moorhens can be seen or heard in among the rushes and reeds. In winter when the water is frozen one cannot help laughing as they slide around on the ice! After about half a mile, just after the notice 'Coastal Park', bear left up the bank again. From here there is an extensive view over an expanse of marsh and scrubland, where a number of birds are usually present, including an occasional ring ouzel at migration times.

In the early morning or late afternoon there is the distinct possibility of seeing a hen harrier or, more rarely, a marsh harrier. The sight of these magnificent birds slowly quartering the ground in search of small mammals, frogs, smaller birds or reptiles, is always exciting. The slowness of their flight when hunting is most noticeable, and this technique enables them to search the ground very closely. The birds also rely on sound, and have very large, owl-like ear openings concealed under their facial feathers. Sometimes when the legs of the harriers are seen to be dangling in flight their unusual length is noticeable. It enables the birds to keep their body clear of vegetation when they grasp prey with their talons.

Bearing right, walk along the top of the bank to a narrow part which leads down on to the flat by a reed-filled pool. A great many teasel plants (*Dipsacus fullonum*) are growing in the drier areas. Reed buntings seem to be everywhere during the spring and summer. At the end of the reed bed turn left and head for a hide, visible in the distance on top of the sea wall. As the hide is approached, the character of the land changes, becoming much more sandy, with patches of sea buckthorn and shrubby seablite (*Suaeda fructicosa/Suaeda vera*).

The small, fleshy leaves of the latter are an adaptation to the sand or shingle habitat and enable the plant to retain water in them.

The hide overlooks a low, rocky, seaweed-covered area, which reaches out into the sea and on which many waders feed. Beyond the visible rocks, where there are mussel beds, flocks of ducks are often present in winter, with teal, mallard and pintails, but more notably common scoter. Over recent years immature eiders have taken to staying throughout the summer.

Return to the car park along the sea wall.

The Devil's Dyke

SUMMARY A 'there and back' walk along a section of the massive Saxon earthwork which stretches some five miles across the Cambridgeshire countryside. An easy walk, in which a fine variety of chalkland plants grows in abundance. A Site of Special Scientific Interest (SSSI), and Ancient Monument, managed by the Cambridge and Isle of Ely Naturalists' Trust and Cambridgeshire County Council.

APPROXIMATE LENGTH OF WALK 7 miles.

BEST TIMES Spring, summer.

LOCATION The village of Reach, near Newmarket in Cambridgeshire. TL570660.

In the village of Reach, start the walk by the signpost that says 'Public Footpath – Newmarket 6¼, Woodditton 7½'. A path leads almost immediately up on to the top of the Dyke, which at this point is covered with a thick scrub of hawthorn, privet and blackthorn. In this, and in other similar scrubby sections along the Dyke, a number of birds nest. These include whitethroats, yellowhammers, long-tailed tits, and turtle doves. The latter is notable as being the only migratory dove seen in Britain; it returns each spring from its wintering grounds in sub-Saharan Africa.

After just under half a mile the narrow track opens out a little, then shortly after, it leads down off the Dyke for a brief distance before climbing up again. In about 100 yards, a much more open area is reached, where there is a fine display of cowslips (*Primula veris*) in spring, and a few isolated blue hyacinths. The fields on either side offer nesting sites for such birds as meadow pipits, skylarks, corn buntings and partridges.

The Dyke is intersected by a road after one and a half miles. Cross this, and climb up on to the earthwork again, where a large noticeboard gives details of the wildlife that may be seen. It also explains the management scheme to clear scrub which, if allowed to encroach on the rich chalkland, would stifle the growth of the smaller plants.

In spring and summer this stretch of the Dyke is a wonderful mosaic of chalkland plants. Purple milk-vetch (*Astragalus danicus*), salad burnet (*Poterium sanguisorba/Sanguisorba minor*), squinancywort (*Asperula cynanchica*), bloody cranesbill (*Geranium sanguineum*), the bright purple-blue of clustered bellflower (*Campanula glomerata*), common rockrose (*Helianthemum chamaecistus*), and dropwort (*Filipendula vulgaris*) are all present. Typical chalkland grasses include torgrass (*Brachypodium pinnatum*) and one of the most easily recognized of all grasses, the delicate shivering flowerheads of quaking grass (*Briza media*). One flower that is not found in this section of the Dyke is the Pasque flower (*Pulsatilla vulgaris*), although it does grow on the earthwork but in the section nearer to Newmarket.

Continue along the Dyke, where the vegetation varies between open grassland and scrub, until the A45 main road is reached. From there, return along the same route.

Wicken Fen

SUMMARY Wicken Fen is a very special place, a
remnant of the Great Fen of East Anglia and the site of
a great deal of important research. It is virtually the
only area of its type to which the public has access
throughout the year. There are two absolutely superb
Nature Trails. One is entirely on boardwalks and is
suitable for wheelchairs and pushchairs; the other is
much longer, is not on boardwalks, and, because of
flooding or excessive trampling, sections of it may be
closed at times. Clearly, waterproof footwear is
advisable for the latter walk. The walk described below
follows the boardwalks, largely because completion of
it is no problem. The excellence of the visitor centre
and the surrounding display area matches that of the
Nature Trails. A National Trust reserve.

APPROXIMATE LENGTH OF WALK ¾ mile.

BEST TIMES Spring, summer.

LOCATION Signposted off the A1123 in the village of
Wicken, Cambridgeshire. TL563705.

From the car park turn left and walk the few hundred yards
down the road and into the visitor and interpretative centre.
After looking round the centre, go outside and walk round
the very informative garden in which is planted a wide range
of the trees and plants of the Fen. These can then be more
easily recognized during the walk.

Turn right along the boardwalk after crossing the ditch
outside the centre. On the left is one of the litter fields. Litter
in this context refers to herbaceous plant material which was
formerly used for animal feed and bedding. Now that this
use has ceased, the field is protected by regular cutting from
the inevitable scrub invasion, and also from the build up of

nutrients that would benefit only the growth of coarser grass and shrubs not typical of open fen. As a result there is a rich fen flora including yellow rattle (*Rhinanthus minor*), marsh thistle (*Cirsium palustre*), yellow loosestrife (*Lysimachia vulgaris*), meadowsweet (*Filipendula ulmaria*) and purple loosestrife (*Lythrum salicaria*). On the right, the banks of the drainage ditch are guarded by reedmace (*Typha latifolia*) and sedges.

Ahead is the wind pump, which helps to maintain the water level in the fen and is thus extremely important. The pathway leads over the drainage ditch, the surface of which is covered with pondweed (*Potamogeton*) and water crowfoot.

The boardwalk now enters an area of fen woodland, in which there are small ponds and areas of shallow water. Some of the ponds used to be old brick pits, dug to extract clay for brickmaking during the last century. They contain a range of water plants, including bladderwort (*Utricularia*), and are fringed with reedmace and yellow irises (*Iris pseudacorus*). Dragonflies and damselflies are attracted to this area, and water boatmen and pond skaters hurry about on the surface of the water. The woodland has a few examples of oak and ash, but more typical are willow, sallow, alder buckthorn and alder. As the walk leads deeper into the fen woodland the surroundings become more jungle-like, with a wonderful wet tangle of sedges and rushes, some marsh marigolds (*Caltha palustris*), woody nightshade (*Solanum dulcamara*), the nationally rare but locally abundant marsh fern (*Thelypteris palustris/Thelypteroides*), and skull cap (*Scutellaria galericulata*).

The boardwalk emerges from the woodland into one of the droves beside a drainage ditch. On the far side of the ditch is a nice succession from the water through reed to sedge, from sedge to scrub, and finally to woodland. Turn right beside the ditch. On the right there is a dense growth of reedmace, sallow and willow, which gives way after a short distance to a huge expanse of sedge.

Follow the walk across the bridge and over the ditch, which is rich in water vegetation – reedmace, water drop-wort (*Oenanthe sp.*), milk parsley (*Peucedanum palustre*), and common reed (*Phragmites australis*). Dragonflies and damsel-flies haunt this area too, and whirligig beetles can be seen on the water. The long drove ahead is, in summer, a mass of flowering plants. Southern marsh orchids (*Dactylorhiza prae-termissa*), ragged robin (*Lychnis floscuculi*), comfrey (*Symphy-tum officinale*), meadow-rue (*Thalictrum flavum*) and marsh marigold can all be seen. A small patch of carr on the right has a ground covering of mosses with a canopy of silver birch, sallow and willow, and it is not uncommon to hear a willow warbler here. A number of shrubs can also be seen, buckthorn and hawthorn among them.

Continue along the drove, noting another litter field on the right. At the far end of the drove on the right is a fine guelder-rose tree. Turn left here, by the waterway known as Wicken Lode. This is an ancient waterway, once much used commercially but now patronized by leisure craft only. Hereabouts is a favourite place for some of the many butterflies for which the fen is noted. Brimstones are common, as is the large skipper.

Just a little way along, the path leads through an area of mature carr, with buckthorn, sallow, bramble, reed and sedge. A few young ashes grow just by the path on the far side of the carr. From here, the boardwalk leads back to the visitor centre.

Throughout the walk, depending on the time of year, a range of birds may be seen. Marsh and hen harriers quarter the open areas of the sedge and litter fields, snipe inhabit the wetter parts, while woodcock can be seen and heard 'roding' over the woods. Woodpeckers, including the more unusual lesser spotted, inhabit some of the larger trees, while kingfishers dart along the waterways. The smaller woodlands attract a variety of small birds such as wood warblers and blackcaps, while the nightingale can be heard on summer evenings. The reeds and sedges give protection and nesting sites to sedge and reed warblers, while wildfowl such as teal, wigeon, mallard, and sometimes greylag geese, visit in the winter.

NORTH
ENGLAND

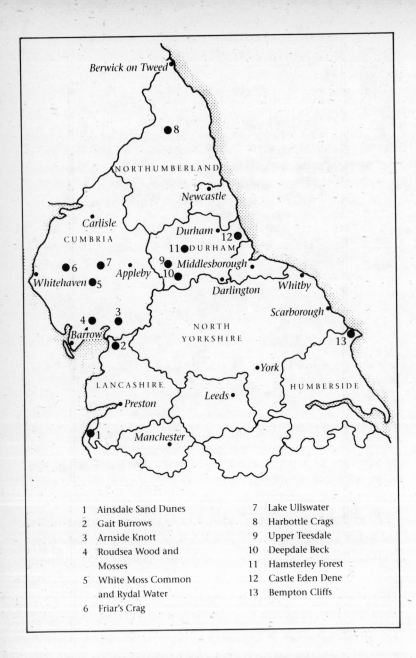

Berwick on Tweed

● 8

NORTHUMBERLAND

Newcastle

Carlisle

CUMBRIA

Durham
● 12

11 ● DURHAM

● 6   ● 7

9 ● Middlesborough

Appleby   10 ●

Whitehaven ● 5

Darlington   Whitby

Scarborough

3 ●

● 4

NORTH
YORKSHIRE

Barrow

● 2

● 13

York ●

LANCASHIRE

HUMBERSIDE

Leeds ●

Preston ●

● 1

Manchester ●

1	Ainsdale Sand Dunes	7	Lake Ullswater
2	Gait Burrows	8	Harbottle Crags
3	Arnside Knott	9	Upper Teesdale
4	Roudsea Wood and Mosses	10	Deepdale Beck
5	White Moss Common and Rydal Water	11	Hamsterley Forest
6	Friar's Crag	12	Castle Eden Dene
		13	Bempton Cliffs

Ainsdale Sand Dunes

SUMMARY A huge area of sand dunes, dune slacks and woodlands, with a wide and very interesting variety of plants and the added attraction of natterjack toads. A National Nature Reserve, in which visitors are asked to keep to the clearly visible and well-marked tracks to avoid damaging the delicate environment. The reserve is well-known for its rich flora, but it must be appreciated that only a small selection of these are likely to be seen by keeping to the tracks. Anyone who wishes to explore away from these tracks must apply for a permit, available from the Nature Conservancy Council, Blackwell, Bowness-on-Windermere, Windermere, Cumbria LA23 3JR.

APPROXIMATE LENGTH OF WALK 6 miles.

BEST TIMES Spring, summer.

LOCATION Car park at Freshfield Station, Lancs. SD292084.

From the railway car park at Freshfield, follow the railway line and the signs pointing to Fisherman's Path. At the end of the row of houses, Freshfield Dune Heath is seen on the right, and is an area of heath, broom and gorse with scattered silver birches and small oak trees.

After about half a mile, cross the railway line and follow the track signposted to the Field Office. Opposite the office (which may or may not be open) there is a stand of balsam poplar (see Coedydd Aber, p. 214). From there, follow the Fisherman's Path signpost which says 'Beach 1 mile, Dune Path ¾ mile'. This sandy track leads between woodland of sycamores, balsam poplar and pine. After a short distance there is a mixed conifer plantation on the right. This has been planted on sand dunes, and as the lack of light precludes any ground flora the outlines of those dunes are still visible. Further along there is some more mixed woodland, this time consisting of oak, hazel, and silver birch on both sides of the track; in contrast to the conifers there is a dense undergrowth of gorse, hawthorn, brambles, a few horsetails and some ferns, with flowering plants such as red campion (*Silene dioica*), and various vetches. Creeping willow is also present here and at other stations through the dunes further on in the walk.

In this area the first bushes of sea buckthorn put in an appearance. Attractive though the grey-green leaves and bright orange berries of this shrub appear, it is something of a menace. Introduced in the 1890s to help stabilize the dunes, it spread rapidly and choked out much of the natural plant life. Much of the buckthorn has had to be removed, and the resulting bare patches have quickly been colonized by other plants.

After about two miles a notice board is reached which explains about the dunes and the plant life of the immediate vicinity, pointing out that the dunes are now stable and that consequently the growth of marram grass (*Ammophila arenaria*) has been restricted, as sand is no longer being deposited (the latter is necessary for the successful spread of marram).

Continue along the pathway, beside which will be found more balsam poplar and some alder trees. At the far end of the path there is a boardwalk leading on to some bare sand dunes. When there are few people about, the boardwalk is a marvellous place to see common lizards sunning themselves. They come creeping up from under the boards and, with care, can be approached quite closely.

At the end of the boardwalk, bear right on to the sand and walk towards the high dunes ahead. On the right, as the top of the small dune ridge is reached, there is a truly magnificent and extensive spread of yellow iris (*Iris pseudacorus*) which is a blaze of colour in June. In the sand nearby are a number of horsetails.

From this point, the white-topped posts of the marked pathway can be seen, following along to the right behind the main dune ridge. There is much marram grass, as would be expected on a dune, and along the path and in among the marram various flowering plants may be found according to the time of year. These include hound's-tongue (*Cynoglossum officinale*), kidney vetch (*Anthyllis vulneraria*), yellow rattle (*Rhinanthus minor*), silverweed (*Potentilla anserina*) and sea spurge (*Euphorbia paralias*). After some distance there is a shallow pool on the right in a dune slack, with a Nature Conservancy Council notice about natterjack toads (see Winterton Dunes, p. 134).

Stay on the track, and after about three to three and a half miles from the start another National Nature Reserve sign-post, saying 'Dune Path North, Shore Road 2½ km', is reached. From here, bear half-right and follow the white-topped posts through some low dunes. Along the path edges more spurge grows, as well as the yellow wild pansy (*Viola tricolor*). In a wetter area on the left of the path early marsh orchids (*Dactylorhiza incarnata*) may be seen. Eventually another shallow natterjack toad pool is reached. Turn right, away from it, and follow the posts through an area thick with sea buckthorn.

Further on, some shallow water with dense growths of pondweed (*Potamogeton*), rushes and marsh horsetails (*Equisetum palustre*) is seen on the right of the path. Another National Nature Reserve information board describes the formation of this type of wet dune slack, which provides a habitat for sedges, rushes, water mint (*Mentha aquatica*), bogbean (*Menyanthes trifoliata*) and yellow irises. It also describes how some of the wet slacks dry out and are then re-excavated to conserve the habitat of the natterjack toad.

In due course, a boardwalk leads across a wetland area, with masses of marsh horsetails on either side. Yet another informative notice board describes the formation of sand dunes and the spread of such plants as evening primrose (*Oenothera biennis*), dewberry (*Rubus caesius*) and Portland spurge (*Euphorbia portlandica*). Continue to follow the marker posts, which lead eventually to a signpost for Pinfold Path, leading to Woodland Path. Follow this, and shortly after there is another National Nature Reserve board. Go through a gap in the fence near this, still following the marker posts, and into a more scrubby area with some young birch. Carline thistle (*Carlina vulgaris*) can be seen here, as well as creeping dewberry, and there is balsam poplar by the trackside.

The path now leads along the edge of a mixed conifer woodland, where there is lily of the valley (*Convallaria majalis*) growing, and some lady fern (*Athyrium filix-femina*). On reaching the road, turn right, and eventually come to a five-barred iron gate with 'No unauthorized vehicles' on it. Go through this. On the right are pine trees, with birch, oak and willows, and underneath are ferns, bracken and brambles. Follow the path into a pine wood, which has little growing in its gloomy depths. After some distance the track emerges on to a road, and the signposts lead back to the field office and thence to the car park.

Gait Barrows

SUMMARY A Nature Conservancy Council reserve for which a permit must be obtained. Permits (free at time of writing) are obtainable by post, or call at the Nature Conservancy Council, Blackwell, Bowness-on-Windermere, Windermere, Cumbria LA23 3JR.
This is an intensely interesting walk on one of the best remaining areas of carboniferous limestone pavement, and an exceptional place for botanists, with a number of uncommon plants and real rarities. Extreme care is necessary on the limestone pavement in wet weather as it becomes dangerously slippery. An extension of the walk includes wet and dry meadows and open water.

APPROXIMATE LENGTH OF WALK 3 miles.

BEST TIMES Spring, summer.

LOCATION Just off the Arnside–Yealand road in Lancs. SD480772.

From the car park bear left down the vehicular road to a gate with a stile beside it; turn sharp left almost immediately, and a few yards ahead there is a sign that says 'No Entry Without Permit'. This sign should be heeded, as the reserve is well supervised and visitors are asked to produce their permits. Proceed along the track through a mixed woodland of ash, oak, hazel and yew with a very varied understorey containing, depending on the area, holly, privet, dogwood, spindle and guelder rose. Little paths and glades lead off the main track, and exploration of these reveals a field layer of lily of the valley (*Convallaria majalis*), bluebell (*Endymion non-scriptus*), primrose (*Primula vulgaris*), yellow pimpernel (*Lysimachia nemorum*), wood anemone (*Anemone nemorosa*), dog violet (*Viola riviniana*), enchanter's nightshade (*Circaea lutetiana*) and, in a few secluded places, the rare fly orchid

(*Ophrys insectifera*). Deer may be seen in the woods – roe deer most frequently, although fallow and red deer are seen occasionally.

Some blocks of limestone can be glimpsed through the woodland, but these in no way prepare one for the main area of pavement later on. After about half a mile the path opens out and an angled T-junction is reached. Take the right-hand road, where the ground is covered with birdsfoot trefoil (*Lotus corniculatus*) in summer. This is one of the areas from which much limestone was removed before reserve status was established, and it is easy to see where the workings took place and almost completely destroyed the unique structure of the pavement. The stone was used locally for walls, buildings and gatestones, and for agricultural lime. Although this particular area of limestone pavement is now protected, some others are not, and the material is still being marketed for use in the construction of rockeries. Anyone who is the least bit interested in conservation should be aware of this, and give thought to the origin of any stone used in rock gardens.

After just under three-quarters of a mile a wide clearing is reached, in which there is a shed. Bear right past an old railway van and follow the track into the main area of pavement. Make a note of the route, as it is easy to become disorientated when wandering around on the pavement itself.

The impact of seeing the expanse of pavement for the first time is memorable. It is unlike any other kind of habitat, and strangely beautiful. Limestone consists principally of the fossilized remains of minute sea creatures. The pavement was raised to the surface by earth movement and left as smooth sheets of rock by the action of ice during the Ice Age. In the 8,000 or so intervening years, rain water (which is weakly acidic) has dissolved some of the stone and given it unique features. The deep fissures and cracks caused by the water action are known as grikes, and the individual blocks of stone formed by the grikes are called clints. The small, gutter-like features that drain water off the clints are called runnels, while the hollows on the surface of the clints, some of which have plants growing in them, are known as solution cups.

As can be seen, the grikes vary in depth – although the deepest are probably no more than about 90 cm (3 feet) – and in width, from just a few centimetres to over 30 cm (1 foot). The most obvious form of vegetation growing from the grikes are small trees – ash, hazel and oak. Although they are small, many of them are quite old, as their root growth, and hence their above-ground growth, has been restricted by the confines of the grikes.

It is, however, the smaller plants growing in the grikes that are of greatest interest at Gait Barrows. It is a real 'hands and knees' job peering into the fissures to see just what is there. Surprisingly, the majority of plants are typical wood-land ones; this is because the atmosphere is damp, humid and sheltered. Ferns are a feature, with the very rare rigid buckler fern (*Dryopteris submontana*) hiding in some of the deeper grikes. Hart's-tongue (*Phyllitis scolopendrium*), hard-shield fern (*Polystichum aculeatum*), and wall-rue (*Asplenium ruta-muraria*) are plentiful, but there is also some of the less common rusty-back fern (*Ceterach officinarum*).

Flowering plants are present in plenty. The most outstand-ing rarity, growing in shallower grikes, is angular Solomon's seal (*Polygonatum odoratum*) – distinguished from the common variety by its square stems. The red helleborine orchid (*Cephalanthera rubra*) is another rarity found on the pavement and in among the scrub at the edges, while herb Robert

(*Geranium robertianum*), lily of the valley (a relative of Solomon's seal), tutsan (*Hypericum androsaemum*), and bloody cranesbill (*Geranium sanguineum*) are less unusual, but add to the overall rock-garden effect of this marvellous habitat.

After looking at the wide expanse of open pavement, take a walk among the surrounding scrub, which yields a further selection of plants – mountain mellick (*Melica natans*), deadly nightshade (*Atropa bella-donna*), the rare pale St John's wort (*Hypericum montanum*), and stone bramble (*Rubus saxatilis*) – the latter a creeping herb with small white flowers on a weak erect stem which bears no prickles.

From the pavement return to the gate near the car park, but instead of going through it, turn down left and follow the track down the hill through a mixed woodland of sycamore, hazel and birch. Wood avens (*Geum urbanum*) can be seen flowering by the trackside. The roadway and surrounding vegetation is a good place to see some of the twenty-seven species of butterfly found in the reserve, including the uncommon Duke of Burgundy fritillary. This butterfly is the only European member of the metalmark family, in which the male has only four functional legs while the female has six. The caterpillar feeds on primrose and cowslip plants. At the bottom of the track, go through the gate and into the very wet meadow. In spring and summer this is a mass of wildflowers – clovers, buttercups, northern marsh and spotted orchids (*Dactylorhiza purpurella* and *D. fuchsii*), and hemp agrimony (*Eupatorium cannabinum*), with ragged robin (*Lychnis floscuculi*), lady's smock (*Cardamine pratensis*) and rushes in the wetter parts.

Where the meadow slopes down to a small, fenced tarn the ground is marshy, and this merges into a fen and then an alder carr surrounding the tarn. Because of the dangerous nature of the ground around the tarn and the fragile environment of marsh and fen, the walk does not enter these areas.

Once in the meadow, turn left and follow the fence to a corner where a wall starts, then turn right and cross the meadow to a gateway in the opposite fence. Turn right again through the gate and follow the wall and then a hedge of hawthorn and privet. Eventually a National Nature Reserve sign by a stile is reached. Climb over the stile into woodland, and then through a gate on the left marked 'Haweswater Reserve'. Go straight ahead down to the water's edge, where in late spring there is a superb display of bird's-eye primrose (*Primula farinosa*) and also butterwort (*Pinguicula vulgaris*) in profusion. Return to the gate, turn left through it and re-enter by the next gate down (also marked Haweswater). Bear right through this and along a muddy track which goes right through the bed of common reed, where there are more bird's-eye primroses, and masses of yellow iris (*Iris pseudacorus*), bog rush (*Juncus stygius*), and some willow.

After a short walk an old building is reached on the left; turn right here on to a broad track which leads through a mixed wood. There are plenty of ferns in the woodland, including hart's-tongue and male fern (*Dryopteris filix-mas*), and, in a field behind a stone wall on the right, an extensive stand of balsam. The path then leads back past the Haweswater gateway to the stile. Retrace your steps back to the car park.

Arnside Knott

SUMMARY This 500-feet limestone hill makes a very pleasant walk, the route going through pasture and woodland with several quite steep climbs. From the top on a clear day there are panoramic views of the Cumbrian hills, the Shap fells and the Yorkshire Pennines. There is a varied flora, and some woodland birdlife, including nightingales.

APPROXIMATE LENGTH OF WALK 4 miles.

BEST TIMES Spring, summer.

LOCATION On the outskirts of Arnside village, Cumbria. SD451773.

Walk back down the road from the car park. On either side, initially, is a mixed woodland containing silver birch, yew, sycamore, hazel and oak, with gorse. Shortly after the road emerges from the wood there is a stile into a field on the right. This field, called Higher Pasture, has a scattering of gorse and bracken with a few trees, including ash, oak and sycamore, and is noted for its limestone flowers, such as thyme (*Thymus drucei*), carline thistle (*Carlina vulgaris*), rockrose (*Helianthemum chamaecistus*), marjoram (*Origanum vulgare*), several orchids, salad burnet (*Poterium sanguisorba/Sanguisorba minor*), and squinancywort (*Asperula cynanchica*). There are also plenty of dog violets (*Viola riviniana*) and wild strawberries (*Fragaria vesca*). Green woodpeckers, yellowhammers and meadow pipits are often seen in this field, while grayling, common blue and Scotch Argus butterflies (the latter in one of only two English breeding sites) are among species that may be present.

At the top of the field, go over another stile and scramble

up a steep stony track bearing right through beech, sycamore, hazel, ash and some juniper. The path emerges on
Knotted Tree Ridge by what is left of the knotted trees (a
garden practice dating from Victorian times). Turn left up
the wide track then turn right by a seat, through some
scrubby woodland where roe deer may be seen, to a trian-
gulation pillar. From there, facing towards the estuary in the
distance, go forward, ignoring the first path crossing, and
take a right turn at the next, then slightly left and over a stile
back into Higher Pasture.

Go half right across the field, skirting a stand of larches,
to a kissing gate in the wall just by a hawthorn bush. Enter
through the gate into Redhills Wood, where there is again a
very good chance of seeing the shy roe deer. Hazel, oak,
yew and ash are the principal trees. Much of the ground
under the trees is covered with brambles, but there are also
bluebells (*Endymion non-scriptus*), wild strawberry, and
violets. Chiffchaffs, blackcaps, tits, and warblers are all seen
in Redhills Wood, while the evenings bring the haunting call
of the tawny owl, and the strange 'roding' flight of the
woodcock.

Take the first turning right up the hill. Some dog's
mercury (*Mercurialis perennis*) grows by the pathway. After
about two miles from the start, the pathway forks; take the
left-hand one downhill. Almost at the bottom turn right and
walk inside the wood but almost parallel with the road
outside it. After a short distance there is a gap in the wall
ahead – go through it and into Yew Grove where, as the
name suggests, there is a fine stand of large yew trees. The
bright red berries of yew are a favourite food for many birds
– redwings, fieldfares, thrushes, blackbirds, greenfinches,
bullfinches, and even the less common and exceptionally
heavy-billed hawfinch – all are present at Arnside Knott.

Yew Grove gives way to mixed woodland again, with a variety of shrubs – blackthorn, spindle, hawthorn and bramble. On the right there is an old quarry, and near this is one of the real rarities of the reserve, red helleborine (*Cephalanthera rubra*). It can be up to 30 cm (1 foot) high and has bright purple-pink flowers, which are rather spiky in appearance.

Further along beyond the quarry there are steep and very unstable scree-covered slopes where conservation measures are being undertaken. There are small sycamore trees on both sides of the path, and a huge yew down the hill on the left. Shortly after that, a main track is joined, followed by a turn to the right up the hill towards a large beech tree.

At the top of the hill, which is quite steep, there is a welcome seat. This is a junction of habitats, with woodland on the one hand, and a certain amount of heath with ling (*Calluna vulgaris*) and tormentil (*Potentilla erecta*), on the other. It is a good place to take a rest and watch for some of the many butterflies for which the reserve is renowned. Among those which may be seen here or in other parts of the reserve are Duke of Burgundy and small pearl-bordered fritillaries, orange-tips, green hairstreaks, small tortoise-shells, dingy skippers, peacocks, painted ladies and brimstones.

From the seat, turn left and then take a right fork through some scrub woodland emerging on top of the hill by the toposcope, which was erected in 1982. The views from here are, once again, absolutely magnificent on a clear day. From the top of the hill take any of the paths to the car park.

Roudsea Wood and Mosses

SUMMARY A National Nature Reserve for which a permit from the Nature Conservancy Council is required. This is obtainable (free at time of writing) by post, or call at the Nature Conservancy Council, Blackwell, Bowness-on-Windermere, Windermere, Cumbria LA23 3JR. The principal interest of this attractive walk through ancient woodland is the clear division between the vegetation growing on the carboniferous limestone ridge and that which is on the more acid Bannisdale Slate ridge. There is also a raised mire or 'moss' with some unusual plants, and between the two contrasting woodland ridges there is a valley mire and tarn. Some of the walk can be very wet and muddy, so stout footwear is advised. A boardwalk leads across a small section at the edge of the raised mire and a further permit is required to explore beyond that – this is normally only issued for scientific research.

APPROXIMATE LENGTH OF WALK 4½ miles.

BEST TIMES Spring, summer.

LOCATION 3½ miles north-east of Ulverston, Cumbria. SD335825 and 351802.

From the car park area by a National Nature Reserve board enter the wood through a small gate. This is an area of mixed woodland on the limestone, with sycamore, ash, oak, silver birch and hawthorn, and a field layer of ferns with some dog's mercury (*Mercurialis perennis*). Follow the main track, and after about 150 yards take the track which is signposted 'Quarry Ride'. The ground here is wetter, with yellow iris (*Iris pseudacorus*), nettles and rushes, and with conifers and a few rowan trees on the left. A second 'Quarry Ride' marker is seen on the left, but ignore that and continue straight ahead towards a boardwalk. Gradually the habitat changes and the trees become more widely spaced until open wet moorland is reached, with heather (*Erica cinerea*), ling (*Calluna vulgaris*), purple moor-grass (*Molinia coerulea*), and a few silver birches and Scots pines.

The boardwalk leads towards a most exciting area of boggy ground, with bilberry (*Vaccinium myrtillus*), bog myrtle (*Myrica gale*), white beak-sedge (*Rhynchospora alba*) and cotton-grass (*Eriophorum sp.*) on either side. This is just the fringe of the raised bog which, where undisturbed, has areas of bog mosses (*Sphagnum spp.*) and other typical bog plants. The lovely liquid call of curlews can be heard from the middle of the bog where the birds are often feeding.

At the end of the boardwalk, however, where the bog has been disturbed, there is some bog moss, sundew (*Drosera rotundifolia*), bog asphodel (*Narthecium ossifragum*), ling, purple moor-grass, and two particularly attractive and not very common plants – bog rosemary (*Andromeda polifolia*) and cranberry (*Vaccinium oxycoccus*). Cranberry is a tiny creeping shrub belonging to the heath family, with alternate dark-green leaves that have grey, waxy-looking undersides and in-rolled edges. The little pink flowers have markedly arched-back petals, which leave the stamens protruding like a tiny beak. Bog rosemary, a member of the same family, is a larger, more upright shrub, with longer, shiny, grey-green leaves ending in a point, with rolled edges and white undersides. The pink or white urn-shaped flowers are in clusters, and grow on quite long stalks.

Return along the boardwalk and turn left after about twenty-five yards on to another boardwalk which leads through a wetter, dense woodland, with silver birch, ash, oak and Scots pine, and masses of bilberry underneath. Cross

Above: Cranberry – a member of the heath family (Roudsea Wood)

Below: Marbled white butterfly on teasel (Cuckmere Haven)

Above: Juniper tree in the re–
markable juniper forest at
Upper Teesdale

Left: Hazel catkins

Above: The six-spot Burnet moth, seen here on scabious, is very common at Barnack Hills and Holes

Right: The rare Spotted Rock Rose, seen at South Stack

Above: Restharrow – common on dry grasslands, especially on chalk and limestone, and on sand dunes (Sandwich Bay)

Below: Low Force waterfalls, Upper Teesdale

Above: Elephant hawk moth

Below: Herb Paris, showing the curious arrangement of the plant's parts in fours and eights – once thought to imbue it with magical properties (Castle Eden Dene)

Above: Bird's Foot Trefoil – a very common and attractive plant of dry grasslands

Below: Cowslips at Upper Teesdale

Left: Wall Pennywort, also known as Navelwort (roadside wall near South Stack)

Below: Marsh Marigold, also known as King-cup – one of the earliest spring flowers of wet places, flowering from March

Above: Guillemots and kittiwakes

Below: Gannets at Bempton Cliffs. Note the blue rope used for 'decorating' a nest

a small bridge, then turn right at a T-junction. The path
leads through more woodland, where holly becomes increasingly common in the understorey, with dog's mercury and
purple moor-grass underneath and a good growth of hair
moss (*Polytrichum*) on the path edges.

Cross another small bridge, just after a notice warning of
a slippery boardwalk, by two big tussock sedge (*Carex
paniculata*) plants, and continue through a woodland which
has a great variety of shrubs such as spindle, sloe, purging
buckthorn, and guelder rose. Ignore a turning to the left
signposted 'Transition North', and continue to a left turn
signposted 'Backbone Ride'. Take that, through yet more
dense wood and scrub, with hazel, spindle, ash, and oak.
Pass the other end of the Transition North track. The ground
is thick with dog's mercury (it is always worth looking
among this for the uncommon herb Paris (*Paris quadrifolia*),
which is present on the reserve (see Castle Eden Dene,
p. 197) and there are silver birches and a number of hawthorns on the left-hand side of the path. Pass another track
signposted 'Transition South'.

The woodland gradually becomes more open, with bigger
oaks, more ash, a number of field maples, and some yew
trees and other conifers. Red squirrels may be seen, as may
roe deer, which are common on the reserve and cause
damage by fraying and browsing. The field layer contains
such plants as yellow pimpernel (*Lysimachia nemorum*), col-
umbine (*Aquilegia vulgaris*), wood anemone (*Anemone nemorosa*), black medick (*Medicago lupulina*), giant bellflower
(*Campanula latifolia*), lily of the valley (*Convallaria majalis*),
and pyramidal orchid (*Anacamptis pyramidalis*), with the most
usual grass being false brome (*Brachypodium sylvaticum*). After
just under two and a half miles there are two large dead trees

on the left, bearing evidence of woodpeckers which are quite common in the wood.

Shortly after the dead trees turn sharp right along an unsignposted track, and when a T-junction is reached turn left down a short, steepish hill. Almost immediately the vegetation can be seen to change. Bracken is present in some quantity for the first time, as well as stitchwort (*Stellaria holostea*), bluebells (*Endymion non-scriptus*), and some yellow irises. There is very little dog's mercury, but more wavy hair grass (*Deschampsia flexuosa*) is present. In places there is purple moor-grass. This sharp change signals the underlying slate of the west ridge of Roudsea Wood.

After coming to a five-barred gate and a National Nature Reserve signpost, return along the same track to the T-junction, where there is a big yew tree on the left, and this time continue straight ahead down a slight slope into a wetter area. Keep on the main track until another junction is reached. Cross this, taking the Valley Ride straight ahead.

After just under four miles another boardwalk is reached. Take the left branch of this into the mire and tarn areas of the valley which divides the two ridges. The boardwalk leads through a wonderful, dense, jungle-like area of birch, willows, sallow, alder, reeds, sedges and rushes, with yellow iris, gipsywort (*Lycopus europaeus*) and ragged robin (*Lychnis flos-cuculi*) growing in and around the water. The species of reed and sedge present include purple small reed (*Calamagrostis canescens*), common reed (*Phragmites australis*), bladder sedge (*Carex vesicaria*), brown sedge (*Carex disticha*), lesser tussock sedge (*Carex diandra*) and cyprus sedge (*Carex pseudocyperus*). Grass snakes may be seen in this area.

Walk along to the end of the boardwalk, then return and turn left at the crossway by a huge tussock sedge. Cross a small bridge and walk on, noting a large yew tree on the right with shoots all over its trunk. Keep on the main track, ignoring a less well-defined one going off to the left. Pass a stone hut with 'Dangerous building' on it on the left. About here there is another area of more acid soil, indicated by the presence of plants such as hard fern. Remain on the Valley Ride, going past a little bridge over a ditch on the left. Eventually come to the main ride again and turn left back to the gate.

White Moss Common and Rydal Water

SUMMARY A delightful walk by Rydal Water, taking in typical Lakeland fell, woodland and farmland, with a wide variety of species of plants and birds among beautiful surroundings. Sections of this walk can be very wet indeed, with some paths actually under water.

APPROXIMATE LENGTH OF WALK 6 miles.

BEST TIMES Spring, early summer.

LOCATION On the Ambleside–Grasmere road, A591. NY348065.

From the car park on the opposite side of the road from Rydal Water, walk down towards the lake and turn right. A pathway leads down towards the River Rothay, which is fringed with alder, willows, ash and some hawthorn. A boggy patch contains some typical wetland plants – bog cotton (*Eriophorum*), meadowsweet (*Filipendula ulmaria*), rushes, spearwort (*Ranunculus flammula*) and bogbean (*Menyanthes trifoliata*) – depending on the time of year. The river is crossed by a footbridge. Stop for a short time on the bridge to enjoy the view, and look for the dippers and grey wagtails that can often be seen in and near the water.

On the other side, follow the signpost to the left towards the Wetland Conservation Area, then turn right on the path leading into it. This is a magnificent area of wetland habitat with an exciting range of plants, including some very handsome sedges. All but a very few sedges can be distinguished from rushes by their triangular stems with solid pith, compared with the rush which has a circular stem filled with rather spongy pith.

The path leads through a dense growth of soft rush (*Juncus effusus*), huge clumps of tussock sedge (*Carex paniculata*), bottle sedge (*Carex rostrata*), delicate lady's smock (*Cardamine pratensis*) with pale mauve flowers, and marsh marigold (*Caltha palustris*), with a few small hazels and willows growing among them. At the first junction of tracks keep straight on. The vegetation becomes increasingly diverse, with yellow iris (*Iris pseudacorus*), lady fern (*Athyrium filix-femina*), marsh horsetails (*Equisetum palustre*), bog cotton (which in fact is a sedge) and bittercress (*Cardamine flexuosa*). Take the next turning left down to the river bank, but be careful, as the water is very deep and the bank can be extremely slippery. The scene, however, is delightful, with a great expanse of water lilies and the beautiful flowers of bogbean – each petal white above and pale pink below, and fringed inside with soft, white, cottony hairs.

From the river bank, return to the crossroads, turn left away from the lake, then continue to bear left towards the woodland. The change from wetland to woodland takes place over a short distance, with the sedges and rushes being replaced by bracken, and the willows by a mixed woodland of ash, sycamore, a few conifers and oak, with the latter predominant. A number of woodland birds may be seen in this and other woodlands during the walk, including wood-peckers and tree-creepers who take advantage of the dead trees, pied and spotted flycatchers, redstarts, and nuthatches. Join a wide pathway which leads up the hill through the woodland to the left. After a short distance there is a large beech tree on the right, with hair moss (*Polytrichum*) growing under it. At the top of the rise there are two Douglas firs and some holly on the left.

Remain on the pathway and, where it forks, keep right until a small open space is reached, with a steep rocky bank partly enclosing a little grassy hollow on the right, and ground that drops away on the left. On the bank and under the rocks are some quite unusual ferns in addition to the male ferns (*Dryopteris filix-mas*) which grow quite profusely. Nestling under rock overhangs are some dainty beech ferns (*Phegopteris connectilis*). They have pale-green stalks and fronds – the latter covered with very fine white hairs. In spite of its name, beech fern is not necessarily associated with beech trees. Another fern in the little hollow is the broad buckler (*Dryopteris dilatata*) – the name coming, it is said, from the kidney-shaped membranes (indusia) that cover the spores on the underside of the fronds. These were thought by some early botanists to resemble shields known as 'bucklers' in Old English. Flowering plants that may be seen in this area include stitchwort (*Stellaria holostea*), yellow pimpernel (*Lysimachia nemorum*), foxgloves (*Digitalis purpurea*) and the charming little marsh violet (*Viola palustris*), which has pale-lilac flowers with deep-purple veining.

Continue up the path to the gate, which has an elder tree on the left and some rowans on the right. Go through the gate and out on to the common, which is open fell country. Immediately ahead, the land rises steeply up the craggy hillside. Turn right down the hill, signposted 'Rydal', and during this section of the walk keep a watch on the sky above the peaks on the right for the ravens, buzzards and peregrines that are occasionally seen. The stony pathway, from which there is a panoramic view of the lake and its surroundings, leads down the hill towards the water, interrupted at several places by little streams that come tumbling down the fellside. At the foot of some of these, just before they cross the pathway, are little boggy areas with bog moss (*Sphagnum*), butterwort (*Pinguicula vulgaris*) and rushes; others have small trees and bushes growing on their banks –

alder, ash and holly. On the slope of the fell, a few dwarf juniper bushes grow, and an attractive little plant with an unattractive name, lousewort (*Pedicularis sylvatica*) – so called because at one time it was believed to give farm stock 'lice' or liverfluke (a flatworm which is parasitic in sheep).

A short distance from where the stone wall on the left ends, a pathway leads down to the lake edge, where there is a boggy area with water mint (*Mentha aquatica*). In spring and summer greylag geese, red-breasted mergansers, and goosanders are seen on the lake, together with a large flock of Canada geese. In winter, whooper swans, pochard and goldeneye have all been reported. Continue on this path by the lake, noting in passing some parsley fern (*Cryptogramma crispa*) growing out of a crevice in the stone wall on the right.

Where the path forks, take the lower one leading to an iron kissing gate into Rydal Woods. This is a mixed wood of ash, oak and sycamore, with hawthorn, bramble, bracken, stitchwort, wild garlic (*Allium ursinum*) and male fern covering the ground in some areas. A great deal of re-seeding is going on under the trees, and visitors are requested not to walk in the fenced-off sections and to keep to the paths. After another iron gate the path continues towards a footbridge over the stream at the end of the lake. In midsummer, just before the bridge is reached, there is an unexpected patch of pink purslane (*Montia sibirica*) on the bank to the right and below the path.

Go across the bridge, and, having safely negotiated the very busy road, turn right along the pavement – noting the ivy-leaved toadflax (*Cymbalaria muralis*) and the common polypody fern (*Polypodium vulgare*) growing in the wall. Turn up left by Rydal Mount. The wall on the right is absolutely covered with maidenhair spleenwort (*Asplenium trichomanes*). Continue up the hill past the church until on the left (and quite easily missed, as I discovered!) is a signpost to Grasmere. Take the turning, and follow the road through a five-bar gate. The track then leads along the side of the hill above the lake, initially through open farmland with scattered trees – an excellent place for seeing jays and green woodpeckers – and then through mixed woodland. Under the trees there are a number of ferns and also some dog's mercury (*Mercurialis perennis*) – the latter usually an indicator of old woodland.

Continue along the path, going through a number of high gates in the fences of fields, until a very rocky stretch is reached after a smaller gate. Where the path divides, take the lower fork to the left, and shortly after the next small gate turn sharp left downhill between stone walls and by a small stream. On the way down, yellow pimpernel (*Lysimachia nemorum*) and another, much larger yellow flower, the Welsh poppy (*Meconopsis cambrica*), bloom in mid-summer. At the bottom of the track on the right, dropping down into a small gorge beside one of the car parks, is an attractive little waterfall. The bottom of the gorge is full of ferns and mosses and more Welsh poppies.

Return to the car park along the main road – a distance of about fifty yards from the gorge.

Friar's Crag

SUMMARY An easy Lake District walk on the shores
of Derwentwater and through the adjacent woodland.
The first part of the walk is suitable for wheelchairs.

APPROXIMATE LENGTH OF WALK 2¼ miles.

BEST TIMES Spring, early summer.

LOCATION Derwentwater is near Borrowdale in
Cumbria. NY264227.

From the car park adjacent to Derwentwater, follow the
tarmac road down past the National Trust information
centre. The road continues within sight of the lake, with a
mixed woodland on the left consisting of oak, sycamore and
beech, with holly understorey. This and other woodland on
the walk provide food and nesting sites for an extensive list
of birds – treecreepers, four species of tits, wrens, mistle-
thrushes and tawny owls. Summer visitors include the
occasional blackcap and garden warbler, with chiffchaff,
redstart, spotted and pied flycatchers, and wood warblers
occurring regularly.

The tarmac road becomes gravel, and where this divides
take the right-hand fork to Friar's Crag, which is a rocky
promontory jutting out into Derwentwater. On it is the
Ruskin Memorial. The view from the end of the little
promontory is a justly famous one. Retrace your steps from
the viewpoint and turn right up a narrow track which leads
round and down to some stone steps to join a broad pathway
near the shore.

Many waterbirds use the lake throughout the year. There
are nesting mallard, red-breasted merganser, goosander, and
greylag and Canada geese. The tiny island of Rampsholme

provides a roost for non-breeding cormorants, while herons may be seen standing motionless at the water's edge. It is well to keep an eye open, especially towards the hills, for the buzzards and ravens that are sometimes seen. Sparrowhawks and peregrines have also been recorded. In winter the resident birds are joined by tufted duck, goldeneye, pochard and the occasional great crested grebe.

Follow the path round the lake edge and across two small bridges which span a wetter area thick with rushes and some lady's smock (*Cardamine pratensis*). Go through the gate into Ings Wood, where there is a wealth of wetland plants such as water avens (*Geum rivale*), yellow iris (*Iris pseudacorus*), rushes and ferns, with alder and willow in the wetter areas, and a mixed woodland of oak, sycamore and yew with some hawthorn understorey. Stitchwort (*Stellaria holostea*), red campion (*Silene dioica*), and great woodrush (*Luzula sylvatica*) are found in the field layer in the drier parts. Woodrush can easily be mistaken for a grass, but nonetheless it is a true member of the rush family, as can be confirmed by examining the stems, which are solid and pithy, not hollow as in a grass. A close look at the leaves reveals longish, very fine white hairs on the edges.

Where the path branches, take the left-hand fork near some lime trees and cross the bridge over Brockle Beck. Anywhere in the woodland some of the larger animals that frequent the area may be seen, although as the walk is so popular their footprints are the most likely evidence of their presence. Roe deer are said to be common, while badger, fox, stoat, weasel and mink are also recorded.

Go through a gate and turn right, noting the ashes, willows and hawthorn, and the bog cotton (*Eriophorum sp.*) in a piece of wet ground over the fence on the right. In the adjacent reed beds, reed warblers can be seen and heard. Go through another gate, and follow the signpost to Calf Close Bay. Turn left, following the sign to the lake edge again, and take the track down on to the shingle. A little more than halfway round the bay, turn off left into the very dark Great Wood, but before doing so, notice the trees a little further on by the lakeside, with their roots exposed to the air. In the clearings in the wood a number of flowers are growing, including bugle (*Ajuga reptans*), violets (*Viola riviniana*) and stitchwort.

On emerging from the darkest part of the wood the track leads along a stone wall beside the Borrowdale Road. Growing on the wall are some nice examples of common polypody fern (*Polypodium vulgare*), maidenhair spleenwort (*Asplenium trichomanes*) and some dog lichen (*Peltigera canina*), while herb Robert (*Geranium robertianum*) is plentiful both on and at the foot of the wall.

On the other side of the road the conical shape of Castle Head, which is an old volcanic plug, dominates the scene. Opposite Castle Head, turn left down the steps into Cockshott Wood and follow the path back to the starting point.

Lake Ullswater

SUMMARY A 'there and back' walk along the hillside
above Lake Ullswater, taking in some typical and very
beautiful Lake District scenery.

APPROXIMATE LENGTH OF WALK 6 miles.

BEST TIMES Spring, summer, autumn.

LOCATION Patterdale village, Cumbria. NY397162.

From the car park opposite the Patterdale Hotel turn right
down the road, then right again on to the public footpath
signposted 'Side Farm'. Cross the fields and the bridge, go
up through the farm yard and turn left on to a path
signposted to Howtown and Sandwick. The path goes along
beside a fine stone wall on the left, behind which is a stand
of handsome sycamores. On the right the ground rises up
the fellside towards Grey Crag and Hare Shaw. Along this
path the occasional grey wagtail may be seen near a tiny
waterfall which drops gently down the hill. The banks of
this are covered with mosses and ferns, and at the base of the
rocks on the left is some of the liverwort, *Conocephalum*.

Continue on this pathway past a clump of larches, keeping
an eye on the high crags to the right, where ravens may be
seen, and above which buzzards often soar. After about half
a mile, pass a farm gate and continue along the main track
off to the right. There is a much smaller waterfall, again
with a collection of mosses and some violets (*Viola riviniana*).

Another gate is reached, near which there is a sign,
'Lakeside path to Howtown'. About 150 yards past the sign
the main track begins to go downhill, but take the smaller
pathway up the hill instead, by another small group of
larches. This small but well-defined path leads gently up the

fellside towards the crags, and from it there are wonderful views of the lake and the surrounding hills. At the higher level above the path the fellside is fairly typical, with some rocky outcrops and a few small shrubs and trees – mostly hawthorn and some rowan. Most of the ground is covered with a close-cropped sward of sheep's fescue (*Festuca ovina*) and common bent grass (*Agrostis capillaris*) with some patches of bracken.

After a short way two paths converge, and just on the right is a small patch of parsley fern (*Cryptogramma crispa*) – a very common plant in the Lake District. It is one of the ferns that produce two types of fronds – the fertile one is long and narrow, and the sterile one is more parsley-like. If there are fertile fronds, look under the rolled edges to see the spores, which are ripe between June and August.

On either side of the pathway there is a little hawthorn scrub with some sedge nearby and one or two pieces of juniper. A short distance along there is another small water-fall with the usual mosses and ferns. The path then leads past a little piece of open water, with bog moss (*Sphagnum*) round the edge and pondweed (*Potamogeton*) growing in the water. Hair moss (*Polytrichum*) is growing in the drier ground near the pool.

With the change of habitat some bilberry (*Vaccinium myrtillus*) is present, together with gorse, much more juniper and some bracken. On the open fellside wheatears sometimes nest under the boulders, and the bushes provide perches for whinchats. The path now leads down a very steep rocky hill between juniper bushes and a few hawthorns. Goldcrests and wrens can often be seen flitting in and out of the scrub.

At the bottom of the hill, turn right on to the main track, where there is plenty of parsley fern in among the large piles of boulders. The path now leads into a delightful damp birch woodland with some juniper, where ferns, mosses and lichens cover the ground and the boulders with a rich carpet of many shades of green; it is a lovely cool place on a hot summer's day. One of the more uncommon plants is the fragile-looking oak fern (*Gymnocarpium dryopteris*), with its slender black stem. The yellow of primroses (*Primula vulgaris*), the mauve of violets, and the delicate, lilac-veined white flowers of wood sorrel (*Oxalis acetosella*) stand out against the green background.

The birches – both living and dead – provide food and shelter for a number of birds. The great spotted woodpecker finds food in the larger, dying trees, while the brilliantly coloured redstart uses trees on the edge of the woodland as perches from which to dart out after insects.

After about three miles a dry stone wall is reached by the side of the path. From here, return along the same track through the woodland to the junction with the steep rocky path which came down the hill between the juniper. Instead of climbing back up the hill, continue on the main track which leads down towards the lake. The country becomes much more open, with rowan trees and bracken. Scree stretches up the hill on the left, and on the right there are holly and juniper bushes.

Continue on this track back to the farm yard, and thence across the fields to the road and the car park.

Harbottle Crags

SUMMARY An upland heather moor with some wetland and impressive outcrops of fell sandstone. Visitors are particularly asked to keep to the way-marked Nature Trail.

APPROXIMATE LENGTH OF WALK 1 mile.

BEST TIMES Spring, summer.

LOCATION Near Alwinton, Northumberland. NT927048.

From the visitor centre follow the track up the hill through a forestry plantation, in which lodgepole pine predominates, to the entrance gate of the reserve.

Inside the gate the heather moorland character of the reserve is immediately apparent. The track is flanked by ling (*Calluna vulgaris*), with some bilberry (*Vaccinium myrtillus*) and a number of silver birch saplings and seedlings. Birds are a feature of the reserve, and the most common one, the meadow pipit, can almost always be seen, characterized by its song flight in which it flutters high into the sky before planing back down to ground again.

As the Trail leads up the hill it is noticeable that the age of the heather cover varies. This is because the hill is managed as a grouse moor – grouse (red and, less often, black) are likely to get up almost anywhere – and controlled burning is carried out annually to provide new heather shoots for the birds to feed on. Thus some of the heather is tall, straggly and old, while other areas are obviously young and vigorous. Grouse feed on the heather (ling) throughout the year: in spring and early summer they enjoy the new green shoots; later in the summer they eat the flowers; in the autumn they take the seeds; while in the winter they look for the new green shoots growing in the more sheltered parts of the plants.

The taller plants offer perching posts for whinchats as they pause between feeding on butterflies and other insects, the former possibly including the small heath. Moths found on the reserve include emperor, fox and northern eggar.

Among the heather on the left of the track in some wetter ground are bushes of the aromatic shrub, bog myrtle or sweet gale (*Myrica gale*). All parts of this plant are dotted with small glands which exude a sweet-smelling, resinous substance. The most unusual feature, however, is that although the vast majority of plants are either male or female, they can vary from year to year. One year a plant may bear male flowers, the next it will have female flowers, or even flowers of both sexes. This phenomenon occurs in only a very few plants – another one is the ash.

The Trail leads on up the hill towards a huge crag, the Drake Stone, which dominates the horizon. Scattered amongst the heather are small groups of silver birch. On the right, at Post Five of the Nature Trail, are an old rowan tree and some saplings, under which in mid-summer can be seen the pinkish flowers of sheep's sorrel (*Rumex acetosella*). Near Post Six is a Scots pine, but trees are relatively scarce, in spite of the fact that thousands of years ago this and other similar hills were covered with forests of oak, birch and pine.

Post Seven of the Trail marks Moss Cairn, said to be where Moss, a sheepdog who worked the hills, is buried. The rocky outcrop is an example of the fell sandstone. Although the principal ground cover is heather, there are small flushes of bog, where bog moss (*Sphagnum sp*.), hair moss (*Polytrichum sp*.) and purple moor-grass are growing, and the heather is replaced by cross-leaved heath (*Erica tetralix*). Around and above Post Seven some of these wetter places have formed pools with mare's-tail (*Hippuris vulgaris*) and common cotton-grass (*Eriophorum angustifolium*) in and around them. At various times throughout the year, examples of sundew (*Drosera rotundifolia*), bog asphodel (*Narthecium ossifragum*) and deer-grass (*Scirpus caespitosus*) can be found. Snipe are liable to take off suddenly from these damp areas and dart away, uttering their alarm call.

As the summit of the hill is approached, the 'benches' of sandstone are clearly visible, and it is easy to see how millions of years ago, when this area was part of an estuary, the rock was laid down in piles – a formation known as 'cross-bedding'. In the vicinity of the huge Drake Stone circular holes in the rock can be seen where millstones were once cut out. Crevices in the rocks afford nesting sites for wheatears, and rooting sites for hard fern (*Blechnum spicant*) and broad buckler fern (*Dryopteris dilatata*).

From the Drake Stone the expanse of open water to the west is Harbottle Lough, which visitors are asked not to approach. From the Stone, however, it is possible to see some of the birds that may be present – teal, mallard, tufted duck and heron. In winter, goosanders, greylag geese, whooper swans and goldeneye have all been recorded. Other birds that frequent the moorland and high crags are ring ouzel and short-eared owls, while the more common kestrel may be seen hovering over the heather.

From Drake's Stone, retrace the route down the hill to the car park.

Upper Teesdale

SUMMARY A walk through beautiful surroundings along the banks of the River Tees from Low Force to High Force Waterfalls, with a fine selection of wild flowers and passing through a remarkable juniper forest. This is reputed to be the best section of the Pennine Way.

APPROXIMATE LENGTH OF WALK 5-6 miles.

BEST TIMES Spring, summer.

LOCATION Bowlees visitor centre, near Middleton-in-Teesdale. NY907283.

From the Bowlees visitor centre walk back to the main road and turn right. Continue for about 500 yards to the phone box, then follow the public footpath sign to the left on the opposite side of the road. Go down through the fields towards the river, over some of the attractive stone stiles, and then through a gap in the stone wall, where the stone has been worn smooth by the touch of thousands of human hands over the years.

The gap gives entry into a delightful open woodland with beech, silver birch, sycamore and Scots pine. Marsh marigolds (*Caltha palustris*) grow in the wetter areas. A bridge (with a dire warning on it!) leads over the river and gives a magnificent view to the right and upstream of the series of broad, relatively shallow waterfalls known as Low Force. Downstream, the river narrows into a rocky gorge. Even if there was no natural history interest, the scenery here is reward enough.

On the far side of the bridge is a section of the Pennine Way. The rocks by a pathside bear various lichens and wood anemones (*Anemone nemorosa*) and celandine (*Ranunculus ficaria*) are dotted about. On the left is a damp meadow, which, in spring, has a mass of marsh marigolds and many plants of lady's smock (*Cardamine pratensis*). Pairs of lapwings are a welcome sight, with the males indulging in their exciting and spectacular display flight. By the river common sandpipers can be seen feeding among the rocks or, if disturbed, flying low in a wide arc over the water with their characteristic flick of the wings to return to the river bank a few hundred yards away.

At intervals along the bank grow clumps or individual trees – willow, silver birch, rowan and alder. Some distance along, the river divides to go round a small island. On the bank in this area a number of attractive wild flowers are found, such as cowslips (*Primula veris*), which grow under the birch trees sometimes; the unusual globe flower (*Trollius europaeus*), a speciality of the area; and dozens of violets (*Viola riviniana*). Further along, where the river opens out again and bubbles over a mass of great boulders and miniature waterfalls, dippers may be seen bobbing up and down in typical fashion. The banks here are low, and on and near them, growing in dampish conditions, the lovely bird's-eye primrose (*Primula farinosa*) flowers in May and June.

After about a mile and a half a flight of steps leads up the side of the valley away from the river. Take these, and a little way from the top the grassland is liberally dotted with delightful wild pansies (*Viola tricolor*) and violets. A pause here to turn and admire the lovely Dales scenery is rewarding.

Ahead, the hillside appears to be covered with gorse bushes, but as the encircling fence (crossed by means of a stile) is approached, the 'gorse' turns out to be a fantastic juniper forest! 'Fantastic' is used advisedly, as it describes well the weird shapes the trees and bushes have taken over the years. Acre upon acre stretches ahead and up the hill on the left.

Juniper is an interesting plant, and one of only three native conifers (the others being yew and Scots pine). As can be seen, the narrow, needle-like leaves are arranged in whorls of three, and they are prickly to touch. Male and female 'flowers' grow on separate bushes. The 'flowers' are, in fact, cones, as might be expected in a conifer. In May and June, the yellowish male cones can be seen in the axils (the angle between leaf and stem) of the leaves towards the tips of the twigs; the dark-green female cones are, as close examination shows, cup-shaped and consist of up to eight scales.

Following wind pollination, the female cones expand, and the scales fuse and grow around the seed which is developing inside, thus forming berries. The female 'trees are seen to bear berries of different colours and shapes. The hard, green ones seen in autumn are first-year ones, which gradually ripen over two or three years into mature, blue-black, fleshy berries which bear a greyish bloom. The juice of these berries is used for flavouring gin.

Amongst the junipers is a good range of ferns, including bracken (*Pteridium aquilinum*), male (*Dryopteris filix-mas*), mountain (*Dryopteris oreades*), and the delicate oak (*Gymocarpium dryopteris*) and beech (*Phegopteris connetilis*) ferns. A certain amount of bilberry (*Vaccinium myrtillus*) is present, and here and there some birch trees. A boardwalk leads through some of the juniper, and as one progresses the sound of rushing water becomes louder and louder. Soon a deep gorge opens up on the right, and quite suddenly and very spectacularly the mighty waterfall of High Force is ahead.

Return to Bowlees by the same route.

Deepdale Beck

SUMMARY A delightful wooded walk by the side of a beck in a steep-sided valley.

APPROXIMATE LENGTH OF WALK 1½–2 miles.

BEST TIMES Spring, summer.

LOCATION From Barnard Castle take the Middleton-in-Teesdale road (B6227) and cross the main bridge, ignoring the turning to Brough. Cross a smaller, narrow bridge, and immediately on the left is a five-bar metal gate with a smaller gate beside it. Park nearby. NZ045166.

In spring the ground immediately inside the gate is covered with a mass of butterbur (*Petasites hybridus*) – a good indication that the habitat is a wet one. The plant is interesting as, except in a few localities in the north of England, the flowers are predominantly male. Occasionally a female flower (distinguished by its longer stalk) is found on an otherwise male plant. In general, however, the butterbur spreads by means of its underground roots. When not in flower the plant can easily be recognized by its huge, rounded and markedly tooth-edged leaves which may grow to a massive 90 cm (3 feet) across. The name butterbur is said to come from the leaves, which were once used for wrapping butter. On the left is a small clump of willow growing near the banks of the beck that runs the length of the valley.

The track leads through an area of rather unattractive forestry working, but there is an encouraging amount of replanting taking place. There is mixed woodland on either side, including some sycamore, with a holly understorey and a delightful range of wild flowers – wood anemones

(*Anemone nemorosa*), honeysuckle (*Lonicera periclymenum*) growing on some of the smaller trees, celandine (*Ranunculus ficaria*), forget-me-nots, red campion (*Silene dioica*) and some early orchids.

Shortly after the forestry working, the valley opens out into a clearing, with masses of butterbur, and some bluebells (*Endymion non-scriptus*) under the trees in spring. Those with sensitive noses will have detected the presence of wild garlic or ramsons (*Allium ursinum*), and this strongly aromatic plant grows in increasing profusion the further one goes. The woodland on the left has been cleared to some extent. There is willow fringing the beck, and on the right there is hazel, elm and oak. A good range of woodland birds is present, and further along curlews can be heard, calling from the fields through which this deep valley runs.

After a few hundred yards the ground on the right becomes very marshy, with fine splashes of colour provided by marsh marigolds (*Caltha palustris*) in spring, and yellow iris (*Iris pseudacorus*) later in the year. Further on again, there is a large area of horsetails interspersed with more butterburs and marsh marigolds. Examination of the marsh marigold leaves will almost certainly show a number of small spire-shelled snails.

The boulder-strewn beck itself is fringed by willow and, in places, alder trees. In the little hollows by the side of the stream small patches of opposite-leaved golden saxifrage (*Chrysosplenium oppositifolium*) are present. Where possible, some of the larger boulders which are not covered by water should be inspected, as a number bear fine examples of the flat, green, irregularly forked branches of the leafy liverwort *Conocephalum conicum*. Close examination will show rather large pores on the surface of the thallus, or leaf-body.

It is possible to cross the beck, of course, but the far bank is very overgrown in places and offers little that cannot be seen more easily on the right-hand bank. However, when a small bridge is reached, it is worth crossing in spring just to be able to stand back and admire the wonderful blue haze created by the bluebells that clothe the right-hand side of the valley.

The track follows the beck along the valley, with various paths leading off to the right and up the steep sides. These can be explored, and it is possible that a glimpse may be obtained of the roe deer which live in the woodland.

After about a mile, return along the same path.

Hamsterley Forest

SUMMARY Although walks through Forestry
Commission conifer forests often lack both variety and
wildlife, Hamsterley is an exception. The well-laid-out
marked walk is full of interest, and there are sufficient
broad-leaved trees to break the monotony of the
conifer plantations. A very pleasant walk, the first part
of which is suitable for wheelchairs.

APPROXIMATE LENGTH OF WALK 2½ miles.

BEST TIMES Spring, summer, autumn.

LOCATION Not far from Barnard Castle in Durham,
on the road between Hamsterley and Wolsingham.
NZ093312.

From the Forest car park walk along the vehicular road past
the Forestry Commission centre, initially on the circular
forest walk. Take a right-hand turn off the road on to a
gravel pathway (signposted Crossfield Walk with white
arrows), go round a five-barred gate and over the bridge
which spans the boulder-strewn and very attractive Bedburn
Beck. The banks of the beck are fringed with a number of
broad-leaved trees, including willow, alder, ash and silver
birch. The beck itself is a favourite place for dippers and
grey wagtails, while trout and sea trout can sometimes be
seen. Other birds that may be present in this area include
summer migrants such as wood warblers, pied and spotted
flycatchers, redstarts, willow warblers and blackcaps.

Continue up the tree-flanked track, noting the bat boxes
on some of the conifers on the right-hand side; these have
been fixed on all but the colder north sides of the trees to
attract the pipistrelles – and possibly noctules – in the forest.
The pathway leads on up a hill, known as Windy Bank

Wood, between stands of conifers – some of which have been marked with identification initials by the Forestry Commission. They include Scots pine, Western hemlock, sitka spruce, Norway spruce, Douglas fir and Japanese larch. There is a healthy population of red squirrels in the forest, so keep an eye out for them – they are most likely to be seen in the larches and pines, as are crossbills.

On the left of the pathway there is a drainage ditch, in which some opposite-leaved golden saxifrage (*Chrysosplenium oppositifolium*) grows at various points, and there is a good growth of rushes, some coltsfoot (*Tussilago farfara*) and also marsh thistles (*Cirsium palustre*). In the gaps between the plantations, bracken and foxgloves (*Digitalis purpurea*) may be seen, while patches of broom grow on both sides of the path.

Wherever there is a muddy path in the clay soil, look for the slots (footprints) of roe deer; the deer themselves may be seen early in the morning and at dusk, but they are shy creatures, and the popularity of the forest walks means that they keep to the denser parts of the woods during the day.

At the brow of the hill bear right where two roads meet. Along this stretch of the road there are some oaks and sycamores and a number of bird cherry trees, easily recognized when in flower by their candlelike spikes of creamy-white flowers. The fruits are small, round and black when ripe. The tree does not grow very tall, and has a dark-brown, peeling bark; the leaves are long and pointed, slightly toothed, and rather wrinkled on the upper surface. It is very much a tree of the north. In late spring it is possible that some of the bird cherries may have been stripped of their leaves and covered in white silk. This is the work of the caterpillars of the small ermine moth.

One of the delights of the pathsides is the presence of little patches of dog violets (*Viola riviniana*), with their heart-shaped leaves and lovely blue-violet flowers with a pale spur. Also growing along the woodland edges are many plants of greater stitchwort (*Stellaria holostea*). Continue along this pathway, ignoring a track to the right after about three-quarters of a mile from the start, which is signposted with a blue marker.

On the left, a little way after the road junction, is an area which has been clear-felled and where there now grows a tangle of bracken, foxgloves and brambles. In spring there are tadpoles in some of the little puddles below the bank in this area. Further on, again on the left, and on a high bank, bilberry (*Vaccinium myrtillus*) grows prolifically under the conifers.

After just under a mile, a metalled road is reached. Follow this down to the right, then very soon fork right beside a five-barred gate with a 'No Vehicles Please' notice on it. A little distance down this track is a fine stand of Grand firs. These imports from British Columbia and the western United States grow to immense heights, and provide good timber. The needles, as can be seen, are flat, of somewhat variable length up to about 5 cm (2 inches), and smell of oranges when crushed.

Follow the track down and over the bridge, then turn right and walk along the metalled road for half a mile or so. Turn right off the road and down to where Bedburn and Ayhope Becks meet near a bridge. Just below the bridge is a balsam poplar tree. This is a delightful spot, with the beck running below the hill on the right, and lined with a variety of broad-leaved trees, which make a pleasant contrast with the previous conifer cover. The trees include alder, sallow, hazel, oak, ash and wych elm. The conditions favour a much greater variety of herbaceous plants than the darkness of the plantations. Among those likely to be seen are wood sage (*Teucrium scorodonia*), dog's mercury (*Mercurialis perennis*), bush vetch (*Vicia sepium*), celandine (*Ranunculus ficaria*), wood sorrel (*Oxalis acetosella*), wood anemone (*Anemone nemorosa*) and wood cranesbill (*Geranium sylvaticum*).

A little way along from the bridge and over the fence on the left are meadows which are rich in flowers, making a wonderful show in spring and summer. Buttercups (*Ranunculus spp.*), daisies, cowslips (*Primula veris*), yellow rattle (*Rhinanthus minor*), vetches, meadowsweet (*Filipendula ulmaria*) and pignut (*Conopodium majus*) are all present at various times.

Just beyond the meadow on the opposite side of the beck is a lovely little waterfall, surrounded by ferns, mosses and liverworts, and with golden saxifrage.

Continue along the beck until the starting point by the bridge is reached, and from there return to the car park.

Castle Eden Dene

SUMMARY A spectacularly beautiful wooded ravine through which a burn cuts its way down to the sea. A very special place for the tree lover. Formerly a local nature reserve managed by Peterlee Council, now a National Nature Reserve. Can be very wet and muddy.

APPROXIMATE LENGTH OF WALK 3 miles.

BEST TIMES Spring, summer.

LOCATION Off the B1281 in Peterlee, Durham. NZ410387.

From the car park near the visitor centre enter the reserve through the gate and go down the hill through dense, beautiful woodland. The variety of trees is superb, with horse chestnut, lime, elm, oak, beech, ash and yew, and glimpses of wild cherry down to the left. There is an understorey of hawthorn and bramble, with a carpet of white garlic (*Allium ursinum*) on both sides of the track. Towards the bottom there are some huge horsetails.

Ignore the turning to the left, and walk on down to a meeting of ways by a bridge under which the Castle Eden Dene burn flows. The atmosphere is damp and humid, with a thick growth of ferns, and alder and willow lining the banks of the stream. The surrounding woodland is of sycamore, larch, ash, wych elm, oak and hazel. Gentle light filters through the dense canopy above – a real haven of tranquillity and rare beauty.

Follow the path to the right by the side of the burn. Dog's mercury (*Mercurialis perennis*), bluebells (*Endymion non-scriptus*), and some rhododendron (*Rhododendron ponticum*) grow here, and some little distance along on the right is a small coppice of hazel and sycamore, with violets (*Viola riviniana*) in the field layer. After about a quarter of a mile there is a little lay-by on the left, bounded by logs, and just beyond that, a small patch of the unusual herb Paris (*Paris quadrifolia*). The curious-looking flower of this plant has four narrow, pointed yellow-green petals, four green sepals, and eight prominent green stamens with eight yellow anthers. In bygone days, the numerical harmony of the plant's parts (four, four, eight and eight) was thought to imbue it with magical and medicinal properties.

Down by the burn, alternate-leaved golden saxifrage (*Chrysosplenium alternifolium*) grows in the damper soil, and the broad fronds of hart's-tongue fern (*Phyllitis scolopendrium*) cover some of the rocks. According to the time of year marsh marigold (*Caltha palutris*), sanicle (*Sanicula europaea*), enchanter's nightshade (*Circaea lutetiana*) and marsh arrow-grass (*Triglochin palustris*) grow here or at other places along the burn.

After just about half a mile, cross the burn by a small bridge, on the left of which is a delightful little hollow crammed with ferns – more hart's-tongue, together with male fern (*Dryopteris filix-mas*) and hard fern (*Blechnum spicant*). About twenty-five yards further on there is an exposed limestone cliff on the left with the most extraordinary curtain of ivy (*Hedera helix*) hanging down in front of it; the damp wall behind the curtain is covered with mosses and liverworts.

Continue up the hill to a sharp hairpin bend – take that, do not go straight on – and follow the path up through a fine stand of beeches. At the top of the hill, turn right at a T-junction then, at a division of the ways, again take the right-hand path by a big horse chestnut tree. In spring there is a charming spread of bluebells and wood anemones (*Anemone nemorosa*) under the trees. An avenue of yews leads to what must surely be one of the most spectacular views in this or any other wood. From this high point above the ravine, one looks across the tree tops to the hillside beyond – a magnificent mosaic of all shades of green, from the delicate paleness of the wych elm and ash, to the deep, almost black-green of yew and other conifers.

Continue along the path, eventually crossing a bridge and going along a little boardwalk to another bridge which spans the gorge; the burn can just be heard a long way below. There are Corsican pines here, which are much appreciated by the red squirrels of the reserve. At the bottom of the track downhill, turn left towards the top end of the valley and walk along the steep side of the gorge under a plantation of yews. Note the number of yews that have fallen due to landslip, and how, on many of these, shoots from the branches continue to grow upwards so that the tree does not die.

At the end of the valley, return over the same route, noting, after about 200 yards, the clearing on the left, which is being left to encourage herbs to grow. Already there are water avens (*Geum rivale*), bluebells, violets, cranesbills, cowslips (*Primula veris*), primroses (*Primula vulgaris*), campions, and forget-me-nots, together with blue moor-grass (*Sesleria albicans*). At the division of the track, take the left-hand path, and when some rough steps up to the left are reached take them and follow on to the left. This leads through some birch and hazel coppicing with gorse on the right. This path leads to the bridge over the gorge and back to the viewpoint over the valley. From there, continue to where the path originally came up the hill, but go straight on up the hill past some sycamores, many of them young, and some rhododendrons. There is a large holly on the right, with wild garlic underneath.

After some distance a golf course can be seen over the fence on the right, and the path leads through a mixed conifer plantation. Turn down to the left where, high up on a tree is a sign which says 'Danger, use path at own risk'! The path opens out between a mature wood of oak, horse chestnut, elm, sycamore and rhododendron. At a cross-roads, turn left down the hill through some fine beech trees to the bridge near the reserve entrance, and from there walk up the hill back to the car park.

Bempton Cliffs

SUMMARY Spectacular sea-bird cliffs, the most southerly on the east coast, and the site of the only colony of gannets on the British mainland. An RSPB reserve. The cliffs are dangerous and extreme care is needed.

APPROXIMATE LENGTH OF WALK 1 mile.

BEST TIMES May to mid-July for nesting birds, but autumn and winter can be rewarding for 'sea watching' and for migrants.

LOCATION Near Bempton village, about 4 miles from Bridlington, Humberside. TA197738.

From the RSPB car park, which is partially surrounded by hawthorn bushes, take the path leading down to the cliffs. More hawthorn, together with some crab apple trees, flanks the path which passes through fields. A great variety of small birds may be seen, both in the bushes and in the fields. Depending on the time of year, corn buntings, whinchats, wheatears, reed buntings, linnets, meadow pipits, and gold-crests have all been recorded, with ring ouzels, redstarts, and spotted and pied flycatchers at migration times.

On reaching the end of the path, turn left, and about 100 yards along the cliff is the first of three railed observation platforms. It is from this that the stunning spectacle of Bempton really makes its impact. The sheer cliffs of glistening white chalk are the highest of their type in the country – in places an impressive 400 feet or more. They provide the range of ledges and crevices required by the different species, and every inch of them, or so it seems, is packed with nesting sea birds.

Above: Old quarry at Cheddar

Right: Usnea lichen in the
New Forest

Above: Sea kale at Cuckmere Haven

Left: Limestone pavement at Gait Burrows

Right: Knotted tree at
Arnside Knott

Below: Lakeside wood at
Lake Ullswater

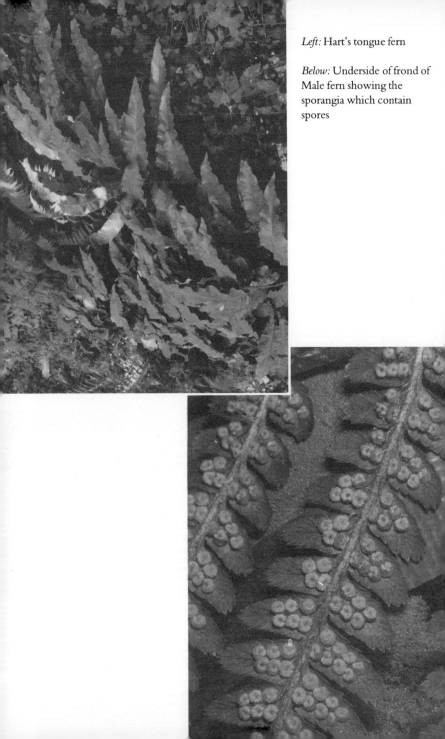

Left: Hart's tongue fern

Below: Underside of frond of Male fern showing the sporangia which contain spores

Right: Royal fern (Studland Heath)

Below: Hair moss with developing sporangia

Above: Sphagnum moss

Below: Thong weed (Embo)

Above: Serrated wrack (Kimmeridge Bay)

Below: Holdfasts and stipes of laminarian seaweeds (Embo)

Left: Goose barnacles on driftwood (Embo)

Below: Alpine club moss (Cwm Idwal)

Right: Limpet, with gouged-out cavity (Cuckmere Haven)

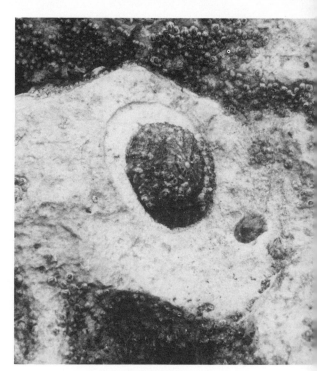

Below: Knot (Ynyslas)

Above: 'Tooth' marks made on rock by limpets as they graze on minute algae (Cuckmere Haven)

Below: Peppery furrow shell, showing the mark made in the mud by the siphon

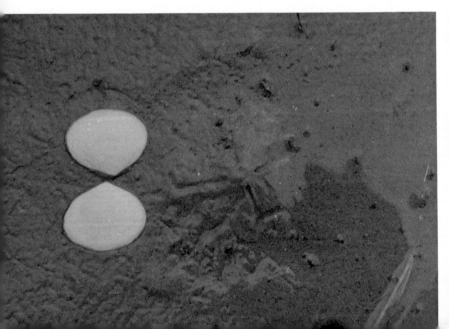

Above: Coot with young

Below: Head of common seal

Above: Female common lizard (Ainsdale Dunes)

Left: Cinnabar moth caterpillars on ragwort

Opposite above: Bird cherry in bloom (Hamsterley Forest)

Opposite below: The river at Coedydd Aber

Left: Waterfall at Coedydd Aber

Below: Cwm Idwal – scratches in the rock caused by the movement of stones embedded in the glacial ice

Right: Ancient tree stump at Ynyslas

Below: River at Cors Caron bog

Above: Warning sign at Cors Caron

Below: Downy birch at Morrone Birkwood

Even before reaching the first platform one becomes aware that many of the 30,000 or so kittiwakes at Bempton must be nesting nearby! The evocative cry, 'kitti-wa-a-ke', is unmistakable. A quick glance confirms that the narrow ledges are crammed with nests, made from mud and seaweed cemented together with droppings (guano).

Watching the birds come and go from their nests can give a clue as to why they choose the apparent hazards of such narrow ledges. It soon becomes obvious that unlike birds such as herring gulls the kittiwake does not thrust straight up into the air when taking off. In order to become airborne it drops downwards for a short distance. A ledge is much more convenient for this type of take-off. If possible, use binoculars to look at the kittiwake's legs. They are short, designed for a life spent almost wholly at sea, and not suitable for pushing off into the air from land. It may also be possible to see that the feet are compact and lack backwardly pointing toes – a useful adaptation for standing on a narrow ledge.

A few nesting fulmars are visible from the first platform, and a very large number of guillemots – some 8,000 nest on these cliffs. Guillemots also prefer narrow ledges, often higher on the cliff than kittiwakes. It is sometimes possible to see a single egg, which is laid on the bare ledge with no nesting material at all. Its unusual shape – like a pear with long, straight sides – helps prevent it falling off the ledge if knocked, as it tends to roll in a tight circle. The sheer cliffs at Bempton are ideal for guillemots (and razorbills) because the fledglings leave the nest before they can fly, taking the short way down by jumping off the ledge. Obviously a straight fall with no protruding ledges is vital for their survival.

The guillemots' life at sea involves long hours on the

surface and much underwater pursuit of food. Like kitti-wakes, they spend little time on land, so their legs are short and, although powerful, are placed noticeably far back on the body, making them clumsy on land. Their wings, adapted for underwater 'flying', are short and stubby, and these characteristics combine to make taking-off by means of a vertical drop essential.

Near the top of the cliff, nesting in deep burrows which they excavate using the strong claws on their webbed feet, are those most endearing of sea birds, the puffins. The image of a puffin with its bill full of fish arranged neatly sideways is familiar, but the means of doing this are perhaps less so. When open, the upper and lower halves of the puffin's beak (i.e. the upper and lower mandibles) are almost parallel; this contrasts with other birds in which the mandibles open at an angle. This parallel opening is achieved by means of an extra bone and a fold of skin in the hinge of the jaw – the fold extending when the beak is open. The birds also have backwardly pointing projections inside the beak which help grip the fish.

A few hundred yards further on along the cliff top is the second observation platform, where more guillemots and some of the 1,500 nesting razorbills can be seen. The latter prefer small crevices and cavities in the rock, and tend to nest higher on the cliff than guillemots and kittiwakes. No nesting material is used, but because of the less vulnerable site the egg is a normal shape. At or near the bottom of the huge cliffs are a number of shag nests, but these are not very easy to see.

Clearly, the nesting birds are the principal attraction of this walk, but the observation platforms offer excellent viewpoints for watching the great variety of migrant and passage birds throughout the year. In late summer waders such as whimbrel, curlew and dunlin may be seen, while from July to September large numbers of sandwich terns and some common terns fly along the coast. In autumn there are regular sightings of common scoters and Manx shearwaters.

About another 500 yards along the cliff top the third observation platform is reached, and from this there are marvellous views of the gannet colony. Between 500 and 600 birds nest on the wide ledges found along this section of the cliffs. The nests are made chiefly of seaweed held together with guano, and sometimes decorated with pieces of rope or fish netting. I watched one bird winging its way back to the cliff trailing a piece of blue rope far longer than its own body length of 90 cm (3 feet). The birds can be seen sitting on their nests incubating the single egg, which incidentally takes approximately forty-five days to hatch – the longest incubation of any bird in the British Isles.

Although birds are *the* feature at Bempton, well over 200 species of wild flowers have been recorded. Many of these are, as might be expected, chalkland species, and most can be seen on either side of the cliff-top path, including rough hawkbit (*Leontodon hispidus*), common scurvy grass (*Cochlearia officinalis*) and field mouse-ear (*Cerastium arvense*). Especially eye-catching are the extensive stands of vigorously growing red campion (*Silene dioica*). The vegetation offers food and shelter for butterflies and their caterpillars. Migrant butterflies such as painted ladies and red admirals are common in autumn, while the resident species include common blue, meadow brown, small tortoiseshell, and the large, small and green-veined whites.

The gannetry is the furthest point of the reserve, so return to the car park along the same route.

WALES

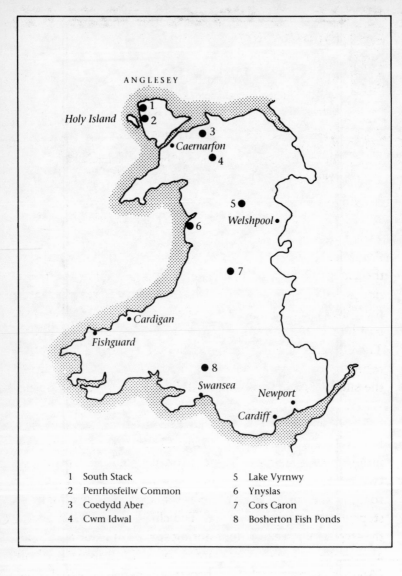

ANGLESEY

Holy Island

1
2
3
● Caernarfon
4

5 ●
Welshpool ●

6

7 ●

● Cardigan

Fishguard

8 ●
Swansea ●

Newport

Cardiff ●

1	South Stack	5	Lake Vyrnwy
2	Penrhosfeilw Common	6	Ynyslas
3	Coedydd Aber	7	Cors Caron
4	Cwm Idwal	8	Bosherton Fish Ponds

South Stack

SUMMARY A dramatic cliff and maritime heathland walk, with fine sea-bird colonies, rare plants, and some extraordinary rock formations. An RSPB reserve.

APPROXIMATE LENGTH OF WALK 4–5 miles.

BEST TIMES Spring and summer, but also autumn and winter for some birds.

LOCATION Follow the signs to South Stack from the A5 in Holyhead. SH205823.

From the RSPB car park walk down to the cliff edge through the extensive area of ling (*Calluna vulgaris*), heather (*Erica cinerea*) and gorse, then follow the path to the right towards the RSPB centre in Ellen's Tower. Common blue and grayling butterflies are often seen in this area. At Ellen's Tower, time spent searching the sea for birds will often result in sightings of Manx shearwaters and gannets during the summer, and, less frequently, of great and sooty shearwaters, and Leach's petrels.

From the cliff edge on the far side of the centre, there is a fine view of one of the towering bird cliffs, with vast numbers of guillemots, some razorbills, and perhaps one or two puffins. Take the steps up and walk along the cliff to the road, at the end of which there is a steep and long flight of steps down to the lighthouse. The cliff face on either side of the steps is a blaze of colour during spring and summer, with a veritable natural rock garden of wild flowers – thrift (*Armeria maritima*), lady's bedstraw (*Galium verum*), and kidney vetch (*Anthyllis vulneraria*). From the steps, closer views of the sea-bird cliffs are obtained, and of the rafts of guillemots and razorbills on the sea. At the bottom, near the bridge across to the stack on which the lighthouse stands, there is a cliff showing huge folds in the rockface, telling of violent earth movements millions of years ago.

Return to the road and continue around the cliff and up towards a stone observation platform. Here, the dramatic beauty of this wonderful coastline can be appreciated in full. To the right are the 400-foot cliffs of Gogarth Bay, rising sheer from the sea. Behind them is a great sweep of brilliant purple heathland leading up to the glistening white rocks and summit of Holyhead Mountain – a most impressive scene. From here, too, it is sometimes possible to see the little band of choughs for which South Stack is famous. These delightful birds sweep up the cliff face, uttering their distinctive call, then swoop down again out of sight. They are easily recognizable by their brilliant deep-red legs and bills. Sometimes, too, they can be seen hunting for insects near the lighthouse steps' car park, apparently unconcerned by the people walking by.

From the observation platform, follow one of the many rough pathways that lead inland behind a rocky hill, and then turn left towards the wireless telegraphy station on Holyhead Mountain. Around this area, look carefully for one of the reserve's rarities, the attractive spotted rock-rose (*Tuberaria guttata*), which flowers in June. It is a small (about primrose-size) yellow flower, with a red spot at the base of each petal.

Follow one of the paths leading towards the wireless telegraphy station, making a detour to look at some open water down to the right, which has various water plants around it. Rejoin a main track that leads to the left of the station, across the open heathland of mixed ling, bell heather, cross-leaved heath (*Erica tetralix*) and gorse, among which in mid-summer many heath spotted orchids (*Dactylorhiza maculata*) are in bloom. The colourful heathland provides shelter and nesting sites for birds such as linnets, wrens, whitethroats and stonechats, and gives some protection from the kestrels and little owls that prey on them. Near the cliff edges, ravens perform their extraordinary aerobatics, making use of the air currents, while peregrines create havoc among sea and land birds alike. Adders and lizards may be seen anywhere on this heathland.

Follow the pathways towards North Stack at the north end of Gogarth Bay, but instead of going down to the lighthouse, turn sharp right down the hill overlooking it, towards a road that can be seen at the bottom, leading back towards the town of Holyhead. Note the telegraph poles beside the road; they are numbered, and at number fifteen (the number can be seen at about head height on the side of the post facing Holyhead) bear right, on to an indistinct track which leads slightly uphill. In this area of heath, woodcock and short-eared owls may be seen during late autumn, and there is evidence of foxes.

Remain on this track until it divides, taking the right fork, which eventually leads down towards some fields between stone walls. Turn right here, and follow along between the walls, where there is gorse and bramble scrub. Goldcrests and warblers may collect here at migration times. The path emerges on to heathland. At a crossroads near a quarry on the left, take the right-hand track towards the wireless telegraphy station. Head for the road which leads to the station, cross it, and return along the outward path, past Ellen's Tower and back to the car park.

Penrhosfeilw Common

SUMMARY A short, more or less circular walk through exceptionally interesting maritime heathland, which includes a rarity. Because of the Common's exposed position on the tip of Anglesey it can be very bracing in a high wind! Although it lacks the large sea bird colonies of nearby South Stack, it is by no means without attraction for the birdwatcher. The coastal views are exceptional. A Site of Special Scientific Interest (SSSI) and RSPB reserve.

APPROXIMATE LENGTH OF WALK 1 mile.

BEST TIMES Spring, summer, autumn.

LOCATION To the south of South Stack Cliffs, near Holyhead on Anglesey. (114)216804

Several broad pathways lead from the RSPB car park, and it does not really matter which one is taken, as all the reserve is easily accessible and the full extent of it is visible. However, the path to the left passes immediately through one of the features of the common – a dense covering of heather and gorse, which in late summer and autumn is a mass of brilliant colour. The principal heather is, in fact, ling (*Calluna vulgaris*), but cross-leaved heath (*Erica tetralix*) and bell heather (*Erica cinerea*) are also present. Two kinds of gorse are found – Western and, in the deeper soil, European.

Ling, heath and heather are so often lumped together under the one heading of 'heather', but they are, of course, different plants. Ling is the only true heather. It is the one with the small, rounded, pale, mauve/purple and occasionally white flowers, with the pale stigma and style of the female protruding. The stalkless green leaves arise in pairs from the stem, and those which grow on the side-shoots are often overlapping. Bell heather, also known as purple or Scottish heather, frequently grows with ling on moors and heaths, often (but not always) near the sea. Its egg-shaped flowers are a very bright crimson-purple – and it is the one that gives that wonderful, deep-purple haze over Scottish hills and moors in autumn. The flowers grow near the tops of the stems, and the leaves grow in whorls of three. Cross-leaved heath has drooping, rose-pink, egg-shaped flowers, larger than those of bell heather. Its leaves are arranged in whorls of four, and this is where it gets both its scientific and common names from. It is commonly found in wetter situations than bell heather or ling.

The two gorses can usually be distinguished by their different growth habit. European or common gorse is the taller, growing up to 2.4 m (8 feet) high (although not on this site) – a straggly but sturdy bush. The flowers are a brilliant golden yellow. Western gorse is much smaller and more compact; the flowers appear narrower, and are not such a brilliant yellow. For anyone who wants to brave close examination of the spines, those of the common gorse are quite deeply furrowed, while the Western gorse ones are either not furrowed at all or only slightly so.

The heather and gorse cover, particularly in the parts of the Common more distant from the sea (and thus more protected), is very dense indeed, but from place to place there are small breaks, where tormentil (*Potentilla erecta*), for instance, is found, as well as heath speedwell (*Veronica officinalis*), and lady's bedstraw (*Galium verum*).

Further down the pathway it soon becomes obvious that the action of the very strong winds that lash this Common has resulted in the heather developing a definite wavelike growth. Further down again, over towards the left-hand side of the Common, there are some very damp, marshy areas.

Growing there in great numbers in spring and summer are the heath spotted orchid (*Dactylorhiza maculata*) (May–July), and the northern marsh orchid (*D. purpurella*). The former has pale-pink flowers with darker stripes and spots, and the latter is a rich deep purple with reddish markings. Also in the marsh areas are the white flags of bog cotton (*Eriophorum sp.*), with sundew (*Drosera rotundifolia*) and bog asphodel (*Narthecium ossifragum*).

When the cliff top is reached, turn right, and continue towards the far end of the Common. As the habitat becomes more exposed to the salt-laden winds, the density of the heath vegetation decreases, and more coarse grasses appear. Flowering plants include masses of thrift (*Armeria maritima*), some sea campion (*Silene maritima*), kidney vetch (*Anthyllis vulneraria*) birdsfoot trefoil (*Lotus corniculatus*), devil's-bit scabious (*Succisa pratensis*), and, much more rarely, the pale heath violet (*Viola lactea*).

Down at the far end of the Common, towards the right, there is quite a large but scattered spread of a plant that grows here and nowhere else – the field fleawort subspecies *maritimus* (*Senecio integrifolius* sub-species *maritimus*), which flowers in early June. It is an unremarkable plant in appearance, with a flower head resembling ragwort, growing on a single stem from a basal rosette. It is often covered in white down.

Further round, on the lower, grassy, more gently sloping cliffs facing back towards South Stack, spring squill (*Scilla verna*) is found.

Birds that breed on the Common include lapwing and redshank, but it is the passage birds that are of greatest interest. Dotterels regularly pass through on migration, as do whimbrel and greenshank, while merlin, short-eared owls and harriers are also seen at migration times.

Return to the car park along one of the pathways.

Coedydd Aber

SUMMARY The Aber Falls at the head of this wooded valley are of themselves worth the walk, but there is much more, including some wonderful Welsh mountain scenery, and a small herd of Welsh Mountain ponies which come down from the higher tops to graze the richer grasses in the valley. Coedydd Aber is a National Nature Reserve, managed by the Nature Conservancy Council; the conifer woodlands on the hillside are managed by the Forestry Commission. The walk follows the marked Nature Trail.

APPROXIMATE LENGTH OF WALK 3½ miles.

BEST TIMES Spring, summer.

LOCATION Off the A55 Bangor–Conway road. SH662720.

From the lower of the two car parks at SH662720 walk along the path above the Afon Rhaeadr Fawr river through the mixed woodland of sycamore, ash, oak and hazel, with alders down by the water. The rock-strewn river has a gravelly bed and is very swift-flowing – the ideal habitat for dippers and grey wagtails. Cross the bridge, and turn right up the hill on the metalled road – this is Post One of the marked Trail, where walkers from the upper car park should start the walk.

On either side of the road is open grassland, with harebells (*Campanula rotundifolia*) in late summer, while the mixed woodland, standing back from the road, forms a dense canopy from summer through to winter, precluding virtually any field layer. However, before the trees are in full leaf, enough light penetrates to allow the growth of typical woodland flowers such as bluebells (*Endymion non-scriptus*), wood anemone (*Anemone nemorosa*) and wood sorrel (*Oxalis acetosella*). Woodland birds are common, and nesting species include nuthatches, blue, great and coal tits, tree-creepers, great spotted woodpeckers, wood and willow warblers, chiffchaffs, and redstarts. Green woodpeckers can be seen probing vigorously among the grass roots for ants.

Much of the woodland on the left of the road is fenced, and near Post Two behind this fence are some balsam poplars. The outline of these trees is much more cone-shaped than the tall, narrow Lombardy poplar, and their name comes from the sticky brown wax which exudes from the opening buds in spring and gives off a powerful but pleasant smell. The leaves are a long, oval shape with a pointed tip and slightly toothed edge, and are a deep-green colour above and white underneath. On the ash tree by the Trail post there is a fine growth of mosses and grey lichens indicating, as might be expected, a clean, moist atmosphere.

By Post Three is a magnificent spreading oak tree, whose great age of over 220 years has been determined by taking a core from the trunk and counting the growth rings. Oaks are probably the best known of British trees – and although a number of species are found in this country, only two are truly native. These are the sessile or durmast oak and the pedunculate or common oak. True specimens of each species are quite easy to distinguish one from the other but, as experience shows, they tend to hybridize, and trees with the characteristics of both are not unusual.

Pedunculate oaks in the open with plenty of room for unrestricted growth usually have wide-spreading branches growing low on the trunk, which is often gnarled. The leaves are paler than the sessile oak, with quite distinct lobes (auricles) at their base, deep indentations at the edges, and are on short stalks. The twigs and leaves are hairless. The acorn of the pedunculate oak is borne on a long stem or pedicle, from which the species takes its name. The boughs of sessile oaks, in contrast, tend to grow from higher up the trunk, the leaves are a much darker green, grow on longer stalks, do not have auricles at the base, show shallower indentations around the edges, and also have a few hairs on the midrib underneath. The acorns do not have a stalk, they grow directly on the twig. In general, pedunculate oaks are found on deep soils in southern and eastern Britain, while the sessile species can thrive in the shallower, poorer soils of the north west. However, this is by no means a strict delineation.

This particular oak tree has many pedunculate features and, as with most oak trees, it provides food and shelter for a variety of creatures. Birds may nest in it, of course, and the caterpillars of at least two moths eat its leaves, and may in some years virtually denude it of foliage in the spring. These are the caterpillars of the mottled umber (with the appropriate Latin name of *Erannis defoliaria*) and the winter moth. The caterpillar of the former is variable in colour, ranging from reddish-brown to a pale yellow-brown, but almost always has distinct yellow patches on its sides. The winter moth caterpillar is bluish-green, with a dark line down the middle of the back and pale yellowish-white lines down either side. The whole creature appears banded. Both caterpillars drop to the ground and pupate there until the moths emerge in late autumn or winter. The males of both species are the familiar type of winged moths, but the females are wingless (or virtually so), and climb up the tree to mate.

Walk on up the road, and as the valley opens out, part of the Aber Falls can be seen at the valley head. Near Post Five there is a fenced experimental plot on the left, from which grazing animals (sheep and ponies) have been excluded. It shows very clearly the effect of grazing, as the enclosed area has a dense growth of woodland grasses, such as wood false brome. The trees within the enclosure have for the most part been planted. One or two bat boxes may be seen on the trees in this vicinity – the species recorded in the valley are pipistrelle and the long-eared. The old cow byre behind the cottage on the left is an information centre containing small displays.

As the road leads around a bend and up an incline, more of the valley is revealed, showing more of the coniferous plantation on the hillside on the left. This consists chiefly of Japanese larch, which differs from European larch in having darker, blue-green needles, rusty-red twigs (compared with the straw-coloured twigs of the European species) and cones in which the scales are reflexed (i.e. bent backwards away from the body of the cone), whereas the scales of the European larch cones are straight. There are also some cedars in the plantation. Almost opposite the conifers, on the right of the road, is a large alder wood, enclosed against grazing animals to allow natural regeneration.

In between the two woodlands is a wide grassy area, which appears to be a favourite grazing ground of the Welsh Mountain ponies when they come down from the high hills. They are one of the nine breeds of British ponies known as the Mountain and Moorland or native breeds (the others are the New Forest, Highland, Fell, Dales, Exmoor, Dartmoor, Shetland and Connemara). Some of the breeds are still as much a part of the natural history of their respective areas as the trees, flowers, birds and other mammals, and it is interesting to look at these Welsh Mountain ponies to see how well adapted they are to the harsh environment of the hills.

First, look at their overall outline, and compare it in the mind's eye with a thoroughbred racehorse. The pony is, of course, much smaller, and is therefore better able to exist on the relatively sparse herbage of the hills. The legs are shorter in relation to the depth of the body than those of the racehorse, and this gives a smaller surface area/volume ratio, resulting in proportionately less body surface from which heat is lost in winter. The legs, too, especially from the knees downwards, are short and quite stocky, ensuring that they are strong enough for the very rough ground over which they need to move. The head is not as tiny as that of some show-ring animals, and this allows a good length of muzzle, so that the cold air that is inhaled has a reasonably large nasal cavity in which to warm up a little before entering the lungs.

The coat in winter is nice and thick, and the mane is also thick and grows long to maintain warmth and to protect the major blood vessels in the neck from the cold air. Similarly the tail is long and thick to protect the pony's rear end; the tail itself tends not to grow from the very top of the end of the hindquarters but from slightly further down, so that when the pony stands, as it always will, with its tail facing the wind and rain, it can clamp its tail down tightly to protect its dock and the thinner skin between the hind legs. A closer look (but not too close, these are not pet ponies!) will show that in certain places, the hair of the coat forms whorls. There is quite an obvious one on the flank, just in front of the hind leg. These ensure that the rain and melting snow are directed away from the more sensitive areas of the body.

Continue along the road, noting, as the end of the valley is approached, the high scree slopes on the left. Carry on through a gateway which leads directly to the Aber Falls. These Falls are a truly magnificent sight, dropping well over 100 feet down the cliffs of Creigiau Rhaeadr Fawr. The bottom of the waterfall is almost completely lost in the mist and spray, and it is not really possible to see the many mosses and liverworts growing on the cliff face.

From the Falls there is a choice – either return to the car park along the same road, or branch off to the steeper and, in places, quite testing, high–level path. For the latter, instead of going through the gate back to the road, follow the fence round to the right, and when another fence is reached turn sharply up the hill – a steep stretch up to a stile at Post Nine. At the stile, a pause to enjoy the view back towards the Falls also gives time to regain lost breath! Buzzards may be seen soaring over the cliffs, and ravens are not uncommon. Other birds that may be seen on the steep slopes before entering the forest include ring ouzels, meadow pipits and wheatears.

Go over the stile into the conifer plantation. From the natural history viewpoint, the walk through the plantation offers a chance to brush up on the difference between various conifers, and to see how the growth of the trees is influenced by the height at which they are growing.

The trees in the first section of the plantation are mostly sitka spruce, whose needles are extremely sharp and have a bluish tinge. The pale-brown oval cones are attractive in appearance, with crinkly, wavy-edged scales. There is also some Japanese larch. The plantation is dense, with virtually nothing growing underneath the trees, but a few mosses and some fungi may be seen along the edges of the path. Birds are not much in evidence, although goldcrests can be heard – if not often seen.

Between Posts Ten and Eleven the trees become noticeably smaller, due to the increasing shallowness and dryness of the soil and the effect of the wind at the greater altitude. By Post Eleven, lodgepole pine is the dominant conifer. It is so named because the American Indians used this species as support poles for their tepees or 'lodges'. The needles of lodgepole pine are short, grow in pairs, are yellowish-green in colour, and twisted. The cones are very unfriendly, each scale bearing a stiff prickle.

At Post Twelve, which at 1,000 feet above sea level is the highest point of the Trail, there is a welcome seat in a wide clearing. As is obvious, the trees at this height are not good specimens; their leading shoots are often broken by the high winds, and they are stunted in growth. In the clearing, however, because more light is available, the variety of ground flora has increased considerably when compared with that in the forest. Bracken is growing, there is some gorse, a strong growth of hair moss and, as the path is followed downhill, bilberry (*Vaccinium myrtillus*) and crowberry (*Empetrum nigrum*) put in an appearance. From this section of the walk there is a wonderful view out to sea on a clear day.

Follow the now-broad roadway down the hill, turning left at the junction near Post Thirteen. The rather soulless conifer plantations now have other trees and shrubs along their fringes – birch, rowan, oak and willow – and by Post Fifteen the woodland is a mixed, largely deciduous one again.

Soon Post Seventeen, where three power lines go over the road, is reached, and a little further down there is a stile to the right, leading to the road back to the car parks.

Cwm Idwal

SUMMARY At over 1,200 feet above sea level, this walk offers the opportunity of seeing some dramatic Snowdonian scenery at close quarters, yet it is not unduly testing. It is, nevertheless, an upland walk, rough in places, so suitable footwear and clothing are advised. The area is of special geological and botanical interest. A National Nature Reserve, the first in Wales, established in 1954.

APPROXIMATE LENGTH OF WALK 4 miles.

BEST TIMES Spring, summer.

LOCATION Close to the A5 near Betws-y-Coed. SH(23)648603.

Take the track signposted Idwal Path, behind the buildings on the side road. Within a very short distance an example of parsley fern (*Cryptogramma crispa*) is seen growing on the bank on the right. Shortly after that a bridge crosses a rushing stream, and from there the path winds its way up the hill, with splendid mountain scenery all around.

The actual reserve of Cwm Idwal is about three-quarters of a mile from the start of the walk, and is entered by means of an iron gate. The view from this point is dramatic, to say the least. Immediately in front and slightly below is Llyn Idwal, a small glacial lake, and behind the lake, surrounding it on three sides, tower the impressive, almost menacing cliffs and crags of Glyder Fawr and Y Garn. Twll Du, the Devil's Kitchen, is the dark cleft in the centre of the cliffs.

Apart from the stunning scenic impact of the *cwm*, or valley, it is especially interesting to the geologist. As a Nature Conservancy Council leaflet explains, the valley was hollowed out of the mountain by glacial action millions of years ago, and is renowned as one of the best of its type in Wales. Twll Du is the bottom of the Snowdon syncline, or fold.

From the gate, turn right amid the huge boulders and rocky outcrops, and walk along beside the fence to a low ridge from which there is a magnificent view of the wide, U-shaped Nant Ffrancon valley opening out below. The valley, also gouged out by glacial action, has a river meandering throughout its length; the lake that once was there was silted up by sediment washed down from the mountains. On the right of the ridge is a large rocky outcrop which offers evidence of ancient glacial movements. The surface of the rock is smooth and rounded, but scarred by deep scratches caused by the stones that were embedded in the glacial ice. This formation is known as 'roches moutonnées', apparently because of an extraordinarily fanciful resemblance to a type of wig!

A short walk to the left from the ridge are some small enclosures which show very clearly the effect of grazing on vegetation. Within the fences there is a strong growth of grasses, rushes and heather, whereas outside there is little but mat-grass (Nardus stricta) which has been very closely cropped by sheep and, during the winter months, by the herd of feral goats that comes down from the higher crags.

From the enclosures, go down the hill to the shingle shore that fringes the lake. Numerous shoals of minnows can be seen darting about in the shallow water at the edge, while further out a glimpse may be caught of trout rising to mayflies. Gulls can often be seen feeding on the smaller fish, while herons and cormorants also visit. Anyone hardy enough to undertake this walk in winter might be rewarded with the sight of goldeneye, pochard and whooper swans.

A close – and lengthy – search may result in finding fossils in the pebbles that make up the shingle. A really fascinating find would be a part of a trilobite – a marine creature somewhat reminiscent of a modern woodlouse, but rounder, with a shield-like head and a segmented body. Another possibility is a bivalve, orthis, which had a scallop-shaped shell.

Continue round the lake until a small stream is reached. It is the Afon Clyd and, as can be seen, it has flowed down a deep gully cut in the mountain face of Y Garn. There is a boggy area around the stream, with rushes, mosses and, in spring and summer, bogbean (*Menyanthes trifoliata*) and marsh cinquefoil (*Potentilla palustris*), the purple flowers of butterwort (*Pinguicula vulgaris*), and the red and green leaves of sundew (*Drosera rotundifolia*). Walk up the stream a short distance and examine the banks, which show clearly in a number of places the horizontal 'soil profile' (i.e. the layers of material under the surface). Under the top soil is a layer of gravel, and under that a thick layer of peat. This is interesting, as peat is normally formed on the *surface* by the degeneration of plant remains. The profile here shows that the peat has been buried, probably by material washed down from the mountain.

The pathway leads on round the lake, climbing a little as it does so, with a bank on the right, and a gentle slope down to the water on the left. Quite a number of specimens of an insignificant-looking plant are found among the grass on either side of the path, but particularly on the bank side. Easily overlooked, because of their dull green colour, they are club mosses – species of *Lycopodium*. Their resemblance to true mosses is, however, superficial. They are small, usually evergreen, much-branched plants, commonly with creeping stems which send up forked branches. Most have little pointed leaves clustered round the stems, which are quite stiff. They bear club-shaped, spore-bearing cones – a primitive reproductive body. The most common club moss found on this walk is the blue-green Alpine variety, which differs from most others by having slightly broader leaves which overlap and cling closely to the stems. The cones are present during July and August.

It is hard to believe that these small, primitive plants are the descendants of huge trees, well over 30 m (100 feet) high, which dominated the vegetation in the Carboniferous period nearly 300 million years ago. The modern club mosses, although so small, still have features in common with their massive ancestors, who also had spore-bearing cones, forked branches and spirally arranged leaves.

The path now goes along beside a mound covered with mat-grass, among which some more Alpine club moss is growing. The mound is of geological importance, as it is an example of a moraine – an elongated, crescent-shaped mound of loose rock which originally fell on the surface of the moving glacier that formed the valley. When the glacier retreated, the mound of rock debris was left, and over thousands of years became covered with vegetation.

From the moraine, leave the path and walk round the base of a small hill on the left until a boggy area is reached. From here, follow the small stream uphill again to a small waterfall. In spring and summer this very narrow rocky gorge with its waterfall contains a surprising collection of plants such as purple saxifrage (*Saxifraga oppositifolia*), alpine meadow rue (*Thalictrum alpinum*), mountain sorrel (*Oxyria digyna*), great woodrush (*Luzula sylvatica*), and the little green spleenwort fern (*Asplenium viride*), with the green stem from which it takes its name.

From the waterfall go on down to the lake – but take care in this area, as it is very boggy. The most common plants are sphagnum moss, various pondweeds, sundews, and rushes. Large shoals of minnows can again be seen in the shallow water at the lake's edge. Continue past the head of the lake, and climb up on to a rocky track which leads round to the left, back towards the entrance to the reserve.

About halfway along this side of the lake, right down to the water's edge once more, one of the many interesting water plants can be seen. This is water lobelia (*Lobelia dortmanna*) which flowers during July and August. The delicately coloured, very pale lilac, two-lipped flowers of this exquisitely dainty little plant are borne on a slender hollow stem which arises from a submerged rosette of leaves. Delicate though it is, water lobelia is reasonably well-adapted to the difficult environment in which it grows. In common with a number of water plants, its leaves are narrow and undivided, thus offering little resistance to the movement of the water. Its roots are strong, ensuring that the plant is firmly anchored. As in all plants, the growth of the roots is dependent on energy released during respiration, and this in turn is dependent on the presence of oxygen which, in the submerged leaves of water lobelia, is carried to the roots through special air spaces.

Also growing in the lake are other water plants typical of similar high-altitude lakes, such as shoreweed (*Littorella uniflora*) – which, as the name suggests, grows at the lake edge – pillwort (*Pilularia globulifera*), autumnal water star-wort (*Callitriche hermaphroditica*), awlwort (*Subularia aquatica*) and alternate water milfoil (*Myriophyllum alterniflorum*). At the lake edge too, is the jointed rush (*Juncus articulatus*) – which can be differentiated from other rushes by running a finger down the leaves, where the transverse joints are easily felt.

Continue around the lake edge to the gate and return along the outward route.

Lake Vyrnwy

SUMMARY A walk near, but not around the shores of, the lake Vyrnwy Reservoir, taking in a variety of habitats including deciduous and coniferous woodland, moorland and meadows. There is one quite steep hill. The RSPB has a very good visitor centre with videos and exhibitions, and there is a hide in the car park.

APPROXIMATE LENGTH OF WALK 3 miles.

BEST TIMES Spring, summer.

LOCATION In the Berwyn hills west of Llanfyllin, reached by the B4393 road to Llanwddyn. SH985215.

From the visitor centre go down the road to the right past the car park. At the fork in the road a short distance on, keep right towards a sign pointing to Llanggadfan. Shortly after this bear right up the hill, following the blue Trail marks. On the right are mature sessile oak and birches. This is just the type of habitat enjoyed by pied flycatchers, and in and around this area a number of nest boxes have been put up by the RSPB to encourage them. Nuthatches are also quite common, and the first indication of the presence of one of these delightful and attractive birds may be the persistent hammering sound of its bill on an acorn which it has placed in a crack in the bark of a tree.

About seventy-five yards or so from the turning on the right, note the birch tree with a mass of witches brooms among its twigs. These, which may be mistaken for birds' nests at first sight, occur where abnormal growth due to biochemical changes has taken place because of the presence of a fungus or a mite. The changes cause many buds which would otherwise lie dormant to develop, with the consequent cluster of twigs.

On the left is an area of scrub – hawthorn, blackthorn and rowan – which gives shelter to redstarts, garden and willow warblers and blackcaps. On the right are some young trees which have recently been planted. As can be seen, they are protected from the unwelcome attention of grazing sheep by plastic sleeves, which will disintegrate in about five years. A number of butterflies frequent this area on warm, sunny days, with the brilliantly coloured peacock being the most conspicuous. Along the verges the bright blue flowers of germander speedwell (*Veronica chamaedrys*) can be seen from March right through until about July, while other flowering plants include tormentil (*Potentilla erecta*), yarrow (*Achillea millefolium*) and sneezewort (*Achillea ptarmica*), with wood sorrel (*Oxalis acetosella*) under the trees. Sneezewort, with its head of strange, white-grey flowers, is allegedly so called because its smell causes sneezing; it was once used to relieve toothache.

Continue up the hill, pausing by the cattle grid to look back across the lake. As can be seen, the habitat changes quite noticeably from one side of the cattle grid to the other. The scrubland is replaced by more open ground, with bracken and a few scattered rowan and ash trees. At the top of the hill there is a rocky outcrop where the succulent red stems and star-like white flowers of English stonecrop (*Sedum anglicum*) can be seen. Go over the stile and round to the hide, from where there is a fine view of the surrounding countryside. Patience is required to see many birds from here, but buzzard, peregrine, merlin, sparrowhawk, kestrel and hen harrier have all been recorded.

Return over the stile and walk on down the hill below a

high bank on the right, above which there is open moorland-type country where yellowhammers may be seen. At the farm on the left, take the right-hand fork towards a conifer plantation. Along the roadside various plants may be in flower, such as foxgloves (*Digitalis purpurea*), heath bedstraw (*Galium saxatile*), milkwort (*Polygala vulgaris*), St John's wort (*Hypericum*), and primrose (*Primula vulgaris*), as well as gorse and some bracken. Butterflies frequent this comparatively sheltered area, with meadow brown and small heaths the most likely to be seen.

On the right, high up above the bank, is a plantation of Japanese larches, and on the left, an area that has been clear-felled, and where bracken and foxgloves are now growing. Among the larches a number of small birds may be heard and, with a bit of luck, seen. There are goldcrest, siskin, wood warbler and chiffchaff. Further down the track, the verge plants include betony (*Betonica officinalis*) and enchanter's nightshade (*Circaea lutetiana*), while the butterflies to be seen include ringlet and speckled wood. It also appears to be a favourite place for pheasants, which are sometimes present in large numbers.

At the bottom of the track there is a large stand of rosebay willowherb (*Epilobium angustifolium*) and an area of small trees and scrub where blackcaps and chiffchaffs may be seen.

Turn right, and just before turning right again up a steep hill, notice a small turkey oak tree growing in the bank. The hill is very steep, and slower progress allows for observation of the different ages of the sitka spruce plantations on either side. On the faces of the high banks of the track, there is a thick cover of gorse, bramble, and ling (*Calluna vulgaris*), with bracken. This vegetation is especially thick in and around the younger conifers, which have not yet shaded it out, and a number of birds have taken advantage of this.

Whinchats, warblers, tree pipits and whitethroats may all be seen in this area.

At the top of the hill there is a choice of two routes through mostly conifer woodland. Take either of these routes, as the two meet later. If, on the chosen route, there is a drainage ditch beside the track, turn over some of the stones and search for signs of life. These are most unlikely to be present, as the acid water running off the conifers drains off into the ditches and establishes a habitat that supports little life.

Where the two tracks meet, go over the stile and down the edge of the meadows, where harebell (*Campanula rotundifolia*), heath bedstraw, and devil's-bit scabious (*Succisa pratensis*) may be seen, as well as some plants of the pink-flowered yarrow close to the roadside. Towards the bottom of the track, there are some alders, where siskins are often seen. The trail joins the road through the village just by the Post Office. Turn left back to the visitor centre.

Ynyslas, Walk 1: The Mud Flats and Salt Marsh

SUMMARY A book could be written about the wealth of wildlife in this part of the Dyfi Estuary. The area is therefore divided into two walks. This one takes in the rich mud flats and salt marsh, and can be undertaken only at low tide (preferably starting on a falling tide). As might be expected, Wellingtons are essential. There is an outstanding visitor centre with displays and a far too tempting bookshop! A National Nature Reserve.

APPROXIMATE LENGTH OF WALK Variable, but up to about 1–1½ miles.

BEST TIME All year.

LOCATION Near Borth, Dyfed. SN609942.

A brief and necessarily simplified explanation of the structure of an estuary and how this affects its inhabitants may be helpful here. An estuary occurs where a river flows into the sea. Most are triangular in shape, and the Dyfi is no exception; it opens out near the sea from a narrower river valley. Obviously there must be some mix of salt and fresh water in an estuary, and this varies according to the state of the tide and the distance of a particular part of the estuary from the sea. The areas nearest the sea will be almost entirely salt water at high tide but will have a great proportion of fresh water at low tide. There is, however, more to it than that. Where the two kinds of water come together the salt water is denser, and this tends to become the bottom layer with the fresh water on top.

Mud flats are a feature of most estuaries, and these are formed by silt which is collected by the river during its faster-flowing passage down from its source. When the river widens out into the estuary, the strength of the flow decreases and it no longer has the energy to carry heavier particles such as stones and gravel, so these fall to the bottom. Finally, it can no longer carry even the fine, silty mud, and this too is deposited, and in time forms mud flats in the lower reaches of the estuary.

Clearly, all this affects the animals in the sand and mud flats. They must be able to adapt to or avoid the consequences of varying salinity in the water. Those that live in the mud flats must be able to deal with a restricted oxygen supply and, as most are within the tidal range, they must be able to adapt to their habitat being both exposed to the air and covered by water.

From the visitor centre, walk down to the water's edge – this is quite a distance at low tide. Some care is needed, as at the bottom of the shore there are some areas of very soft sand into which it is quite easy to sink. Although this wide stretch of sand may appear almost devoid of life, this is certainly not the case. The most obvious clue to the hidden world of the sand lies in the thousands upon thousands of worm casts that can be seen from the middle shore downwards. These are made by lugworms (*Arenicola*), one of the commonest species of worms, which live in tubes in the sand. The tubes are U-shaped, and the casts are formed by the excretion from the rear end of the worm of sand which it has eaten and from which it extracts organic food material. Logic suggests that there must be some indication of where that sand came from, and indeed there is. Within a few inches of every worm cast will be found a small depression which marks the mouth end of the tube.

It is interesting to have a look at the lugworms if possible. They have haemoglobin (the oxygen-carrying pigment) in their blood, and this enables them to survive in an environment where oxygen is in short supply for long periods. It will be noticed that most worms are dug from a layer of sand that is blackened to a greater or lesser degree. The depth of this 'black layer' varies, but the discoloration is caused by the deposit of organic material below the surface and by the activity of bacteria, which results in a low oxygen content in the sand. Ragworms (*Nereis sp.*) and catworms (*Nephtys sp.*) are also found in the sand, but these are free-living worms which move through the sand and sediment by means of many leg-like appendages called parapodia.

The lower shore is also littered with cockle shells (*Cerastoderma edule*), some of which are empty, but some still contain the living creatures. Normally they live just under the surface of the sand, and obtain both food and oxygen by means of a fleshy siphon which projects above the surface when the tide is in; waste material is eliminated through a second siphon. Cockles bury themselves under the surface by means of a stout, muscular 'foot' but, rather surprisingly perhaps for such sedentary creatures, they can also move over the surface of the sand – although not exactly at a gallop! When the cockle is on the surface, the foot is protruded then bent in the middle so that the tip touches the sand. The creature suddenly straightens the foot then rolls over several times. A careful search will probably reveal a cockle on the surface with a distinctive furrow in the sand beside it, showing where it has moved. Another common bivalve that can be found in this area is the pink tellin, which is about 2 cm (¾ inch) across, and very prettily striped.

From the obviously sandy part of the estuary, move over to the right to the mud flats and salt marsh. Here, the lower part of the shore is quite clearly very muddy, and divided up by dozens of winding and quite deep channels. The most noticeable creatures, especially in and around the channels are four molluscs – two bivalves, the peppery furrow shell (*Scrobularia plana*) and clam (*Mya arenaria*), the gastropod edible periwinkle (*Littorina littorea*), and the tiny laver spire shell (*Hydrobia ulvae*).

There are plenty of white peppery furrow shell valves lying on the surface, but evidence of the living creatures buried in the glutinous mud requires closer scrutiny. In the water of the channels the tips of the very long, white siphons are sometimes visible just above the muddy surface. Usually, however, the only evidence of their presence is the shallow grooves, radiating from a small central burrow and made by the siphon as it searches for food.

The edible periwinkle is a familiar sight, but the tiny laver spire shell may be less so. This minute (only 0.5 cm (¼ inch) long) creature is present in numbers well into the millions, and is usually found in clutches. It browses on the muddy surface sediment. The spire shell is a remarkable little creature, and when it is covered by water it floats upside down on the surface, feeding on tiny particles of debris.

Several crustaceans can be seen on the mud flats. Most obvious are the shore crabs (*Carcinus maenas*) which tend to shelter under the seaweed and rocks in the channels, but many are also found in among the vegetation. In the spring it is easy to recognize female crabs, as they will almost certainly be carrying masses of yellow-orange eggs under their bodies. At other times of year, when the underside of the creature is examined it will be seen that the female has seven segments folded underneath the body, compared with the five of the male, and that the last of the segments has a rounder tip.

Some crabs are found minus a limb. This may be accidental, but it may also be a defence mechanism deliberately performed by the animal itself, in almost the same way as a lizard will shed its tail. If a crab gets a limb trapped among boulders, or is coming off second best in a fight with another crab, it can, by a sudden contraction of muscle, cause a limb to break by the base of the second segment. A membrane develops to cover the broken surface, and at the next and successive moults of the horny shell the limb will grow, and eventually achieve normal size.

It will be seen that in areas of the middle shore the mud flats are dotted with tiny holes. These are the ends of the U-shaped burrows of the shrimp-like crustacean known as *Corophium*, which is only about 0.75 cm (⅓ inch) long.

Up the shore, away from the lower reaches of the mud flats, the vegetation becomes denser, and the plant species change the higher up one goes. This is an example of plant succession and it has resulted in the development of a fine salt marsh. Zones of plants can be seen relatively easily, and it is apparent that the different zones spend differing times covered, or nearly covered, by the tide.

The green filamentous seaweed *Enteromorpha* is the first plant to colonize the mud and begin to stabilize it. Patches of this can be seen at Ynyslas, although the amount varies considerably from year to year. More silt collects round the *Enteromorpha* and forms a habitat for the first of the land plants to move in. This is the strange-looking, salt-tolerant, succulent glasswort, or marsh samphire (*Salicornia europaea*), with its bright green, fleshy stems and leaves. The construction of these enables the plant to retain water. Their rounded outline offers less resistance to the water, and their dense root system anchors them firmly in the substrate.

Associated with the glasswort in the lower shore is some of the tough, stiff and sharp-edged cord-grass (*Spartina anglica*). It too can stand long periods of immersion, as it has salt glands around the edges and at the bases of its leaves which enable it to eliminate salt. It also assists in stabilizing the mud flats by reducing the flow of the currents and thus allowing more deposition of silt. In among the cord-grass there is a large population of laver spire shells and edible periwinkles and, when the tide is in, fish such as young bass and mullet, and sand goby are also seen.

The next plant to arrive is the annual seablite (*Suaeda maritima*), and as the distance up the shore increases, this is followed by sea aster (*Aster tripolium*), thrift (*Armeria maritima*), sea meadow grass, common salt-marsh grass (*Puccinellia maritima*), sea plantain (*Plantago maritima*), sea rush (*Juncus maritimus*), sea spurrey (*Spergularia marina*), and finally, at the top, the plants that can stand salt immersion least well – red fescue grass (*Festuca rubra*), long bracted sedge (*Carex extensa*), common reed (*Phragmites australis*), sea club-rush (*Scirpus maritimus*) and scurvy grass (*Cochlearia officinalis*).

It can be seen that although *Enteromorpha* initially forms a zone on its own, successive zones as one goes higher up the shore do not always consist of single species but of a mixture, most especially at the fringes of the various zones. At the very top the plants, although maritime, cannot stand anything but brief immersion.

In addition to being a superb place for plant and marine life, the estuary attracts rich bird life to feed on many of these species. Waders are there in good numbers – dunlin, curlew, oystercatcher and ringed plover are commonplace, with knot, grey plover, bar-tailed godwit, greenshank and redshank also present. Shelduck are always present, feeding especially on the laver spire shells, while winter visitors include mergansers, goldeneye, pintail, teal, and small numbers of white-fronted geese. Such a collection attracts raptors such as hen harriers and short-eared owls, peregrines and merlins.

Obviously, no definite route or length has been set for this walk. When the different areas of the habitat have been seen, return to the car park.

Ynyslas, Walk 2:
The Sand Dunes and the
Submerged Forest

SUMMARY This walk follows the dune Nature Trail
through the Ynyslas sand dunes, but makes quite a
long detour along the beach towards Borth to include
the submerged forest.

APPROXIMATE LENGTH OF WALK 3 miles.

BEST TIMES Spring, summer.

LOCATION As for Ynyslas, Walk 1.

Ynyslas is one of the best places in which to see how sand
dunes are formed, from the youngest at the top of the shore
to the oldest. However, it is convenient to start the walk
from the visitor centre and go through the dunes in the
reverse direction – from the oldest to the youngest. As this
is not really the best way to understand dune succession, a
brief explanation of how it happens should help the visitor
to appreciate the various points of interest as they occur
during the walk.

Sand dunes are formed initially by sand blowing up against
some obstruction on the upper shore above high-tide mark.
The obstruction may in the first instance be rotting seaweed
thrown up by the sea. As the sand accumulates around the
seaweed not only does a tiny dune form (at right angles to
the direction of the prevailing wind) but the seaweed eventually breaks down, forming some humus. In due course
plant seeds are able to establish themselves in the humus and
grow, and in time they bind the sand together and make a
more permanent structure. At Ynyslas some of the dunes
have been formed by sand accumulating on shingle ridges.

The most important colonizer of these embryo dunes (as they are called) above high-tide mark is marram grass (*Ammophila arenaria*). It has an extensive root system which helps to bind the sand together, and although it is often buried by the increased amounts of sand which are trapped around it, its shoots are actually stimulated by this and it grows up through the sand, both upwards and sideways, thus spreading stability. When this occurs the dunes are known as 'mobile', because they frequently change shape as more sand collects. However, they are permanent enough to enable other plants to begin colonizing – plants such as sea spurge (*Euphorbia paralias*), Portland spurge (*E. portlandica*), hairy hawkbit (*Leontodon taraxacoides*) and groundsel (*Senecio vulgaris*). There is still, however, a high percentage of marram grass.

Further away from the shore the dunes become less subject to additional deposits of sand and the diversity of plants increases markedly. Mosses move in and provide ground cover, while plants such as rest-harrow (*Ononis repens*) and ragwort (*Senecio jacobaea*) can grow. The amount of marram decreases. However, some sand is still deposited so this area is known as semi-fixed dunes.

Finally, the dunes furthest from the shore are known as fixed dunes. They have an almost total cover of mixed vegetation, but the amount and vigour of the marram decreases, as it grows best where it has to force its way up through the shifting sand.

The walk begins at the visitor centre. From there, follow the post marked with an arrow towards the vehicle barriers at the entrance to a sandy hollow, and proceed on to a boardwalk of sleepers. This leads first through an area of semi-fixed dunes, with marram, sea spurge, ragwort, groundsel and hawkbit. A little way along on the right there is a dune whose side is totally devoid of plants because of people sliding down it.

Just before the next Trail post, which marks the beginning of the mobile dunes, there is a stand of rosebay willowherb (*Chamaenerion angustifolium*) and there may also be some plants of centaury (*Centaurium erythraea*). The mobile dunes have an abundant growth of marram, but there are extensive patches of bare sand. At the end of the boardwalk there is a shingle ridge, and it is plain to see that the sand is accumulating on and among this. At least one plant can be seen on the shingle, and that is sea sandwort (*Honkenya peploides*).

Walk down over the shingle on to the sand and turn left. Along here and in the vicinity of the strand line a number of plants may be seen. These include sea rocket (*Cakile maritima*), which has pale, pinky-mauve flowers and fleshy leaves, and less commonly, prickly saltwort (*Salsola kali*), which also has fleshy leaves but with vicious prickles, and a very extensive root system. Both are salt tolerant, and are able to extract fresh water from the salt water. Sand accumulates around them, and they form embryo dunes, but these are almost always transitory.

Walk along the sand to the left, but instead of turning up left into the dunes again where the sand dune Trail leads, continue along the beach towards Borth. Quite a number of things may be washed up on the shore. At certain times of the year there are great numbers of necklace-shaped ribbons of sand-like material, 2.5 cm (1 inch) or more in width which, on closer examination, reveal a honeycomb structure. This is an egg mass of the necklace shell, and each of the honeycomb cells is an egg capsule. Sometimes literally millions of delicate, sand-encrusted tubes, about 15 cm (6 inches) long and 0.5 cm (¼ inch) in diameter will be found – these are the tubes of worms such as the sand mason (*Lanice conchilega*).

About half a mile along the shore the first signs of the extraordinary submerged forest can be seen. This does vary, however. Sometimes much of it is covered with sand, at other times considerable portions of it are visible. It consists of stumps and trunks of ancient oaks and pine and, where areas of peat are exposed, of pieces of hazel, birch and willow. The trunks and stumps are seaweed encrusted, and many show signs of the presence of the common piddock – a bivalve which drills into wood – while the peat beds contain peppery furrow shells.

From the submerged forest, return along the beach and turn right to rejoin the Nature Trail where it leads up to a high boardwalk and lookout platform. To the right, on the way up, look across at the huge 'blowout' or valley of almost bare sand. This was caused by the passage of many feet and the action of the wind but it has been replanted with marram grass, which is gradually stabilizing it once more. The high platform is an excellent place from which to see the succession of sand dunes, from the embryo dunes high on the shore to the fixed dunes which are almost completely covered with plants.

Follow the pathway, and in the fixed dunes a great variety of grasses can be seen. The most common ones are red fescue (*Festuca rubra*), common bent (*Agrostis tenuis/capillaris*) and spreading meadow grass (*Poa subcaerules*). There are also many flowering herbs such as ribwort plantain (*Plantago lanceolata*), heath dog violet (*Viola canina*), common centaury, lady's bedstraw (*Galium verum*), rest-harrow, and ragwort. Towards the far end of the boardwalk a number of shrubs – elder, hawthorn, bramble and blackthorn – can be seen.

At the end of the boardwalk, steps lead down into a flat, grassy area, with patches of shrubs and small fixed dunes. This is known as a dune slack, and in winter some of it is under water. It is a most exciting area from a botanical viewpoint, and a wonderful place for orchids – with northern marsh orchid (*Dactylorhiza purpurella*), early marsh orchid (*D. incarnata*), common and heath orchid (*D. fuchsii* and *D. maculata*), and marsh helleborine (*Epipactis palustris*). The latter was unknown on this site before 1965 but by 1982 there were an incredible 170,000 spikes!

In the wetter area there is much marsh pennywort (*Hydrocotyle vulgaris*), silverweed (*Potentilla anserina*) and grey willow (*Salix cinerea*). On the sides of the dunes hereabouts there is the striking yellow biting stonecrop (*Sedum acre*), wild thyme (*Thymus drucei*), bird's-foot trefoil (*Lotus corniculatus*) and soft cranesbill (*Geranium molle*). Mosses, liverworts and horsetails are also present.

Of course, plants are not the only species that live in and among the dunes. Butterflies are a feature, and these include common blue, meadow brown, dark green fritillary and peacock, as well as moths such as the cinnabar and burnet. Banded snails are very common, while the mammalian population includes rabbits, voles, hedgehogs and the very rarely seen polecat. Birds, too, are present in some numbers, with skylarks, linnets, stonechats, wheatears and meadow pipits among the most common.

From the dune slack, follow another boardwalk through more fixed dunes, which are also covered with vegetation, back to the visitor centre.

Cors Caron

SUMMARY A National Nature Reserve. Bogs have a particular fascination for some naturalists, and Cors Caron is an outstanding example. Not only is it a magnificent raised bog with all the accompanying bog plants, but over forty species of birds nest there, and more than 160 have been recorded within its boundaries. The most exciting prospect is that of seeing a red kite. Among the mammals, the polecat and otter are both present. The part of the walk along the Old Railway Nature Trail, is usually dry, but anyone wishing to undertake the section of the walk on the bog itself will certainly need Wellingtons. *A permit is required for all parts of the reserve other than the Old Railway Trail.* This is obtainable (free at time of writing) from The Warden, 'Minawel', Pontrhydfendigaid, Ystrad Meurig, Dyfed, SY25 6BN.

APPROXIMATE LENGTH OF WALK 4 miles.

BEST TIME All year.

LOCATION Beside the B4343 on the Tregaron–Pontrhydfendigaid road in Dyfed. SN696632.

Cors Caron is a raised bog, with a convex dome of peat covered with bog plants. Like most of its type it was formed over an original shallow lake. Floating aquatic plants gradually covered the surface and, as plant litter built up, rooted plants, starting with reeds, invaded the water and over centuries a peat fen developed. As the peat accumulated over an area that was increasingly dominated by sedges, rushes and grasses, it dried out slightly and allowed the invasion of alder, birch and pine to form a carr. Later still, because of increased rainfall, the water level rose and the trees died out.

At this stage, certain species of bog moss (*Sphagnum*) began to invade, and in due course the whole of the centre of the bog became carpeted with these mosses, leaving carr on either edge. Because of attractive conditions the bog mosses continued to grow in the centre of the bog, and eventually it assumed its present convex shape. In fact there are three raised bogs at Cors Caron – the south-east, west, and north-east. Because of the highly fragile nature of the bogs, especially the centres, the route remains on the boardwalk provided in that area.

From the roadside lay-by at SN696632 go over the stile and turn left along what was an old railway line. Walk along this through scrub for about a mile until a gate is reached on the right, which leads to the south-east bog and then on to a boardwalk. Please stay on the boardwalk throughout its length to avoid damaging the bog.

The walk leads out into the bog, where at this point it is covered with ling (*Calluna vulgaris*) and purple moor-grass (*Molinia caerulea*), under which grow a number of mosses and lichens. There are a few scattered trees of downy birch and rowan. After about 400 yards, follow the boardwalk to the left. Here, there are tussocks of deer-grass (*Scirpus caespitosus*), together with cross-leaved heath (*Erica tetralix*), bog mosses, hare's-tail cotton-grass (*Eriophorum vaginatum*) and bog asphodel (*Narthecium ossifragum*). Other plants found include bog rosemary (*Andromeda polifolia*), more ling, common cotton-grass (*Eriophorum angustifolium*), tormentil (*Potentilla erecta*) and several lichens (species of *Cladonia*).

Further along the boardwalk, near the highest point of the bog, the habitat changes to what is called a pool and hummock complex – an area of boggy pools and small hummocks of vegetation. What can be seen will depend on the time of year and the water level, but the species recorded include various bog mosses, ling, lichens, and the round-leaved sundew (*Drosera rotundifolia*). Continue round the boardwalk to where it rejoins the original one, and turn left down to the bridge over the River Teifi. As the river will be met again from time to time, this is a good place to list the plant species that can be seen on or near it. They include yellow water-lily (*Nuphar lutea*), bog pondweed (*Potamogeton polygonifolius*), several species of water starworts (*Callitriche spp.*), and alternate-flowered water milfoil (*Myriophyllum alterniflorum*). From here, the rounded dome of the great west bog is very apparent.

Just a little way inland and to the right of the river, is one of a number of 'flashes' or permanent backwaters, which are very important both botanically and as a habitat for wintering wildfowl. They contain relatively nutrient-rich water, and because much of the water comes from the nearby hills they have a high proportion of lime. Do not attempt to walk into the flash, as the bottom is extremely soft.

The principal plants to be seen in and around the water are water horsetails (*Equisetum fluviatile*), alternate-flowered water milfoil, bog pondweed, water crowfoot (*Ranunculus pseudofluitans*), yellow water-lily and water starwort. Grasses around the edge are tufted hair-grass (*Deschampsia oaespitosa*) and purple moor-grass, and there are also soft rush (*Juncus effusus*) and reed canary-grass (*Phalaris arundinacea*).

The water acts as an attraction for a number of dragonflies and damselflies. Birds that may be seen on the water during the winter include mallard, whooper swans, wigeon and teal. At all times, keep a good look out for the sight of a magnificent red kite flying over the reserve.

Return to the bridge, cross the river, walk along to the right for a short distance, then cross another bridge back on to the river bank. From this point, a number of red-topped posts can be seen, which mark the route through the flood plain of the river. The area is dominated by rushes and sedges, including soft rush, sharp-flowered rush (*Juncus acutiflorus*), slender tufted sedge (*Carex qcuta*), and grasses such as purple moor-grass. Marsh marigold (*Caltha palustris*) may be found in some places, with meadow buttercup (*Ranunculus acris*), marsh cinquefoil (*Potentilla palustris*), and various species of forget-me-not.

Continue following the red-topped posts across the flood plain until the route leads back to the right towards the hills and a boardwalk leads across another section of bog – this time the north-east bog. Follow the boardwalk to the gate in the fence, go through it and turn left along what is part of the Old Railway Nature Walk. A short distance along on the left is a fine high observation tower from which there are glorious views over the bog and the surrounding countryside.

The record book in the tower will tell of the birds seen from this viewpoint. In the pool and scrape in front and below, wildfowl and waders may be present, while buzzard, sparrowhawk, peregrine and merlin may be seen out over the bog. To the right there is a tributary of the river, where otters are sometimes seen. They feed on migrant trout and salmon. In the willows near the tributary a number of smaller birds find shelter and nesting sites – willow tit, pied flycatcher, willow warbler and tree pipit among them.

From the tower, walk back to the right along the Old Railway Nature Walk. Note the fine growth of the lichens – species of *Parmelia* and the bearded *Usnea* – on the willows. Some hundred yards or so past the gate out on to the bog, there is another gate, beyond which a boardwalk enables members of the public without permits to see some of the bog plants. It is worth looking at this, if only to smile at the salutary warning notice which says more in a delightful cartoon about the dangers of stepping off the boardwalk than a whole paragraph of written warning!

Between the boardwalk and the fence the ground is reasonably dry and holds bilberry (*Vaccinium myrtillus*), deer grass, purple moor-grass, bell heather and a little ling. On the other side the ground is much wetter and is covered with bog mosses, together with bogbean (*Menyanthes trifoliata*), marsh willowherb (*Epilobium palustre*), marsh cinquefoil, cotton-grass and white beak-sedge (*Rhynchospora alba*).

Return to the Railway Walk, past a clump of alders, and notice on the left of the track a wetter area, with such plants as meadowsweet (*Filipendula ulmaria*), rushes, reed canary-grass (*Phalaris arundinacea*), and a few marsh marigolds which grow in the ditches. The next section has more willows and, on the left, a very thick patch of thistles and nettles. This is an excellent place for butterflies and their caterpillars. Species seen may include small copper, green-veined white, common blue, small heath and peacock. Anywhere along this track where it is warm and sheltered, adders and common lizards are likely to be seen sunning themselves.

The habitat changes somewhat, and the track is fringed with a denser scrub of hawthorn, blackthorn, hazel, small oak, sallow, and ash, with a field layer of celandine (*Ranunculus ficaria*), whitlow grass (*Erophila verna*) and dog's mercury (*Mercurialis perennis*). A variety of woodland birds is often present in this scrub, including grasshopper warblers, pied flycatchers, wrens, blackcaps and robins. After about a mile from the observation tower, the starting point is reached.

Bosherton Fish Ponds

SUMMARY An easy walk around these artificially created fish ponds in limestone valleys which are cut off from the sea by a sand bar. A great variety of plants, insects, and birds. A National Trust reserve managed jointly with the Nature Conservancy Council as part of the Stackpole National Nature Reserve.

APPROXIMATE LENGTH OF WALK 3 miles.

BEST TIMES Spring, summer.

LOCATION Take the B4319 from Pembroke, then the turning to Bosherton village. SR966948.

From the car park, which is signposted from the village, go down the steps to the lake edge, turn left and cross the causeway leading over the arm of the lake. There are huge expanses of water-lilies on the surface, while in the clear water the very thick growth of stonewort (*Chara sp.*) can be seen on the lake bottom. Stoneworts, or brittle-worts as they are sometimes called, are a group of freshwater algae which grow principally in lime-rich waters such as these. The plants eventually become covered with a scaly layer of lime, and are then very brittle, hence their alternative name. Coots, of which there are a great many in the Ponds, find the stoneworts an attractive food source.

Damselflies and dragonflies are very common over and near the water – the blue damselfly and the Emperor dragonfly both being present. The latter has the largest wingspan of any British dragonfly, at 11.5 cm (4½ inches). The abdomen of the male is a bright, almost metallic blue with a black band down the middle of the back and black rings around it. The females are smaller than the males and are slightly greener in colour, but may become more blue when older. The male is an aggressively territorial insect, attacking intruders and often tearing pieces out of their wings.

A little time spent watching the water, particularly from near the bank, may result in the sighting of a pike, which feed on the many shoals of small roach found in the pond. The latter are members of the carp family, and are silvery-coloured, round-backed fish with reddish eyes. Curiously, they have no teeth in their jaws. They do, however, have sets of teeth on bones in the back of their throats which help them crush the small aquatic animals on which they live.

On the far side of the causeway, turn right and follow the shore line. Here the path is flanked by scrub and small trees including hawthorn, ash, gorse and sycamore, with calcicole plants such as slender St John's wort (*Hypericum pulchrum*), black bryony (*Tamus communis*), wild thyme (*Thymus drucei*) and ploughman's spikenard (*Inula conyza*). Butterflies are attracted to this area on warm sunny days, and among those which may be seen are orange-tip, peacock, and speckled.

Walk on around the path, which soon leads up a slope on to a headland from which there are delightful views of the ponds. On this headland there is a larger area of scrub including blackthorn, hawthorn, privet and bramble, with some of the bushes covered in traveller's joy (*Clematis vitalba*). The scrub here and along the lake edge affords nesting sites and shelter for sedge and willow warblers, and reed buntings.

The path leads down from the headland to another causeway across the water. Reeds, pondweed, fleabane (*Pulicaria dysenterica*), purple loosestrife (*Lythrum salicaria*) and water mint (*Mentha aquatica*) can all be seen by the water's edge. Follow the path round to the Green Bridge, where there is an information board. Do not cross the bridge at this stage, but continue straight ahead along the 'Permissive Walk' which goes along the eastern arm of the pond. As can be seen, the water vegetation is somewhat different, with bur-reed (*Sparganium*) and spiked water milfoil (*Myriophyllum spicatum*), and a thick surface covering of pondweed (*Potamogeton*).

The path goes through an attractive mixed deciduous woodland with sycamore and ash. On the left-hand side in particular, there is a great number of enormous specimens of hart's-tongue ferns (*Phyllitis scolopendrium*). Ivy-leaved toad-flax (*Cymbalaria muralis*) and common polypody ferns grow on the banks, and long-tailed tits flit through the trees. At many points where the path goes very close to the water, dragon and damselflies are present in numbers.

Further around the pond, a group of buildings is reached. Go through an archway with a footpath sign, up a shallow flight of steps beside a large house, and on to a terrace. From here there are more splendid views of the lakes and, down below, there is a large reed bed and alder carr, where coots, reed warblers, mallard, teal and moorhen may be seen.

From the terrace, return to the Green Bridge, and cross it, following the signpost to Broadhaven. To the right of the path are the lakes and to the left the sand dunes of Broad-haven, which protect the lakes from the sea. Ignore the Stackpole Head signpost, and instead continue on to a sign pointing to Bosherton; this leads to a path which follows the lake on the opposite side from the outward walk. Around here there is sometimes a large flock of coots – I counted over forty. Other waterbirds that have been recorded include herring gulls, heron and, in winter, pochard, tufted duck, smew, goosander and goldeneye.

The homeward journey passes along the edge of a larch

plantation, and also a mixed woodland where a variety of birds may be seen, including tree-creeper, chiffchaff, black-cap, and goldcrest. At the end of the path, turn right over a small wooden bridge and back to the car park.

SCOTLAND

1 St Abb's Head
2 Pass of Killiecrankie
  and Linn of Tummel
3 Loch Muick
4 Morrone Birkwood
5 Rassal Ashwood

6 Beinn Eighe
7 Embo
8 The Big Burn Walk at
  Golspie
9 Duncansby Head
10 Invernaver

St Abb's Head

SUMMARY Primarily a sea-bird cliff walk, but there is also plenty to interest the botanist. A National Nature Reserve and Site of Special Scientific Interest (SSSI) owned by the National Trust for Scotland and managed in co-operation with the Scottish Wildlife Trust. The cliffs are dangerous.

APPROXIMATE LENGTH OF WALK 4 miles.

BEST TIMES May–July for breeding birds; autumn for migration.

LOCATION Off the B6438, near Coldingham, Berwickshire. (67)913673.

There is a very good visitor centre just below the car park and on the way to the cliffs, as well as an equally good cafe. Follow the Trail signs along the road or the pathway beside it. Silverweed (*Potentilla anserina*) grows in profusion along the path, and there is wall-rue fern (*Asplenium ruta-muraria*) on the stone wall by the road. Turn left at the sign 'Footpath to St Abb's Head' and walk down through the gates to the cliff edge. Across the rocky Starney Bay, immediately ahead on emerging from the path, rises the massive cliff face of the White Heugh – well named, as it is white with guano (bird droppings) deposited over the years, by countless thousands of guillemots, herring gulls, kittiwakes and razorbills. At the height of the breeding season the sea below is absolutely alive with birds.

Turn left along the cliff-top path. The grass-covered cliff face, here slightly less precipitous than elsewhere on the reserve, is bright with thrift (*Armeria maritima*), and in spring early purple orchids (*Orchis mascula*) and primroses (*Primula vulgaris*) can be seen among the grass. The only stand of bracken on the entire reserve also grows on the cliff face. On the rocky shores of Starney Bay a number of waders may be seen, depending on the time of year. These include purple sandpiper, redshank and turnstone.

On the bank along the path leading round to the northern side of the White Heugh, keep a look out for purple milk-vetch (*Astragalus danicus*), which has a crowded head of violet flowers born on leafless stalks, and short-stalked pinnate leaves. As the northern face of the White Heugh is approached, the ear tells one long before the eye that there must be a huge kittiwake colony! Every available ledge on the sheer face seems to hold a kittiwake or the occasional herring gull. A fine view of the birds can be had from the path, which seems at times uncomfortably near the vertical drop to the rocks below!

The northern face of the White Heugh, where sheep do not graze, has a population of Scots lovage (*Ligusticum scoticum*) – an uncommon plant with purplish, ribbed stems, shiny, bright green leaves, and a head of small, clustered white flowers. Visitors are not recommended to attempt to find this plant, as the headland is very dangerous indeed except for the most experienced.

From just beyond the White Heugh the reserve widens out, and the walker can wander at will within the boundary fence. Inland, although only a short distance from the cliffs, the short turf supports a number of flowering plants such as tormentil (*Potentilla erecta*), lady's bedstraw (*Galium verum*), heath bedstraw (*G. saxatile*), harebell (*Campanula rotundi-folia*), slender-flowered thistle (*Carduus tenuiflorus*), milkwort (*Polygala vulgaris*) and silverweed (*Potentilla anserina*).

Those who choose to stay near the cliffs will find splendid viewing points on small hilltops, where sea watching is a rewarding pastime. Parties of gannets go to and from their breeding sites on the Bass Rock along the coast, while during migration times great and Arctic skuas and Manx and sooty shearwaters are seen regularly. Migration times also bring exciting rarities; those recorded include greenish and yellow-browed warblers and red-breasted flycatchers. On some of the hills the rocky outcrops are covered with English and biting stonecrop (*Sedum anglicum* and *S. acre*). The coastal views are quite breath-taking in places.

After approximately three-quarters of a mile the reserve narrows once more and the path leads steeply down to Horsecastle Bay, where a variety of seaweeds and seashore lichens are seen. The pathway leading over the stile and behind the hill just beyond the bay is relatively protected, and is a good place for seeing some of the reserve's butter-flies, such as common blue, meadow brown, and small tortoiseshell.

After just under two miles the lighthouse is reached. Keep on past this, past the small car park and out on to the cliff edge once more. This is the place where, if you think you have seen huge sea-bird colonies near the start of the walk, it is time to re-assess! The 300-feet-high cliffs here are *covered* with birds. Kittiwakes and guillemots are the most common, plus some razorbills and most of the reserve's small number of puffins.

After viewing these fabulous cliffs, turn inland once more, walk to the road, cross over, and walk down the steep hill towards the Mire Loch. Here an interesting phenomenon may be observed. Huge flocks of kittiwakes come from their nests to bathe in the fresh water, splashing about with every evidence of enjoyment before returning to their nests on the cliff faces. These birds, plus others such as swans, coots, moorhens and mallard, have appreciably enriched the waters of the loch with their droppings. As a result there is a covering film of microscopic algae on the surface which prevents light reaching the lower layers of the water and inhibits the growth of water plants. Thus although the loch edges are fringed with bur-reed (*Sparganium*), yellow iris (*Iris pseudacorus*), marsh thistle (*Cirsium palustre*) and great reed-mace (*Typha latifolia*), there is virtually no growth of water plants further out.

From the loch, return either along the road or by re-tracing the route round the cliffs.

Pass of Killiecrankie and Linn of Tummel

SUMMARY A wide range of habitats provides plenty of interest in this walk, which begins in the deep wooded gorge of the River Garry, continues to its confluence with the River Tummel, and thence through the different types of woodland in the Linn of Tummel. The variety of habitat is matched by the fascinating range of plants, birds and animals (including otters) that inhabit this historic area.

APPROXIMATE LENGTH OF WALK 4 miles.

BEST TIMES Spring, summer.

LOCATION The Pass of Killiecrankie visitor centre outside Killiecrankie village near Pitlochry. NN914610.

From the Pass of Killiecrankie visitor centre go down the steep steps, which lead through mixed, largely deciduous woodland with hazel, rowan understorey and a field layer including rosebay willowherb (*Chamaenerion angustifolium*), cow-wheat (*Melampyrum pratense*) and St John's wort (*Hypericum*). A fine view of the gorge and river is obtained from Soldier's Leap, where a soldier, fleeing for his life after the Battle of Killiecrankie in 1689, is said to have jumped the eighteen and a half feet across the River Garry.

From the Leap, follow the pathway marked 'Linn of Tummel' down the hill and along and above the River Garry. The path goes through more mixed woodland, with beech, sycamore and plenty of oak. Along the path edge and in the woodland are a great number of different species of plants, depending on the time of year. These include wood anemone (*Anemone nemorosa*), lesser celandine (*Ranunculus ficaria*), golden saxifrage (*Chrysosplenium*) in the wetter parts, wood sorrel (*Oxalis acetosella*), white campion (*Silene alba*), stitchwort (*Stellaria holostea*), wood forget-me-not (*Myosotis sylvatica*), wild garlic (*Allium ursinum*), herb Robert (*Geranium robertianum*), hedge woundwort (*Stachys sylvatica*) and bluebell (*Endymion non-scriptus*). Nearer the river, water mint (*Mentha aquatica*), marsh marigold (*Caltha palustris*), water avens (*Geum rivale*), and meadowsweet (*Filipendula ulmaria*) may be found.

When the road at the end of the pass is reached, follow the signpost to Linn of Tummel over the bridge. Pause on the bridge to admire the superb views up and down the gorge. Once over the bridge turn left, noting the huge beech tree on the bank, and then follow the pathway through more mixed woodland containing sycamore, oak, ash, hazel and, on the river side, some alder.

At a division of the ways, take the downhill path, with alder trees on the left, some beeches, and more woundwort and some dog's mercury (*Mercurialis perennis*) underneath. In a short distance Post One of the Linn of Tummel Nature Walk is reached, near to which is a clump of big oak trees. Go on down towards the river, noting the mixture of trees, including beech, ash, birch, hazel and sycamore. In late summer woundwort, lady's bedstraw (*Galium verum*), some rosebay willowherb and bird's-foot trefoil (*Lotus corniculatus*) can be found underneath. Earlier in the year, dog's mercury flowers, together with wood sorrel and wood anemone.

Approach the river bank quietly. In this lovely setting among the alders there is a little sandy beach where bird and animal tracks may be seen, even if some of the creatures themselves are shy. Grey wagtails and mallard, however, are commonly seen, but the presence of the secretive otter is usually only apparent because of the signs 'it leaves. Otter prints may show the animal's five toes, but very often the print of the inner one is missing. If the print is very clear, the web that joins the toes may be visible. The track of the adult forefoot is almost circular, and about 6–7.5 cm (2½–3 inches) long, while that of the hind foot is longer, measuring up to about 10 cm (4 inches). The droppings (spraints) are most likely to be seen on some protuberance such as a boulder, or under a bridge, and can be recognized, if fresh, by their black, tarry, mucilaginous appearance and oily smell. When older, they become grey and rather crumbly.

From the river, climb up the steps, noting the hair moss (*Polytrichum*) on the right, and come to Post Four of the Trail by a large beech tree on the right, surrounded by birch and oak, with violets underneath in late summer. A short distance on, Post Five clearly marks a meeting of different habitats. On the left is a plantation of Douglas firs, on the right is an oak-dominated wood, and the remainder is mixed woodland with some larch trees. The conifers are much appreciated by the red squirrels, which are quite common in the area but not very easily seen. As with the otters, their presence is obvious only because of the signs they leave – in this instance larch and Douglas fir cones from which they extract the seeds by biting off the scales, starting, as they must, from the bottom, and leaving a very frayed-looking object.

From this junction, follow the path down to the river bank. As can be seen, the habitat has changed, with the introduction of more bracken under the scrub, and with sycamore and ash trees as well as oak. Anyone with time to spare might sit here or hereabouts and keep watch on the river and its banks, as there are definite signs of otters in the vicinity.

Return to the main track and turn left, signposted 'Coronation Bridge'. The change of habitat is much more obvious along here, with more acid-loving plants appearing – notably some ling (*Calluna vulgaris*) and bell heather (*Erica cinerea*). On the right, the woodland up the hill has become more like the ancient forest, with splendid specimens of Scots pine, birch, rowan, hazel and oak. Scots pine is easy to spot, as the bark of its trunk has a lovely pinkish tinge, especially near the top. The Scots pine needles grow in pairs, are blue-green and only about 4 cm (1½ inches) in length. Goldcrests are likely to be heard in this area, and tree-creepers and crossbills may be spotted high in the trees. Under the trees bracken is common. There is also some bilberry (*Vaccinium myrtillus*), and common polypody fern (*Polypodium vulgare*) grows on the bank by the sides of the path.

Ignore for the moment the signpost pointing up the hill, and continue on round the river bank to take a close look at the waterfall. It is not a high one but tumbles down over the huge boulders of the river bed and is a good place for dippers.

Return to the signpost up the hill and this time follow it, eventually coming to a clearing in the forest – an enchanting, peaceful place covered with bracken and other ferns, mosses and lichens, strewn with fallen timber and guarded by tall pines and oaks. This is a place to sit, watch and listen. Goldcrests twitter quietly in the tree tops, and a slight rustle in the undergrowth or the sound of a snapped twig could herald the arrival of the shy roe deer. A noisier arrival could be that of one of Britain's largest birds – the capercaillie.

Continue along the track, passing a fine stand of huge Douglas firs together with some blocks of Norway spruce and Western hemlock. In a mature Douglas fir the bark is thick with deep fissures, often with orange-brown coloration in the cracks. The needles grow singly on the twigs and, if pulled off, do not leave the little peg seen in some other conifers; all that remains is a small, round scar. The egg-shaped cones are like no other; there is a three-pointed bract on the outside of every scale. Norway spruce (the Christmas tree) has softly pointed, mid-green needles, which *do* leave a peg when pulled off. The cones are very long with straight scales, and always hang downwards. Western hemlock is quite easy to recognize as its needles vary considerably in length. The leading shoot (i.e. the one at the top of the tree) is invariably drooping, and the numerous cones are small, brown, and egg-shaped.

Follow the signs down the hill, and turn left down some steps. Dog's mercury appears again, plus bracken, wound-wort and cleavers (*Gallium aparine*). A small, very over-grown burn is crossed by a footbridge. Push aside some of the vegetation to reveal a number of mosses and liverworts on the stones, and some watercress (*Rorippa nasturtium-aquaticum*). Golden saxifrage is present in early spring. Some small thickets of hazel grow nearby, showing signs of earlier coppicing.

The path leads on down beside a field on the right and a wood dominated by sycamore on the left. Springtime sees a profuse growth of ground ivy (*Glechoma hederacea*) and, further along, a number of woundwort plants and some St John's wort. The path leads back to Post One of the Trail, and from there, return over the bridge and back to the visitor centre along the path by the River Garry.

Loch Muick

SUMMARY A circular walk round the shores of Loch Muick amid majestic Highland scenery, with views of the famous mountain, Lochnagar. A straightforward walk, but sections are rough and rocky so stout footwear is advised. This is part of the Balmoral Estate and is managed by it in conjunction with the Scottish Wildlife Trust.

APPROXIMATE LENGTH OF WALK 8 miles.

BEST TIMES Spring, summer.

LOCATION At the end of an unclassified road from Ballater, Deeside. NO311852.

From the car park at the Spittal of Glenmuick (Muick, incidentally, is pronounced 'mick'), walk down the road to the excellent visitor centre in among the conifers. Much can be learned about the reserve from the displays. Outside the centre, crossbills, redpolls, siskins and spotted flycatchers nest in the mixture of larch, spruce and pine.

Crossbills are not the easiest birds to see, as they tend to feed on the conifer seeds towards the tops of the trees. However, the conspicuous colour of the handsome male does help a little, especially if the sun shines on its rich red-to-orange plumage. They are very early nesters, starting in February, probably because their staple diet is in good supply then. The fledging period for crossbills is unusually long, and the youngsters grow very slowly. They take all of three weeks to fledge (compared to just over a fortnight for other members of the finch family), and their beaks do not assume the adult crossed mandibles until after a month or more. The chicks' slow growth can be attributed to their food. Most finches live on an easily digested and high-protein diet of insects. Crossbills, however, are fed a regurgitated mixture of partly digested conifer seeds with just a few insects, and as the seeds are less nutritious, the chicks' growth rate is slower. Late in the year, crossbills of all ages feed on aphids, but as they cannot take these with their crossed beaks they use their tongues.

From the visitor centre, follow the road towards the loch. The view from the path (and indeed from almost anywhere throughout this walk) can be absolutely breathtaking, with the huge mountains towering over the loch, their peaks often lost in cloud or mist. On the right, the land slopes away to the wide valley of the River Muick where curlews are often present. Alpine lady's mantle (*Alchemilla alpina*) grows in some numbers along the side of the path, together with harebells (*Campanula rotundifolia*), known as bluebells in Scotland, and the minute, bright blue flowers of milkwort (*Polygala vulgaris*), while in the drainage ditches and small boggy areas butterwort (*Pinguicula vulgaris*), pondweed (*Potamogeton*) and bog asphodel (*Narthecium ossifragum*) are common.

The path leads on past a turning up to the left until a large clump of conifers, including Scots pine, is reached, also on the left. In spring and early summer it is worth leaving the path here and sitting quietly on a boulder in the wood to watch the spotted flycatchers, for whom this is a favourite nesting place.

On leaving the woodland, cross the road and walk down to the loch edge – the ground can be boggy in places. There are frequently common sandpipers on the shore, as well as pied wagtails, but there are few true water birds. Mallard and teal are sometimes seen, goosanders may also be present, and perhaps a red-throated diver. The scarcity of water birds is partly explained by the fact that the loch is poor in nutrients, and consequently does not have much plant life. It is also deep, without many shallows at the edges, and therefore is not very attractive to birds. The only plant likely to be seen is the strange, lime-encrusted stonewort, *Nitella*, which has whorled branchlets on a main stem.

Return to the path and continue along the south-east shore of the loch. From time to time little burns, rocky and moss-encrusted, come bubbling down the bracken- and heather-covered hillside, and around some of these the ground is carpeted with alpine lady's mantle. Wheatears perch on some of the boulders on the rough hillside, and the lucky visitor may see an occasional mountain, or blue, hare straying down from the high moorland above. Except in winter, its coat is an unusual grey-brown colour with a distinct bluey tinge – hence the alternative name. Mountain hares moult three times a year: from brown to white in autumn, from white to brown in spring, and a less obvious brown-to-brown moult between June and early September.

Continue round the loch until reaching the spectacular Black Burn. Here, a broad torrent of water rushes down the boulder-strewn burn from the mountain above, passes under the wooden bridge and onwards to the loch. Stunted birches (almost all that remains of the original Caledonian forest that once blanketed the area) and aspens grow by the burnside. After crossing the bridge, take the track to the right. It becomes quite narrow and rough, but is not difficult to follow. The vegetation above and below the track consists largely of ling, with bilberry (*Vaccinium myrtillus*), crowberry (*Empetrum nigrum*) and some tormentil (*Potentilla erecta*). In the damper areas there are patches of the brilliant red bog moss (*Sphagnum*), and small rowan trees cling precariously to the rocky soil. Adders and lizards are common on this reserve, and use the path or the boulders on the hillside for sunbathing on warm days. From this section of the path, the highest point of the walk, the view back down the glen is less dramatic, but is nonetheless of great beauty.

The track leads gradually down to the head of the loch, where the great summit of Broad Cairn (over 3,000 feet) is often lost to sight in the clouds. Below it, the Dubh Burn rushes down nearly 1,000 feet from the Dubh Loch, losing its force as it spreads out into many little streams which flow gently into Loch Muick. A series of bridges crosses the various streams, before the path wends its way back along the shore towards a conifer wood surrounding a large lodge.

Turn left up the hill just at the entrance to the wood. At the wood edges are some downy birch trees, with some wild thyme (*Thymus drucei*) on a few of the barer patches of ground, and plenty of hard fern (*Blechnum spicant*) growing out of the crevices between the rocks. A small waterfall is crossed by a bridge, and the path eventually rejoins a wide, gravelled track leading back towards the visitor centre. While walking along this side of the loch, search the skyline of the hills on the opposite side with binoculars; red deer are often to be seen there, and, more rarely, a golden eagle may be soaring high above the hilltops.

This is a comparatively sheltered area where the hill rises steeply from the loch edge, and a number of butterflies and moths are likely to be seen in a good year. Most common among the butterflies is the pearl-bordered fritillary, but the dark green fritillary (which has dark green on its hind wings) may also be present. The caterpillars of both these feed on violets. The caterpillars of three moths in particular may be seen feeding on the heather: the northern eggar moth, the emperor moth and the fox moth. The caterpillars of the northern eggar moth are large, brown and hairy (and its pale cocoon is very noticeable among the heather). The emperor caterpillar is very strikingly coloured but difficult to see, as its green body with black bands and pink spots blends remarkably well with its food plant, the heather. There is a distinct possibility of seeing the male emperor moth, however, which flies by day. It is a splendid-looking creature with four large 'eyes' and red tips to the fore-wings. The caterpillar of the fox moth is relatively easy to spot in autumn, when it is dark brown with yellow-orange rings, but in spring it is difficult to distinguish from that of the northern eggar.

Many hard ferns grow in the stone wall that fronts the bank on the left-hand side of the roadway, and the right-hand side, reaching down to the loch below, is covered with bracken, and a few small birches.

Among the heather, four different 'berry' plants – bilberry, crowberry, bearberry (*Arctostaphylos uva-ursi*) and cowberry (*Vaccinium vitis-idaea*) – can be found, and it can be quite challenging to distinguish between them. A short foray from the road where it crosses the bridge over the Alt-an-Dearg Burn is a convenient place for this. It may come as a surprise to learn that bearberry, cowberry and bilberry all belong to the heath family; crowberry is the odd one out. Bearberry and cowberry are easy to confuse, but bearberry is a prostrate shrub with trailing stems, while cowberry grows to a height of about 15 cm (6 inches). The leaves of both are small, but cowberry leaves tend to be lighter in colour and are broadest in the middle, while those of bearberry are broad at the tip. Bilberry is a deciduous shrub, growing up to a maximum of 45 cm (18 inches) high, and has distinctive four-angled green twigs. Crowberry, in spite of not being a heather, is the most heath-like of the quartet! It has narrow, rolled-edge, shiny leaves which spiral tightly up the reddish stem, and at a quick glance it could easily be mistaken for a heather.

The road continues along the loch edge, and when the boathouse on the right is reached, turn down past it and return across the river valley to the clearly visible visitor centre.

Morrone Birkwood

SUMMARY This area of pure downy birch with juniper is a marvellous example of a sub-alpine woodland on basic (alkaline) soils with a number of calcareous flushes. It can be wet underfoot. Visitors are particularly asked not to stray from the clearly defined pathways. This means that a number of interesting plants may not be seen, but it is very important not to damage this rare habitat. A National Nature Reserve.

APPROXIMATE LENGTH OF WALK 2½ miles.

BEST TIMES Spring, summer.

LOCATION On the edge of Braemar, to the south-west. NO143911.

A short time spent sitting in the car in the car park, especially in early morning or at dusk, may be rewarded with quite close views of red deer, mountain hares and, less commonly, roe deer.

From the entrance to the car park, walk up past the house on the right and take the right fork where the road divides. Beside the path is some dwarf juniper, ling (*Calluna vulgaris*), bell heather (*Erica cinerea*) and, in the damper areas, bog asphodel (*Narthecium ossifragum*), butterwort (*Pinguicula vulgaris*) and cross-leaved heather (*Erica tetralix*). Some of the downy birch trees can also be seen.

Downy birch is distinguished from silver birch by its greyer or brown bark, and as the name indicates it has very fine downy hairs, which are found on the twigs and on the leaves. On the leaves the hairs are often seen only on the veins underneath. The wings of the seed are as broad as the seed itself, whereas the seed of the silver birch has wings twice as broad as itself.

At a junction of tracks, there is a Nature Conservancy Council cairn. Take the track straight ahead which leads alongside a fenced enclosure, keeping the fence on the left. As can be seen, the exclusion of deer from the enclosure has resulted in a much denser growth of vegetation there than outside. There are a number of wood ant nests in this area. Hard fern (*Blechnum spicant*) is present in some abundance, and there are also lousewort (*Pedicularis sylvatica*), milkwort (*Polygala vulgaris*), cow-wheat (*Melampyrum sp.*) and wild thyme (*Thymus drucei*). In the mud along the path deer slots and deer droppings are often seen.

After a short distance a little burn crosses the path. There is a boggy area beside it with striking red bog moss (*Sphagnum sp.*), yellow mountain saxifrage (*Saxifraga aizoides*), more bog asphodel and, in the drier areas, some alpine lady's mantle (*Alchemilla alpina*) and bilberry (*Vaccinium myrtillus*).

The path leads out on to more open heathland, with ling, some bell heather and cross-leaved heather, the occasional plant of petty whin (*Genista anglica*), and a little dwarf juniper. Another attractive small burn crosses the pathway, with a magnificent show of yellow mountain saxifrage, bog cotton (*Eriophorum*), and green bog moss. After the burn, take the right-hand track where the path divides. Look carefully among the vegetation along here for some stagshorn club moss (*Lycopodium clavatum*) (see Cwm Idwal, p. 222) with cones borne on branched stems which do indeed resemble stag's antlers. In barer patches among the heather, there are also clusters of the red-tipped lichen, *Cladonia floerkeana* – the red tips on the grey-green stalks being the fruiting bodies.

Remain on the clearly defined track (which can be very wet in places), heading towards a fenced conifer plantation. When the fence is reached walk alongside it towards the gate and stile at the corner. Note the number of horsetails (*Equisetum*) in among the heather. By the stile, turn left along a broad track, which leads through more heather and juniper and past another Nature Conservancy Council cairn. There is a tiny lochan on the right and a large aspen tree near it. More alpine lady's mantle grows along the path, with some devil's-bit scabious (*Succisa pratensis*) and yellow mountain saxifrage.

Soon a much more heavily wooded area is reached, which is the main area for downy birch, some of it within an enclosure on the left. On the right is Morrone Hill, with great limestone crags. Within the birchwood there is a great deal of dwarf juniper and a number of wet flushes and hollows, the whole exhibiting a marvellous flora. Because of the restrictions, however, much of this cannot be seen. Just for the record, the plants within the wood include common wintergreen (*Pyrola minor*), chickweed wintergreen (*Trientalis europaea*), water avens (*Geum rivale*), wood cranesbill (*Geranium sylvaticum*), Scottish asphodel (*Tofieldia pusilla*), alpine cinquefoil (*Potentilla crantzii*) and some rare sedges. The grasses most commonly seen are sweet vernal (*Anthoxanthum odoratum*), wood fescue (*Festuca altissima*) and various bents.

At the end of the enclosure, turn left down the hill and back to the car park.

Rassal Ashwood

SUMMARY This is of particular interest, as the lime-loving ashwood is set in the Western Highlands – a region where acid soil predominates. Rassal Ashwood is the most northerly of its kind in Britain. It is a Nature Conservancy Council reserve.

APPROXIMATE LENGTH OF WALK Variable, up to 1–1½ miles.

BEST TIMES Spring, summer.

LOCATION Near Lochcarron in the Western Highlands. NG843433.

About ten miles out of Lochcarron there is a Nature Reserve signpost on the right of the road. Park in a pull-in several hundred yards past the sign, and walk back up the hill towards the woodland. A number of flowers grow in the grazing land through which one walks – field scabious (*Knautia arvensis*), eyebright (*Euphrasia officinalis*), and the lilac-blue flowers of field gentian (*Gentianella campestris*). In the wet ground outside the wood and around the many little rivulets which run down the very steep hill, there is butterwort (*Pinguicula vulgaris*), and the attractive yellow mountain saxifrage (*Saxifraga aizoides*), which has red spots on its petals. Black bog-rush (*Schoenus nigricans*) is present, as is broad-leaved cotton-grass (*Eriophorum latifolium*). The presence of both these plants indicates that the underlying soil is not the usual acid type so widespread in the Highlands. It is unexpectedly lime-rich, as it is part of an unusual limestone strip in the north-west Highlands.

There is no boundary fence around this part of the wood, nor are there any formal pathways, so the visitor is left to wander at will through this interesting reserve. The unusual nature of the ground becomes immediately apparent on entering the wooded area; it is uneven and hummocky due to the underlying limestone pavement. The ash trees are huge and some are lichen-encrusted. Lichen also grows underneath them and in the surrounding grass – much of it dog lichen (*Peltigera canina*). The grasses include some of the bromes (*Brachypodium spp.*), cocksfoot (*Dactylis glomerata*) and common bent (*Agrostis capillaris*). In addition to the dominant ashes there are some very solid hawthorns, with blackthorn, hazel and rowan.

As both ash and rowan (also known as mountain ash) are present, this is a good place to look at the differences between these two trees. On this site the ash trees are much larger than the rowan and so it is easy to tell them apart, but saplings can be less easy, due to the similarity of the leaves at first glance. The twigs of ash cannot be mistaken for anything else at close quarters – indeed, it is possible to identify them by feel alone. This is because the side shoots on the twigs are paired and the nodes (i.e. the sections of the stem from which the buds grow) are flattened. Another identifying feature is the blackness of the buds. In contrast, the buds of rowan grow singly and alternately on the sides of the twig. Both trees have compound leaves (i.e. the leaf is made up of a number of leaflets), but the midrib of the rowan is reddish-green whereas that of the ash is pale green, and the rowan leaflets have very distinctly toothed edges while those of ash are very much less obviously toothed.

Ash is one of those strange plants that change sex. Most ash trees have both male and female flowers, but it is not uncommon for a tree to be either wholly male or wholly female, or for a tree to be female one year and bisexual or male the next.

Growing between and under the trees are a number of flowering plants such as enchanter's nightshade (*Circaea lutetiana*), early purple orchid (*Orchis mascula*), wild strawberry (*Fragaria vesca*), primrose (*Primula vulgaris*), yellow pimpernel (*Lysimachia nemorum*), dog violet (*Viola canina*), large stands of yellow iris (*Iris pseudacorus*), ragged robin (*Lychnis flos-cuculi*) and that most elegant and lovely of flowers, grass of Parnassus (*Parnassia palustris*), which of course is not a grass at all, its white petals delicately marked with pale-green veins. The presence of this plant again confirms the nature of the underlying limestone.

The wood is also rich in birds, with tree-creepers, willow warblers, mistle thrushes and various tits, to name just a few.

Leave the ashwood and climb further up the hill, where the vegetation changes to the more common acid grass and heather moorland with large areas of bracken, and unusually large spreads of hair moss (*Polytrichum spp.*). Much of the area is boggy, with rushes and cotton-grass. The reserve is bounded on two sides by the very deep and steep-sided Alt Mor Gorge, which should not be approached from the reserve except by experienced and properly equipped climbers.

Return to the car park by the same route.

Beinn Eighe Mountain Trail

SUMMARY The first part of this walk is a very steep and testing trail, leading 1,800 feet up the side of the mountain, and should not be undertaken by anyone who is not reasonably fit or who is unaccustomed to serious hill walking. Suitable footwear, warm clothing and some food are recommended. A magnificent walk with dramatic views, demonstrating not only some Caledonian forest, but how vegetation changes with increasing height. A National Nature Reserve, and designated as a Biosphere Reserve of international importance by UNESCO.

APPROXIMATE LENGTH OF WALK 4 miles.

BEST TIME May–August.

LOCATION Car park on the side of Loch Maree, about 2½ miles from Kinlochewe, Ross and Cromarty. (19)002651.

From the car park, follow the Trail signs through the tunnel under the road, and up beside the Allt na h-Airidhe burn. Alongside the path are heather (*Erica tetralix*) and ling (*Calluna vulgaris*), bilberry (*Vaccinium myrtillus*), some broom, and a few silver birch and small Scots pines. The burn itself has plenty of bracken growing on the banks, and the gravel bed is very suitable for the spawning of salmon and sea trout which come up from the sea through Loch Maree.

A short climb leads into the heart of the ancient woodland (see Glas Leitire Walk, p. 279), with Scots pines and more birches, rowans and holly. This is the Glas Leitire pinewood, in which some of the 'granny' pines are over 350 years old. These ancient trees are large, with gnarled trunks and a heavy crown, and are surrounded by younger trees which are straighter and have much smaller crowns.

Under the trees on both sides of the path are patches of boggy ground containing bog moss (*Sphagnum*) – including some spectacular patches of the red species – and hair moss (*Polytrichum*), bog asphodel (*Narthecium ossifragum*), some horsetails, bog myrtle (*Myrica gale*) and bog cotton (*Eriophorum*). Bracken grows in the drier parts, with some hard fern (*Blechnum spicant*), bilberry and cowberry (*Vaccinium vitis-idaea*). A number of fungi appear in this area in late summer and autumn, the most conspicuous being some of the *Russulas*.

Although they are unlikely to be seen in daylight, roe deer live in this densely covered woodland, while pine martens and wild cats have been recorded. As might be expected in a native pinewood, the Scottish crossbill is present in some numbers.

The path climbs steeply up through the pinewood and emerges on to more open ground, where the going becomes very tough indeed, zigzagging up over rock and scree some 1,050 feet in just over a third of a mile. Anyone not liking the look of this should return immediately, as it is the start of the toughest section of the climb. At about 820 feet a big rocky outcrop, the Trumpet Rock, is reached. This is a good place to stop, rest, and survey the magnificence of the surrounding country. Below, on the far side of the road, is the great expanse of Loch Maree, backed by the huge mass of Slioch.

The vegetation becomes sparser with increasing height, and more stunted, as might be expected. Stumpy heather is the most common plant, providing shelter and food for a few red grouse and winter food for red deer. Growing among the rocks by the path are a few examples of the curious fir club moss (*Huperzia selago*) (see Cwm Idwal, p. 222), while mosses and lichens find shelter in among the heather. Anyone who reads the Nature Conservancy Council leaflet will learn that the 1,000-foot cairn marks the end of the steepest section of the path – at a point halfway to the top of the trail. However, any feelings of jubilation are premature as a short distance further on, one is confronted by a near-vertical rocky outcrop! Admittedly it is not particularly high, and there are both hand and footholds, but anyone carrying, as I was, a load of camera gear, may find it testing!

Once up this rocky outcrop the going is easy, and the conservation cairn at 1,800 feet is reached without difficulty. It is truly a strange landscape. Plant life is scarce, and what there is clings precariously to the rocky substrate to gain protection from the hostile environment. Deer-grass (*Scirpus caespitosus*), sedges, and heath rush (*Juncus squarrosus*) are relatively common, as is dwarf juniper, while crowberry (*Empetrum nigrum*) and alpine bearberry (*Arctous alpina*) can be found. The lovely mountain azalea (*Loiseleuria procumbens*) is also a plant of this inhospitable landscape. Once again the views are awe-inspiring. Above and to the left is the stark, almost forbidding ridge of Beinn Eighe, its shiny quartzite scree lending it a snow-covered aspect even in mid-summer. The literature tells of an astonishing thirty-one peaks of 3,000 feet being visible from this point on a good day.

From the conservation cairn, the path leads across the plateau below Meall a' Ghiubhais, following a line of stone cairns. On the left after a short distance is Lunar Loch – named to commemorate the moon landing in 1969, and appropriately so, as this can fairly be described as lunar-type landscape! The grey-white rock is quartzite, the reddish stone is Torridonian sandstone. Surprisingly, perhaps, in this apparently barren environment, the loch itself is by no means lifeless. Floating bur-reed (*Sparganium angustifolium*) covers the far end of the water, while palmate newts can be seen in the shallowest water around the edges, and frog spawn is not unknown. Caddis fly larvae are quite plentiful, and the common hawker dragonfly is often seen. This is ptarmigan and mountain hare country, and also red deer territory, although so popular is the walk in good weather that neither is likely to be seen except at dawn or dusk. Golden eagles may be seen soaring high over the hills, while ravens tumble and display around cliff faces. Burns race down the bleak mountainside, including An t-Altt which supplies the Allt na h-Airidhe burn where the walk began some 1,700 feet below. The water at this level is pure and sparkling, and delicious (and safe) to drink.

After crossing the plateau, the path begins the descent down the mountain – a descent which is markedly less steep than the ascent. Cairns mark the height above sea level, the first being at 1,500 feet. The path leads down a valley, which is comparatively sheltered and allows the growth of lusher vegetation. There are a few rowan trees growing between the 1,500- and 1,000-foot mark. Among the longer, stronger heather (compare this with the stunted plants of the ascent) may be found the attractive dwarf cornel (*Chamaepericly-menum suecicum*), a plant of Arctic regions which belongs to the dogwood family. It grows only about 15 cm (6 inches) high, and has four white petals and opposite pairs of stalkless, pale-green leaves. In autumn the flowers are replaced by bright red berries. On the way down, keep a good look out for club mosses, of which there are a number of specimens.

At about 1,000 feet the yawning cavity that is the Allt na h-Airidhe Gorge can be seen to the right. On the left, a great cliff rises above the path, and from it a few pine trees grow in improbable niches on the face. Just past this impressive cliff is a small enclosure in which some planting and draining took place in the 1970s.

As the path leads round to the right a closer view can be had of the great gorge – but real care must be exercised as the cliff edges are both slippery and crumbly. The burn runs along the bottom of the massive fault, and in it aquatic insects live, providing food for dippers. Dead trees in the gorge offer shelter for beetles and larvae, which are fed on by great spotted woodpeckers, and also by pine martens.

Follow the pathway down the hill towards the woodland, where the vegetation changes once more. In addition to the trees, the banks are covered with bilberry, and a careful search in July and August may reveal creeping lady's tresses (*Goodyera repens*), an uncommon creeping orchid with white, unspurred flowers which give off a rather unpleasant smell. Another rarity of this area is the chickweed wintergreen (*Trientalis europaea*), a delicate little plant, about 10 cm (4 inches) high, with a head of white to pale-pink flowers with five to nine petals. The path eventually leads to the conservation cabin on the Glas Leitire Nature Trail, completing the Mountain Trail, then leads on down the hill back to the car park.

Beinn Eighe:
Glas Leitire Walk

SUMMARY The shorter and less demanding of the two
walks on Beinn Eighe, amid scenery of almost
overwhelming grandeur in the West Highlands,
overlooking Loch Maree. The pathway is steep and
very rough in places, and good strong footwear is
advisable.

APPROXIMATE LENGTH OF WALK 1 mile.

BEST TIMES Summer and autumn.

LOCATION As for the Beinn Eighe Mountain Trail.

The pathway begins in the car park by the culvert which
passes under the main road. The Allt na h-Airidhe burn
flows down the hillside, through the culvert and into Loch
Maree. As can be seen, the bed of the burn is a mixture of
brown sandstone and white quartzite boulders, but there are
also stretches of gravel in which salmon and sea trout spawn
in late autumn. The fish provide welcome food for otters.

The track leads up the hill to the right, and is flanked on
both sides by ling (*Calluna vulgaris*), some of which is over
fifty years old, and bilberry (*Vaccinium myrtillus*) – often
called blaeberry in the Highlands. There are young Scots
pines on the right, but a pine stump, also on the right, shows
growth rings indicating that it was growing there at the time
of the Jacobite Rebellion in the sixteenth century. This part
of the Beinn Eighe reserve is a remnant of the old Caledonian
pine forest which once covered so much of the Highlands,
and can be recognized as such by the presence of pine trees
of different ages and shapes and the very thick ground cover.

Cowberry (*Vaccinium vitis-idaea*) and bilberry grow among the heather, and in the damper places there are some red bog mosses (*Sphagnum sp.*) and insectivorous sundew (*Drosera rotundifolia*). The yellow flowers of bog asphodel (*Narthecium ossifragum*), which turn orange before withering, bloom in the summer, as does another flower of wet and boggy places, the little pink lousewort (*Pedicularis sylvatica*). Hair moss (*Polytrichum*) and hard fern (*Blechum spicant*) occur in some of the drier places. The pathway between cairns three and four is very steep and rough, then levels out a little.

From just above cairn four and to the right, a magnificent panoramic view across Loch Maree opens out. Immediately opposite is the massive peak of Slioch (3,200 feet), and to the right of that, the silvery river Fasagh flows steeply down Gleann Biannasdale to the loch.

Continue climbing up through the heather–clad hillside to cairn six, where the effects of red and roe deer browsing on the young Scots pines can be seen nearby. Deer need calcium and phosphorus when they are calves and for the growth of antlers, and these two minerals are present in the young trees.

The conservation cabin, a welcome shelter in bad weather, marks the half-way stage of the walk, and is also just below the highest point of the Trail at about 360 feet. Birds are not a great feature of this part of Beinn Eighe, but careful searching with binoculars over the peak of Slioch could reveal a golden eagle. Further down on the mountain itself, herds of red deer may be seen, or perhaps some of the feral goats that have made a wild home in this part of the Highlands. Also from this vantage point, some of the geological structures of Slioch are visible, notably the wavy line where the upper Torridonian sandstone meets the lower Lewisian gneiss. To add to the geological interest, in front of the cabin is a plinth showing samples of the different layers of rock in the area. The top is quartzite, in which can be seen the burrows of marine worms dating back some 600 million years. Beneath that is the dark layer of Torridonian sandstone which is even older (800–1,000 million years), and the bottom layer is the oldest of all, the banded Lewisian gneiss of 1,200–1,600 million years ago.

Follow the track down the hillside through woodland that changes as the height above sea level decreases. Initially, the familiar pine forest is dominant, but after cairn eight, birch takes over as the most common tree and the undergrowth is dominated by thick bracken. Some of the comparatively few species of birds are likely to be seen from here onwards. Common birds such as tits, wrens and robins are present in average numbers, but the rarer ones, such as crossbills, twites and siskins, are seen on occasion. The path passes another smaller burn (the Allt an Torach), where, among the grass, are tormentil (*Potentilla erecta*), devil's-bit scabious (*Succisa pratensis*), rushes and some hard fern. A typical birchwood sight is the growth of bracket fungi on a number of the dead trees. In clearings where the bracken has not so far encroached, some attractive flowers may be seen – woundwort (*Stachys sylvatica*), sanicle (*Sanicula europaea*), and wood anemone (*Anemone nemorosa*). Just opposite cairn ten, on the bank, a small crevice marks a disused pine marten's den. Although they are elusive, there are a few of these rare and lovely animals on the reserve.

On the lower slopes the birches are joined by rowans, and as the ground becomes wetter and boggier a number of alder trees are found. At cairn eleven, a boardwalk leads over a bog in which frogs, toads and newts may be seen. After crossing the boardwalk, the main road is reached, and this should be crossed with great care, as it is very busy in the summer months.

From the far side of the road, go down to the shores of Loch Maree. Along the shore and on the banks are other species of trees which form part of the pine forest – alder, birch, rowan, and some holly. Sections of the bank are covered in really fine specimens of *Thuidium* moss.

The car park is just a few hundred yards ahead.

Embo

SUMMARY Embo is a most attractive beach on the coast of Sutherland near the Dornoch Firth. It has a small sand dune system, and the beach is part-sand, part-rock – the latter containing rock pools with boulders under which a variety of shore creatures may be found. It is a very good sea-bird watching point, especially from the small jetty.

APPROXIMATE LENGTH OF WALK 2 miles.

BEST TIME All year.

LOCATION Through Grannie's Heilen Hame caravan site at Embo, near Dornoch in Sutherland. NH819925.

From the buildings at the top end of the caravan park walk down on to the beach and turn right. At the top of the beach, between this point and the jetty further along, a number of typical dune and maritime plants grow – thrift (*Armeria maritima*), sea rocket (*Cakile maritima*), marram (*Ammophila arenaria*) and sea lyme grass (*Elymus arenarius*). This is the sandy part of the beach, with a few rocky outcrops, and there are varying amounts of flotsam and jetsam washed up according to the tide and the weather.

Some of the more interesting animals sometimes washed in attached to pieces of driftwood are clutches of goose barnacles. These creatures *appear* to be bivalve shells, attached to driftwood or pier legs, etc., by a long fleshy stalk. In fact, when examined they prove to have five thin, translucent, whitish plates with a blue tinge. They are misleading animals altogether, because they also look like molluscs but are actually crustaceans, belonging to the same family as crabs. Unlikely though it seems, goose barnacles have body parts which are more or less equivalent to the head, thorax and abdomen arrangement of other crustaceans. The long stalk is a much enlarged equivalent of the crustacean head, while the part between the main plates is the thorax; only the abdomen has been almost lost during evolution. When the goose barnacle is feeding, the two main shell plates open, and the animal protrudes six pairs of jointed and typically crustacean legs which are used for catching and filtering food.

When the main rocky shore is reached, wander slowly down towards the sea. At the top of the shore, many of the pools are full of the bright green seaweed, *Enteromorpha*, which has narrow tubelike fronds. Sometimes there is some of the membranous red seaweed, *Porphyra*, growing on the rocks, and this is extremely slippery if stepped on. A little further down, there is some channelled wrack (*Pelvetia canaliculata*) and further down still, a wide zone of spiral wrack (*Fucus spiralis*). Where this is growing in pools, the spiralling from which it gets its name is plain to see. On the landward (and thus more sheltered) side of some of the rock shelves is quite a prolific growth of knotted wrack (*Ascophyllum nodosum*). Lower still, a small band of serrated wrack (*Fucus serratus*) is found.

The pools have a number of seaweeds in them, including the red *Ahnfeltia plicata*, with a fine, wirelike texture, and *Griffithsia flosculosa*, which is also rather stiff. In a few pools, the green seaweed *Codium*, with dark-green fronds which are circular in cross-section, is found.

Near the low-water mark in certain places there is a thick growth of sea thong (*Himanthalia elongata*), although sometimes only the buttons from which the long thongs grow can be seen. Right down at the bottom, and only partially revealed at low tide, is the kelp zone, with the big fronds of oarweed (*Laminaria digitata*) and Foslie Frond (*L. hyperborea*). The very attractive blue-rayed limpet is found feeding on these kelps.

A great many barnacles (the more usual acorn ones, not the goose barnacles) live on the rocks, as well as a very heavy crop of mussels.

Having investigated the lower shore while the tide is out, it can be very interesting to spend some time higher up the shore turning over a few rocks in the pools (and replacing them so as not to destroy the habitats of the creatures under them). Under many of them, small shore crabs are found, together with tiny, flat-sided crustaceans which dart under some other shelter, swimming on their sides. These are various species of a creature called *Gammarus*. Clinging to the under-surface of some of the rocks are chitons, or coat-of-mail shells, which are flattened, oval-shaped animals with eight articulated shell plates on their backs. If disturbed, the creature rolls up in just the same way as a woodlouse, and in so doing protects the soft body underneath.

In some of the pools there will be a starfish, often under seaweed and near the mussels. One only has to watch a starfish for a little while, or to turn it over on its back, to see that it is not the immobile creature that it at first appears to be. It can move, and it is highly predatory. It moves by means of structures called tube feet, which can be seen on the underside of the animal – they are the little line of protuberances in the centre of each arm. They work by a kind of hydraulic system which enables the starfish to protrude them when needed and to retract them when it is not moving. Some starfish have little suckers on the end of the tube feet, which are used for attachment to the rock. In the centre of the underside is the mouth of the starfish. From this runs a short gut or stomach which has pouches, two of which extend into each arm. These, together with the tube feet, are used in the most extraordinary fashion when the starfish attacks a mussel. As everyone who has tried it knows, mussels are not easy to open; they are able to hold their two shells together by means of powerful muscles. However, the starfish attacks the mussel by moving on top of it, then with part of each arm still on the rock it uses its tube feet to exert a continuous very strong pull on the two shells. Eventually the mussel cannot resist any longer, and a small gap opens between the two sides of the shell. Immediately this happens, the starfish extrudes its stomach through its mouth, inserts it into the gap, and digests the contents of the shell.

When the rocky shore has been examined, the end of the jetty is a marvellous place from which to scan the sea in search of birds. Sea ducks are almost always offshore at Embo – particularly eiders, and quite frequently long-tailed ducks, while common scoters are occasionally seen. Red-throated and northern divers may also be present in the autumn. On the shore, turnstones and purple sandpipers are often busy among the rocks.

From the jetty, go down on to the beach on the far side from the one just described. Although only a matter of yards apart, this beach differs quite markedly from the other one. It is predominantly sandy, although there are some outcrops of low rock, covered with *Enteromorpha* and a great deal of knotted wrack – the latter showing that the area is much more sheltered.

When the tide is some way out, a number of pools remain, some near rocks but most in the sand. It is fun to watch the flat periwinkles moving about in these, leaving a distinct trail behind them in the sand. Also in and around the pools and distributed quite widely on the beach are the coils of sand that signal the presence, underneath, of lugworms, which live in sand-lined tubes (see Ynyslas, p. 230).

It is a pleasant walk to the next point, with an increasing amount of rock at the bottom of the shore, on which curlew, purple sandpipers, turnstones, and ringed plover are nearly always present. It is not unusual in late autumn to hear and see skeins of greylag geese flying overhead, most of them coming from nearby Loch Fleet to feed on the fields behind the dunes. About half way round the bay, a fresh water outlet runs down from between the sand dunes, and near this there is always a large mixed flock of gulls, usually with a few curlews. It is always worth keeping an eye out to sea, where more sea ducks and divers are frequently seen. Return to the caravan park.

The Big Burn Walk at Golspie

SUMMARY The gorge through which the Big Burn runs has been described as the most beautiful of its type in Sutherland. The walk follows the gorge right up to and past a delightful waterfall before returning through a variety of habitats.

APPROXIMATE LENGTH OF WALK 4 miles.

BEST TIMES Spring, summer.

LOCATION Golspie in Sutherland. Park just beyond the Sutherland Arms garage on the A9. (17)837003.

From the car park take the path under the big chestnut tree, and follow it down a flight of steps to the bridge over the burn. Wild garlic (*Allium ursinum*) grows in profusion beneath a canopy of sycamore, horse chestnut, rowan, and some fine beech trees up the bank on the left.

Over the bridge the pathway leads through a delightful area of woodland interspersed with little glades, with a small picnic area on the left, surrounded by larch and silver birch. Just near the bridge on the burn banks are some willows and one or two lime trees. Lining the path, too, are a number of trees, some of them labelled, including ash, bird cherry and hawthorn. Bluebells (*Endymion non-scriptus*), red campion (*Silene dioica*) and primroses (*Primula vulgaris*) carpet the ground, while a number of the trees are covered in lichens. There are some pedunculate oaks and some more silver birch on the left. Woodland birds are common in this area, and spotted flycatchers are among the nesting species.

After about half a mile, look across and up to the left to a huge sand cliff on the far side of the gorge. In its sheer face is an active colony of sand martins. These charming birds use their very tiny feet to excavate deep nesting tunnels, which are between 60 cm-1.2 m (2–4 feet) long. When the long fledging period of about three weeks is over, the youngsters indulge in juvenile 'games' of pursuing each other, and in high-speed aerobatics in which their parents sometimes join. Also on the cliff face are several pairs of fulmars.

The path now leads across the deep gorge by means of another bridge, then almost immediately back again over another. From the second one, an attractive little waterfall is visible, and down below, grey wagtails are often present on boulders in the middle of the burn. Coal tits, too, are seen in this area, distinguishable from the rather similar marsh tits by their white cheeks and neck napes.

After just over a mile from the start, where the pathway divides, follow the red signpost (the trail is liberally sprinkled with various coloured posts which can be a little confusing!) towards a steep flight of steps, then turn immediately right over a bridge. Follow the lower of two tracks from here close to the banks of the burn to a wooden viewing platform, which quite suddenly and dramatically gives a superb view of the Big Burn Waterfall, dropping some fifty feet into the plunge pool below. The platform also affords fine views down the burn, which is densely fringed on both sides by alders, ash, ferns and wild garlic, and in some of the rock crevices and in damper areas with golden saxifrage (*Chrysosplenium alternifolium*). Dippers are likely to be seen, bobbing up and down on the rocks in the middle of the stream. The overhangs of the banks offer good sites for the birds' domed nests.

Retracing your steps from the platform – notice the large growth of *Thuidium* moss on the bank on the right – turn sharp right up the steep flight of steps. Here the habitat changes noticeably, with a field layer of bilberry (*Vaccinium myrtillus*) and banks of rhododendrons. Hard ferns grow on the banks, and there are great spreads of hair moss (*Polytrichum*) and some stitchwort (*Stellaria*). A bridge leads over the waterfall, with rhododendrons on one side and sycamore trees on the other.

Turn left over the bridge by the seat and enter a rather gloomy conifer plantation, which has some wood sorrel (*Oxalis acetosella*) growing along the edges. Where the path divides, stay on the lower one, and where a blue signpost points in both directions, turn back to the right at a hairpin bend, going through more conifers. Ignore the bridge, and shortly afterwards pass some steps on the right. Continue past a few Scots pines with a sign 5JA on them and remain on the upper track, where there are rhododendrons on the right.

Another area of mixed woodland is reached on the right, with a common lime tree (which is labelled), together with some oak and a few more conifers. Cross over a tiny burn which runs under the path. There is a wych elm (labelled) on the left. This can most easily be separated from the English elm by the difference in the bark, with that of the English elm being more obviously divided into cracked squares. In spring the bluebells under the trees in this area are a magnificent sight. There is an equally beautiful view of the gorge. Near some beeches on the right is another car park; continue past a sycamore tree and a seat. Yet another plantation of conifers is reached and the trees, mostly sitka spruce and larch, are heavily encrusted with lichens. The pathway emerges from the plantation into an open glade with bracken, more bluebells in spring, and red campion. There are some oak trees, and more conifers on the left.

Follow the red signpost and turn left quite steeply downhill to a T-junction; turn left here and follow the yellow sign. There is a large American oak nearby. Return to the car park on the original pathway.

Duncansby Head

SUMMARY One of the most northerly bird cliffs on mainland Britain, giving close-up views of many nesting birds, as well as more distant views of seals (common and grey). Quite a good place for sea-coast wild flowers. Spectacular cliff views, especially of Duncansby Stacks.

APPROXIMATE LENGTH OF WALK 1 mile.

BEST TIMES Spring, summer.

LOCATION Turn off the A9 in the village of John o' Groat's – signposted. ND402734.

Even before leaving the car sea birds can be seen, as fulmars are almost always in view nesting on the cliff ledges immediately opposite the car park, and there are invariably numbers of them flying to and fro along the cliff edge, with their distinctive, stiff-winged flight.

From the car park, cross the road and walk up towards the lighthouse. A fence leads down beside the lighthouse (outside the wall). Follow this fence, which leads down to the cliff edge and along to the right.

At first, the drop of the cliff face is so sheer that it is virtually impossible to see the nesting birds. However, hundreds upon hundreds of them can be seen flying in and out from the nests below – fulmars, guillemots, razorbills, a few puffins, kittiwakes – and the sea appears at times to be almost black with rafts of auks. There is also a constant passage of the various species of gulls.

With so many birds, eggs and nestlings, predators are very much in evidence. From almost any part of the cliffs, great skuas can be seen, creating havoc wherever they go. One of their favourite feeding ploys is to chase and harry the smaller birds and force them to drop whatever food they are carrying. Eggs and unwary nestlings are easy prey, and the skuas also hunt adults down in the air, using their powerful claws. Adult auks on the water are sometimes attacked, and when one skua makes a kill, another very often joins in the resulting meal. All this can be seen from the cliffs at Duncansby, and however unattractive it may seem, it has to be remembered that the skuas need to eat! An interesting sidelight on this predatory creature is that it is the only bird to live at both north and south poles.

The handsome (and lethal) peregrine is also in attendance, stooping with incredible speed to strike its prey with the claw of its foot. In winter the occasional merlin comes to the coast, harrying the meadow pipits which are common on the moorland behind the cliffs.

Growing among the rough grass which reaches right to the cliff edges are a number of attractive wild flowers. Spring squill (*Scilla verna*) is present in good numbers, as well as sea and red campion (*Silene maritima* and *S. dioica*), masses of attractive thrift (*Armeria maritima*), which also grows on the cliff face, buttercups, and – in a rather unlikely setting – primroses (*Primula vulgaris*), which can be found flowering as late as mid-June.

Further round the cliff top, where deep, fjord-like indentations occur, there are wonderful views of the cliff faces on each side, and the nesting birds are visible at quite close quarters. Shags' evil-smelling nests of rotten seaweed are to be seen (but fortunately not smelled) right at the bottom of the cliffs, often only just above the splash zone. Shags are one of the earliest breeding birds, and may start as early as February. Next up this 'high-rise' bird colony are the nests of kittiwakes, followed by the guillemots and the razorbills.

It is easy to see that apart from the puffins, of which there is only a small colony at Duncansby, the fulmars occupy the nesting positions nearest the top of the cliff face. From several positions around the cliff-top path a close-up view of these lovely birds is possible. Even without binoculars their strange 'tube' noses are clearly visible. They are constructed of plates of horny material joined together by discernible sutures, with the horny tube on top. Several theories have been put forward about the function of the tube. Some authorities suggest that it is some kind of air-speed indicator, others believe it functions as a nostril for scenting, while others, including the late James Fisher, state that it is used in preening, with oil from the stomach trickling down it and being distributed over the feathers.

That fulmars produce an oily fluid in their stomach is certainly not in dispute, as anyone who has approached an adult or young one on the nest too closely will testify! Without apparent preparation or hesitation the bird will vomit the appalling-smelling oily fluid in the direction of the intruder. Their range is as much as 1.2 m (4 feet), and anyone who thinks that, having avoided the first discharge, it is safe to proceed, should take note of what James Fisher wrote with certainty born of experience: 'Second barrels, and even third barrels, are quite usual . . .'

Soon the first of the huge offshore 'stacks' – great blocks of rock which have been detached from the mainland – can be seen, its top level with the cliff path. It seems to be a favourite place for puffins and razorbills, and good views of these two birds can be had there.

Only about half a mile from the lighthouse the coastline curves inwards to a rock-strewn bay. From here the famous Duncansby Stacks – a group of massive rocky outcrops – dominate the coastline. They too have their complement of sea birds, and parts of them are white with guano. This bay, which has a number of smaller offshore rocks that are exposed at low tide, is a favourite basking place for seals. Grey seals are frequently seen here, but it is not unusual to see common seals (or at least not before the virus hit local colonies). Telling the two species apart should be quite simple, but the younger ones can sometimes lead to confusion. The profile of the adult grey is straight and the head much flatter than that of the common seal. The latter has a distinctly rounded head, with a 'dished profile', i.e. there is a concave line from forehead to nose. Common seals often bask with hind flippers and heads raised. A further point of difference (which is hardly likely to be seen from a cliff top!) is that the common seal's short muzzle has V-shaped nostrils, while the longer muzzle of the grey has nostrils that are almost parallel.

Although it is possible to walk further along the cliff, the best of the birds have now been seen and a return can be made along the same route. However, by way of variation it is possible to follow a well-defined grassy track across the moorland back to the car park. Curlews nest on this moorland and are often heard giving their haunting, bubbling call.

Invernaver

SUMMARY The outstanding feature of this walk is the extraordinary mixture of plants to be seen within a relatively small area. Calcicole and calcifuge plants grow, if not side by side, at least near to each other, and because of the very exposed position, several arctic-alpine plants are found almost at sea level.

APPROXIMATE LENGTH OF WALK 8 miles.

BEST TIMES Spring, summer.

LOCATION Take the Tongue road (A836) from Bettyhill in Sutherland. Take the first right some miles after crossing the bridge, and park in a pull-in just near a signpost to Torrisdale. NC679610.

From the pull-in, it is a good idea to look at the lie of the land across the river valley and estuary before going down to the footbridge, as it can be quite confusing when on the level. Immediately at the bottom of the hill is the Borgie River, on the far side of which is an area of wet, marshy ground, criss-crossed by smaller streams. On the far side of this is a wider tributary, and beyond this the land rises steeply to a plateau of fields, then more steeply again to the moorland above. To the left, the river enters the sea at Torrisdale Bay, which is backed by a storm beach and sand dunes.

Go down the steep hillside to the footbridge over the river. On the way down, a number of attractive small plants grow among the bracken, coarse grass, gorse and ling (*Calluna vulgaris*). These include lousewort (*Pedicularis sylvatica*), milkwort, and common spotted orchids (*Dactylorhiza fuchsii*). Cross the footbridge (do not be discouraged by the barricade at the far end – that is to stop the stock from the marsh crossing over!). Negotiate the marshy area – the route taken will depend on the water level in the small streams, but head for the bottom of the hillside on the opposite side of the river valley. The marsh is covered with rushes, tussocky grass, and some bell and cross-leaved heather (*Erica cinerea* and *E. tetralix*).

On the far side, turn left along the bottom of the hill towards the sea, following a grassy track which is wet in places, making an ideal habitat for butterwort (*Pinguicula vulgaris*). In the spring and summer, dozens of wheatears may be seen perching on the rocks of the hillside, amongst which they nest. Look over to the right towards the river estuary, as some mergansers may be on the water and there are often a few greylag geese. Further along the track a few white-topped posts indicate the route. On the hillside above these, gorse is growing, with dwarf juniper and some thrift (*Armeria maritima*). As the sand dunes are approached, ringed plover frequently run along the edge of the water.

Follow the path to the beach, then turn right and walk up through the sand dunes towards the hillside ahead. The dunes are initially covered with marram grass (*Ammophila arenaria*), but as the distance from the beach increases they become more established with mosses, including shaggy moss (*Rhytidiadelphus triquetrus*), lichens, white clover (*Trifolium repens*) and wild thyme (*Thymus drucei*). In some of the dune slacks curved sedge (*Carex maritima*) may be seen.

After just about a mile, start climbing up the side of the hill towards the moorland above. There is no pathway, so just choose the best route up the rock-strewn hillside. Note how the sand is blown up the hill and how the plants tend to stabilize it, with the habitat changing gradually from maritime plants such as sea campion (*Silene maritima*) and thrift, to moorland, with dwarf juniper and some ling.

At the top, keep walking parallel with the shore until the mouth of the River Naver can be seen ahead, then turn inland. Again, there are no pathways, and it is left to the individual to wander about and see all that this remarkable place has to offer. The top of Invernaver is basically moor-land, but growing among the heather, ling, crowberry (*Empetrum nigrum*), bearberry (*Arctostaphylos uva-ursi*) and creeping willow (*Salix repens*) are spreads of alpine bistort (*Polygonum viviparum*), the glorious colours of yellow and purple saxifrages (*Saxifraga aizoides* and *S. oppositifolia*), and moss campion (*Silene acaulis*), contrasting with the delicate white of mountain avens (*Dryas octopetala*) with its yellow stamens. Most of these plants would not normally be expected at this level or near the sea.

Some distance inland there is a small loch with a few birches round the edge (the force of the gales in all but the most sheltered areas such as this ensures that most of Invernaver is treeless) and, further on, a number of boggy patches with bog cotton (*Eriophorum spp.*), bog mosses (*Sphagnum spp.*) and great sundew (*Drosera anglica*) – the latter differs from the more common round-leaved sundew in having oblong leaves measuring up to 4 cm (1½ inches) in length.

Return to the car park along the same route.

HELPFUL BOOKS

Bang, Preben, and Dahlstrom, Preben, *Guide to Animal Tracks and Signs*, Collins, 1974

Barrett, John H., and Yonge, C. M., *Pocket Guide to the Seashore*, Collins, 1958

Campbell, A. C., *Country Life Guide to the Seashore and Shallow Seas of Britain and Europe*, Country Life, 1976

Fitter, Richard, Fitter, Alastair, and Farrer, Ann, *The Grasses, Sedges, Rushes and Ferns of Britain and Northern Europe*, Collins, 1984

Fitter, R. S. R., and Manuel, Richard, *A Field Guide to Freshwater Life in Britain and North-West Europe*, Collins, 1986

Heinzel, Hermann, Fitter, Richard, and Parslow, John, *The Birds of Britain and Europe*, Collins, 1972

Howarth, T. G., *Colour Identification Guide to British Butterflies*, Warne, 1973

Jahns, Hans Martin, *Guide to the Ferns, Mosses and Lichens of Northern Europe*, Collins, 1980

Phillips, Roger, *Grasses, Ferns, Mosses and Lichens of Great Britain and Ireland*, Pan Books, 1980

Rose, Francis, *The Wild Flower Key*, Warne, 1981

USEFUL ADDRESSES

Cambridgeshire and Isle of Ely
   Naturalists' Trust
1 Brookside
Cambridge CB2 1JF

Cornwall Trust for Nature
   Conservation
Five Acres
Allet
Truro
Cornwall TR4 9DJ

Devon Wildlife Trust
35 New Bridge Street
Exeter
Devon EX4 3AH

Dorset Trust for Nature
   Conservation
39 Christchurch Road
Bournemouth
Dorset BH1 3NS

Exmoor National Park
   Committee
Exmoor House
Dulverton
Somerset TA22 9HL

Forestry Commission
   (Headquarters)
231 Corstorphine Road
Edinburgh EH12 7AT

Hampshire and Isle of Wight
   Naturalists' Trust
71 The Hundred
Romsey
Hampshire S05 8ZB

Kent Trust for Nature
   Conservation
PO Box 29
Maidstone
Kent ME14 1YH

Lake District National Park
   Authority
National Park Office
Brockhole
Windermere
Cumbria LA23 1LJ

Lincolnshire and South
   Humberside Trust for Nature
   Conservation
The Manor House
Alford
Lincolnshire LN13 9DL

National Trust
42 Queen Anne's Gate
London SW1H 9AS

National Trust for Scotland
5 Charlotte Square
Edinburgh EH2 4DU

Nature Conservancy Council
   (Headquarters)
19–20 Belgrave Square
London SW1X 8PY

Norfolk Naturalists' Trust
72 Cathedral Close
Norwich
Norfolk NRI 4DF

Northamptonshire Trust for
 Nature Conservation
Lings House
Billing Lings
Northampton NN3 4BE

Northumberland Wildlife Trust
Hancock Museum
Barras Bridge
Newcastle-upon-Tyne NE2 4PT

Nottinghamshire Wildlife Trust
310 Sneinton Dale
Nottingham NG3 7DN

Royal Society for Nature
 Conservation
The Green
Nettleham
Lincoln LN2 2NR

Royal Society for the Protection
 of Birds
The Lodge
Sandy
Bedfordshire SG19 2DL

Scottish Wildlife Trust
 (Headquarters)
25 Johnston Terrace
Edinburgh EH1 2NH

Somerset Trust for Nature
 Conservation
Fyne Court
Broomfield
Bridgwater
Somerset TA5 2EQ

GLOSSARY

ANTHER The structure at the top of the stamen (q.v.) which contains pollen.

ARTICULATED An articulated joint is one which is movable.

AURICLE When used botanically, the term describes an earlike lobe or pair of lobes on the base of leaf blades in some plants.

BRACT A small modified leaf which has a flower in its axil, i.e. the angle between the leaf and the stem; also the whorl of small leaves found at the base of a main umbel (q.v.). Bracts also occur in conifer cones.

CALCAREOUS Describes soils that have developed on chalk and/or limestone, and are thus rich in calcium carbonate.

CALCICOLE A plant that grows only on chalk/limestone soils.

CALCIFUGE A plant that prefers acid (non-calcareous) soils.

CANOPY The uppermost layer in the four-part ascending structure of a wood, consisting of large mature trees and their branches.

CARAPACE The hard exterior 'shell' of crustaceans, such as crabs.

CARR Wetland scrub/woodland usually consisting of alder, willow, and/or buckthorn.

CLIMAX VEGETATION The final, more or less stable stage in plant succession (q.v.). In Britain and Europe this is normally the forest.

COPPICING The cutting back to ground level of trees to encourage the growth of additional shoots. In 'coppice with standards', the majority of trees are cut back, but a selected few are not; these latter develop into 'standard' trees with (usually) one main trunk.

COROLLA The collective term for the petals of a flower.

DECIDUOUS Trees that shed their leaves in the autumn.

FIELD LAYER The second layer in the four-part ascending layers of a woodland, consisting of ferns and herbaceous plants.

FILAMENT The stalk that bears the anther (q.v.).

GROUND LAYER The lowest layer in the four-part ascending layers of a wood, consisting chiefly of mosses, liverworts, and fungi.

HALOPHYTE Plants able to tolerate salty conditions.

HOLDFAST The structure by means of which seaweeds are attached to the substrate. Holdfasts are not roots.

HYBRID A plant or animal whose parents were genetically different.

HYPHAE In fungi, the above-ground fruiting body and the underground rootlike mycelium consist of a mass of tiny threadlike filaments known as hyphae.

INSECTIVOROUS PLANTS Plants such as the butterwort (*Pinguicula sp.*) and sundew (*Drosera sp.*) which are able to digest insects.

MAST Term used to describe the seeds of some trees, notably those of beech.

NITROGEN-FIXING Some plants, particularly those belonging to the pea family, are able to obtain the nitrogen necessary for their survival from the air rather than from the soil or water, as is the case with the majority of plants. This is done for them by bacteria which live in nodules (small lumps) on their roots, and which obtain nitrogen from the air in the soil.

ORGANIC MATERIAL The breakdown products of living organisms.

PHOTOSYNTHESIS The synthesis of food materials by green plants, using water, carbon dioxide, and the energy of the sun. This energy is absorbed by the green pigment, chlorophyll. Parasitic plants such as the broomrapes lack this pigment.

PINNATE Used to describe a leaf in which separate leaflets are arranged along the leaf stalk, usually in opposite pairs and often with a terminal leaflet.

POLLARD Hard pruning of a tree in which the young branches are cut back nearly to the trunk.

SEPALS The outer whorl of floral leaves surrounding the petals (q.v. corolla) of a flower. They are usually green.

SHRUB LAYER See understorey.

SLOTS The footprints of deer.

SPADIX An erect spike of florets (small flowers), such as is found in the cuckoo pint/lords and ladies (*Arum maculatum*).

SPATHE A large bract (q.v.) surrounding the flowering parts of some members of the lily, daffodil, or iris families.

STAMEN The male organ of a flower, consisting of the filament (q.v.) and the anther (q.v.).

STIGMA The surface, often sticky, at the top of the style (q.v.), which receives the pollen prior to germination.

STIPE The stem-like structure of seaweeds and some fungi.

STIPULES A leaf-like structure at the base of the stalk of a leaf.

STYLE The sterile, stalk-like portion of a carpel (part of the female organ of a flower), which bears the stigma (q.v.).

SUCCESSION In botany, the progressive change in plant populations during development from the initial colonization to the climax vegetation (q.v.).

SUCCULENT Leaves or stems that are capable of storing water and have a fleshy appearance.

UMBEL The term used to describe the flowering head of a plant in which there is a main stem or stems from which several branches bearing the flowers all arise from one point.

UNDERSTOREY The third layer in the four-part ascending layers of a wood, consisting of shrubs and small trees.

VEGETATIVE A means of asexual reproduction. More specifically in botany it refers to asexual reproduction by means of runners, for example, or a portion of the parent plant breaking off and growing into a new plant. Examples include corms, bulbs and tubers.

INDEX

—